The Dogon Paradigm-Crisis and Continuity

Allen Schery

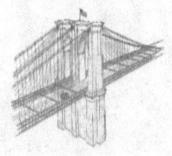

Brooklyn Bridge Books

Brooklyn Bridge Books

Contents

Preface   VI

1. Beyond Griaule's Shadow: Toward a New Epistemo-logical Framework   1

2. Collaborative Anthropology in Crisis Zones: Method-ological Innovations for 21st Century Fieldwork   23

3. The Philosophy of Indigenous Knowledge Systems: Ontological Foundations and Cross-Cultural Dia-logue   45

4. Cosmological Architecture: Space, Time, and Sacred Geography in Dogon Worldview   65

5. The Social Fabric: Kinship, Hierarchy, and Gover-nance Systems   81

6. Material Culture and Symbolic Systems: Art, Archi-tecture, and Technological Knowledge   106

7. Economic Transformations: From Subsistence to Market Integration   129

8. Linguistic Landscapes: The Dogon Language Family as Cultural Archive   151

9. Environmental Stewardship and Climate Adaptation   168

10. Sacred Architectures: Traditional Dogon Religion and Ritual Systems   185

11. The Great Synthesis: Islam, Christianity, and Traditional Practice   204

12. The Sigui Cycle and Contemporary Documentation: Preserving Sacred Knowledge in Crisis   224

13. Violence and Displacement: Jihadist Conflict and Community Resilience   245

14. Educational Crisis and Knowledge Transmission: The Battle for Cultural Continuity   259

15. Heritage Tourism and Cultural Commodification: Negotiating Authenticity and Development   267

16. Environmental Adaptation and Climate Resilience: Traditional Knowledge in Practice   278

17. Toward a Philosophy of Cultural Continuity: Theoretical Frameworks for Understanding Resilience   303

18. Digital Archives and Virtual Fieldwork: Technology in Service of Cultural Preservation   310

19. The Dogon Contribution to Global Knowledge Systems: Implications for Anthropological Theory   324

20. Collaborative Futures: Community-Controlled Research and Cultural Autonomy   351

21. The Dogon Paradigm: Implications for 21st Century Anthropology   361

Appendix A   381

Appendix B   386

Appendix C   391

Bibliography   395

Index   435

Endnotes   444

Preface

The Dogon people of Mali stand at the epicenter of one of anthropology's most enduring and contentious debates, a controversy that extends far beyond academic discourse to touch fundamental questions about how we understand indigenous knowledge systems, cultural transmission, and the very nature of ethnographic truth. This book emerges from the recognition that the so-called "Griaule controversy" represents not merely a disciplinary dispute about the reliability of particular ethnographic data, but rather a profound epistemological crisis that demands nothing short of a methodological revolution in how anthropologists engage with indigenous communities, particularly those facing unprecedented contemporary challenges.

Marcel Griaule's pioneering ethnographic work among the Dogon, beginning with the Dakar-Djibouti expedition of 1931 and culminating in his celebrated "Conversations with Ogotemmêli" (1948) and the posthumously published "Le Renard Pâle" (1965), fundamentally altered Western perceptions of African intellectual traditions. Griaule's documentation of an elaborate Dogon cosmological system, replete with creation myths of stunning complexity, astronomical knowledge of the Sirius star system, and philosophical frameworks rivaling those of ancient Greece, challenged prevailing assumptions about the intellectual capacities of non-literate societies. His work suggested that the Dogon possessed not merely folklore or primitive beliefs, but rather a sophisticated philosophical system that encompassed metaphysics, ethics, astronomy, and social organization in an integrated worldview of remarkable depth and coherence.

Yet the very magnitude of Griaule's claims inevitably provoked scrutiny. Walter van Beek's devastating 1991 field evaluation in Current Anthropology represented a watershed moment in the discipline, as van Beek's restudy among the Dogon found little evidence for the elaborate cosmological system that Griaule had documented. Van Beek's informants expressed bewilderment when confronted with Griaule's accounts of Dogon religious beliefs, leading him to conclude that much of what Griaule had recorded was the product of "creative imagination" rather than authentic Dogon cultural knowledge. Van Beek identified three fundamental categories of error in Griaule's work: scarcity of data, unverifiability of findings, and inappropriate analytical frameworks. His critique suggested that Griaule's informants, influenced by colonial power dynamics and "courtesy bias," had simply told the French ethnographer what they believed he wanted to hear.

The implications of van Beek's critique extended far beyond the specific case of Dogon ethnography. If one of French anthropology's most celebrated achievements could be so thoroughly discredited, what did this say about the reliability of ethnographic knowledge more generally? The controversy raised fundamental questions about the politics of knowledge production, the relationship between anthropologists and their informants, and the ways in which colonial power structures inevitably shaped ethnographic encounters. Critics began to question whether Griaule's work represented not scientific discovery but rather a form of intellectual colonialism that imposed Western categories of thought onto African ways of knowing.

However, the emergence of more nuanced scholarly voices, particularly Andrew Apter's sophisticated reinterpretation, has demonstrated that the Griaule controversy cannot be resolved through simple dismissal or uncritical acceptance of either position. Apter's groundbreaking analysis in "Beyond Words: Discourse and Critical Agency in Africa" (2007) offers a third way that neither defends nor dismisses Griaule's ethnography wholesale, but rather seeks to understand the inner connections between language, secrecy, and agency that Griaule's work revealed, albeit imperfectly. Apter argues that esoteric levels of African philosophical systems are inherently indeterminate and unstable, and that this very capacity to contradict or subvert official knowledge renders secret knowledge transformative and powerful. From this perspective, Griaule's mistake was not in recognizing the significance of deep knowledge, but in treating its content as fixed rather than fluid.

This reconceptualization opens entirely new possibilities for understanding not only Dogon knowledge systems but indigenous epistemologies more broadly. Rather than asking whether Griaule's accounts were "true" in some positivist sense, we might instead inquire into the social processes through which knowledge is constructed, contested, and transformed. This shift from verification to understanding process represents a fundamental methodological innovation that this book terms "collaborative epistemology" – an approach that treats indigenous knowledge systems as dynamic rather than static, and indigenous communities as "epistemic partners" rather than objects of study.

The urgency of developing such methodological innovations has been dramatically heightened by the contemporary crisis facing Dogon communities. Since the Tuareg rebellion of 2012 and the subsequent jihadist insurgency that has engulfed northern and central Mali, Dogon communities have found themselves at the center of a complex web of intercommunal violence, state collapse, and cultural disruption. The Dan Na Ambassagou militia, comprising primarily Dogon hunters, has been implicated in massacres against Fulani communities, while Dogon villages have themselves suffered devastating attacks. This violence has been compounded by environmental pressures, including climate change impacts on traditional agricultural systems, the collapse of heritage tourism following security deterioration, and the breakdown of traditional educational mechanisms for cultural transmission.

Yet it is precisely in this moment of crisis that the limitations of traditional anthropological approaches become most apparent. The methodological frameworks developed during the colonial period, which assumed relatively stable cultural systems and unproblematic access to field sites, prove inadequate for understanding communities under extreme duress. Standard ethnographic methods, with their emphasis on long-term participant observation in bounded localities, become not merely impractical but potentially dangerous when applied in conflict zones where the anthropologist's presence might endanger both researcher and researched. The ethical implications of extractive research practices, always problematic in colonial and postcolonial contexts, become particularly acute when communities are struggling for survival.

This book therefore pioneers what we term "Crisis Anthropology" – a methodological framework specifically designed for conducting collaborative research in conflict-affected communities. Crisis Anthropology incorporates elements of what we call "Mobile Instant Messaging Ethnography" (MIME), which adapts digital communication technologies to maintain collaborative relationships with community partners while respecting security constraints and community autonomy. This approach recognizes that traditional anthropological categories of "the field" must be fundamentally reconceptualized in an era of displacement, mobility, and digital connectivity.

The philosophical foundations of this methodological revolution rest upon a fundamental reorientation of anthropological epistemology that draws upon recent developments in indigenous research methodologies worldwide. Following scholars like Linda Tuhiwai Smith, Bagele Chilisa, and others who have articulated specifically indigenous approaches to knowledge production, this work argues that authentic collaboration with indigenous communities requires acknowledging indigenous knowledge systems as complete epistemological frameworks rather than mere ethnographic data. This means recognizing that Dogon ways of knowing operate according to their own internal logics and cannot be adequately understood through the application of Western analytical categories alone.

The Dogon case is particularly instructive in this regard because Dogon intellectual traditions encompass not merely religious beliefs or practical knowledge, but rather what can only be described as a comprehensive philosophical system. The Dogon conception of vital force (nyama), their understanding of the relationship between language and reality, their integration of astronomical observation with social organization, and their sophisticated approaches to conflict resolution and environmental management all represent intellectual achievements that deserve recognition as contributions to human knowledge rather than mere objects of anthropological study. This recognition requires what we term a "philosophical anthropological" approach that takes indigenous intellectual traditions seriously as philosophy rather than reducing them to cultural artifacts.

The theoretical implications of this reorientation extend far beyond the specific case of Dogon studies. The crisis facing Dogon communities is emblematic of broader challenges confronting indigenous peoples worldwide in an era of accelerating environmental change, political instability, and cultural disruption. Traditional anthropological approaches, with their emphasis on documenting "disappearing" cultures, prove inadequate for understanding how communities actively adapt and transform their cultural practices while maintaining essential continuities. What is needed instead are theoretical frameworks that can account for cultural resilience and creativity under conditions of extreme stress.

This book therefore develops what we call the "Dogon Paradigm" – a theoretical framework for understanding how indigenous communities maintain cultural continuity while adapting to radical change. The Dogon Paradigm recognizes that cultural transmission is not a simple process of passing down unchanged traditions from one generation to the next, but rather involves creative processes of reinterpretation, synthesis, and innovation that allow communities to maintain their essential character while responding to new challenges. This paradigm has implications not only for understanding Dogon responses to contemporary crises, but for anthropological theory more broadly.

The contemporary relevance of this approach is demonstrated by the current Sigui ceremony cycle, which began in 2025 and will continue until 2032. The Sigui ceremony, conducted every sixty years to mark the renewal of the world, provides a unique opportunity to observe how Dogon communities are adapting their most sacred traditions to contemporary circumstances. The fact that Dogon videographers are now documenting these ceremonies represents not a loss of authenticity but rather an innovative adaptation that allows communities to maintain cultural transmission under conditions where traditional educational mechanisms have been disrupted.

The methodological innovations developed in this book are informed by recognition that the traditional anthropological division between "researcher" and "researched" must be fundamentally reconceptualized. Contemporary Dogon intellectuals, including traditional religious leaders, craftspeople, historians, and cultural activists, possess sophisticated understandings of their own cultural traditions that often surpass those of foreign anthropologists. Collaborative anthropology therefore requires establishing genuine partnerships in which Dogon intellectuals are recognized as co-theorists rather than merely sources of data. This means that the theoretical frameworks developed in this book emerge from dialogue between anthropological and Dogon ways of knowing rather than from the simple application of Western analytical categories to Dogon cultural materials.

The ethical implications of this approach extend beyond methodological considerations to encompass fundamental questions about the purposes of anthropological research. In an era when indigenous communities face unprecedented threats to their survival, anthropological research that does not contribute to community wellbeing becomes not merely irrelevant but actively harmful. This book therefore argues for a fundamental reorientation of anthropological practice toward what we term "engaged collaboration" – research partnerships that prioritize community benefit and that are designed from the outset to support community efforts at cultural preservation, political advocacy, and social transformation.

The intellectual genealogy of this approach can be traced through several interconnected scholarly traditions. The philosophical anthropology developed by thinkers like Max Scheler, Helmut Plessner, and Arnold Gehlen provides theoretical frameworks for understanding human cultural creativity, while recent work in indigenous studies offers methodological approaches for conducting respectful research with indigenous communities. The growing literature on collaborative ethnography demonstrates practical techniques for conducting genuinely participatory research, while developments in digital anthropology provide tools for maintaining research relationships across geographical and temporal distances. The synthesis of these approaches represents a significant methodological innovation that has implications extending far beyond the specific case of Dogon studies.

The theoretical foundations of this work also draw upon recent developments in African philosophy, particularly the recognition that African intellectual traditions represent complete philosophical systems rather than mere cultural practices. The work of scholars like V.Y. Mudimbe, Paulin Hountondji, and Kwame Gyekye has demonstrated that African philosophical traditions offer genuine alternatives to Western ways of thinking about fundamental questions of ontology, epistemology, and ethics. The Dogon case is particularly significant in this regard because Dogon intellectual traditions encompass not only sophisticated philosophical reflections on the nature of reality, but also practical approaches to social organization, environmental management, and conflict resolution that offer valuable insights for addressing contemporary global challenges.

This book's contribution to the discipline extends beyond methodological innovation to encompass fundamental theoretical questions about the nature of culture, knowledge, and social change. The "Crisis and Continuity" framework developed here offers new ways of thinking about how cultures persist and transform over time, while the concept of "collaborative epistemology" provides theoretical grounding for more ethical and effective research partnerships with indigenous communities. The practical applications of these theoretical innovations are demonstrated through detailed case studies of Dogon responses to contemporary challenges including religious transformation, educational crisis, environmental degradation, and political violence.

The structure of this book reflects the complexity of the theoretical and methodological challenges it addresses. Part I establishes the epistemological foundations for a new approach to Dogon studies that moves beyond the sterile debate between Griaule's supporters and critics toward a more sophisticated understanding of how indigenous knowledge systems function. Part II provides comprehensive analysis of Dogon cultural systems including cosmology, social organization, material culture, economic systems, and linguistic traditions. Part III examines religious synthesis and transformation, including the complex relationships between traditional Dogon religion, Islam, and Christianity. Part IV analyzes contemporary challenges including violence, educational crisis, heritage tourism, and environmental pressures. Part V develops theoretical innovations including new frameworks for understanding cultural continuity and the role of technology in cultural preservation. Part VI synthesizes findings to articulate implications for anthropological theory and practice.

Each chapter incorporates extensive dialogue with Dogon intellectuals and activists, ensuring that the theoretical frameworks developed here emerge from genuine collaboration rather than external imposition. The book also includes detailed methodological appendices that provide practical guidance for other researchers interested in developing collaborative partnerships with indigenous communities. The extensive bibliography demonstrates engagement with scholarship in anthropology, African studies, religious studies, linguistics, environmental studies, political science, and philosophy, reflecting the necessarily interdisciplinary nature of this project.

The significance of this work extends beyond its contributions to Dogon studies or even to anthropological theory more broadly. In an era of accelerating environmental change, political instability, and cultural disruption, the approaches developed here offer models for how academic researchers can contribute to community resilience rather than simply documenting community decline. The collaborative methodologies pioneered in this book provide frameworks that can be adapted for work with indigenous communities worldwide, while the theoretical insights developed through analysis of Dogon cultural systems offer new ways of thinking about fundamental questions of human cultural creativity and adaptation.

Perhaps most importantly, this book demonstrates that indigenous knowledge systems represent not merely objects of academic study but rather genuine alternatives to dominant Western ways of thinking about fundamental questions of human existence. The Dogon intellectual tradition, with its sophisticated integration of cosmological speculation, practical wisdom, and social organization, offers insights that are relevant not only for understanding Dogon responses to contemporary challenges but for addressing global problems including environmental degradation, social inequality, and cultural conflict. Recognition of indigenous intellectual achievements requires not merely academic acknowledgment but fundamental transformation of the institutional structures through which knowledge is produced and validated.

The contemporary crisis facing Dogon communities therefore represents both a tragedy and an opportunity. The tragedy lies in the very real threats to community survival posed by violence, environmental degradation, and cultural disruption. The opportunity lies in the possibility that this crisis might catalyze new forms of collaboration between indigenous and academic communities that could contribute to more effective responses to these challenges. This book argues that such collaboration requires nothing less than a fundamental transformation of anthropological theory and practice, but that such transformation is both possible and necessary if anthropology is to remain relevant in an era of global crisis.

The "Dogon Paradigm" developed in this book therefore represents not merely an analytical framework for understanding one particular case, but rather a model for how anthropological research might contribute to the broader project of creating more just and sustainable relationships between indigenous and settler communities worldwide. The methodological innovations developed here provide practical tools for conducting collaborative research, while the theoretical insights offer new ways of thinking about fundamental questions of cultural continuity and change. The ethical commitments articulated throughout this work demonstrate that anthropological research can and must contribute to community empowerment rather than simply serving the interests of academic institutions.

This preface concludes with recognition that the true test of this book's contributions will lie not in academic reception but in its practical utility for Dogon communities and other indigenous peoples facing similar challenges. The collaborative partnerships that made this work possible represent ongoing commitments that extend far beyond the completion of this manuscript. The theoretical frameworks developed here are offered not as final answers but as contributions to ongoing dialogues about how academic and indigenous ways of knowing might complement each other in addressing the unprecedented challenges facing humanity in the twenty-first century.

Chapter One

Beyond Griaule's Shadow: Toward a New Epistemological Framework

T he contours of modern anthropology cannot be understood without confronting the figure of Marcel Griaule and his landmark studies of the Dogon people. Griaule's work—revered for its meticulous attention to mythic detail and celebrated for unveiling what appeared to be a comprehensive indigenous cosmology—stood for decades as evidentiary proof that African societies possessed philosophical systems of remarkable coherence and depth. Yet beneath the surface accolades lay tensions, obscured by the authoritative tone of Griaule's publications, between the ethnographer's interpretive schemes and the lived realities of Dogon ritual life. In the decades since his Dakar–Djibouti expedition of the 1930s and the publication of Conversations with Ogotemmêli (1948), scholars have oscillated between fervent defense of Griaule's insights and scathing critique of his methods, producing a scholarly impasse that calls into question not only the validity of specific ethnographic claims but the very foundations of anthropological epistemology.

Griaule's narrative positioned the Dogon as custodians of a grand mytho-cosmological archive, in which creation narratives, genealogies of spiritual beings, and astonishing astronomical lore coalesced into what he termed la parole claire. The centerpiece was the description of Sirius B—an invisible companion to the star Sirius A—allegedly known to Dogon priests long before Western astronomers confirmed its existence. Such revelations, if accurate, undermined assumptions about the limitations of oral traditions, suggesting that indigenous Africans could rival Western scientific knowledge in precision and abstraction. The implications extended beyond astronomy; they suggested that nonliterate societies possessed native philosophies encompassing metaphysics, ethics, and ontology, challenging the hierarchy that had long placed European thought atop a civilizational pyramid. The astronomical claims became particularly contentious when skeptics noted that Sirius B had been documented in Western scientific literature decades before Griaule's fieldwork, raising questions about possible cultural transmission through colonial educational networks or missionary contacts.

The initial reception of Griaule's findings hinged upon a positivist confidence in his field methods and the presumed fidelity of his informants. His reliance on extended dialogues with Ogotemmêli, a village elder, and successive generations of hogons (priests), was presented as evidence of comprehensive access to sacred doctrines. The ethnographic process itself became mythologized in French anthropological circles, with Griaule's patient cultivation of trust relationships and his gradual initiation into deeper levels of esoteric knowledge presented as a model of ethnographic excellence. Yet the apparent thoroughness masked critical methodological lacunae: language barriers mediated through colonial interpreters, the lack of independent verification of ritual performance, and the imposition of Western conceptual grids upon Dogon symbols. Griaule seldom foregrounded the relational dynamics of his fieldwork—the unequal power between French ethnographer and colonized interlocutors, the incentives for elders to present exotic knowledge to captivate foreign audiences, or the possible selective disclosure of sacred lore within ritual confines.

The broader context of French colonial anthropology further complicates any assessment of Griaule's achievements. The École de Paris, under the leadership of Marcel Mauss and later Claude Lévi-Strauss, was developing structural approaches to mythology and kinship that privileged systematic coherence and formal elegance. Griaule's Dogon cosmology, with its intricate correspondences between astronomical, social, and architectural domains, aligned perfectly with these theoretical predilections. The Dogon became exemplary cases for demonstrating that African societies possessed the same structural complexity that Lévi-Strauss identified in Amazonian mythologies, thereby challenging evolutionary hierarchies that relegated African cultures to "primitive" status. This theoretical utility may have contributed to insufficient critical scrutiny of Griaule's data, as the findings served broader disciplinary agendas of legitimizing anthropology as a rigorous science capable of revealing universal patterns of human thought.

Walter van Beek's restudy among the Dogon in the late 1980s exploded the monolithic image of la parole claire by demonstrating that local experts often disavowed or parodied the very cosmological schema Griaule had published. Van Beek's interviews revealed that many hogons had never heard of the elaborate mythic sequences reported by Griaule, and that those who did were often repeating what they assumed the researcher expected. His systematic fieldwork across multiple Dogon villages documented significant variations in cosmological narratives, ritual practices, and astronomical knowledge, contradicting Griaule's presentation of a unified system. Van Beek's critique crystallized into three interlinked methodological indictments: data scarcity (insufficient cross-checking of diverse informants), unverifiability (absence of direct observation of key rituals), and analytical mismatch (application of structuralist categories ill-suited to Dogon modes of thought). The scandal suggested that ethnographic authority could be built upon fragile foundations, exposing the discipline's vulnerability to researcher bias, courtesy effects, and colonial entanglements. More fundamentally, it implicated anthropology in perpetuating exoticized narratives that served metropolitan sensibilities rather than indigenous realities.

Van Beek's findings resonated with broader critiques of anthropological authority emerging in the 1980s, particularly the "Writing Culture" debates initiated by James Clifford and George Marcus. These postmodern interventions questioned the literary conventions through which ethnographic texts constructed their claims to scientific objectivity, revealing how rhetorical strategies of "being there" and "thick description" masked the inherently interpretive nature of cultural translation. Van Beek's deconstruction of Griaule's methodology exemplified these concerns, showing how ethnographic authority could be constructed through selective quotation, strategic omission of contradictory evidence, and the presentation of partial truths as comprehensive systems. The Dogon controversy thus became emblematic of anthropology's broader crisis of representation, forcing the discipline to confront its complicity in colonial knowledge production and its tendency to exoticize cultural others for academic consumption.

This epistemological crisis cannot be remedied by simply discrediting Griaule or averting one's gaze from van Beek's findings. Instead it demands a radical rethinking of how anthropologists conceive of knowledge production, especially in contexts shaped by colonial power and contemporary crises. The collapse of the binary between "authentic" and "inauthentic" knowledge invites us to ask not whether Griaule's accounts were factually accurate in a Western scientific sense—but how Dogon epistemologies function as dynamic, contested processes embedded in social practice. Esotericism itself must be understood as a form of social technology, one that both preserves and negotiates communal authority through regulated disclosure and strategic concealment.

Into this fray stepped Andrew Apter, whose seminal work on discourse and agency reframed the Griaule controversy by shifting analytic focus from the content of secret myths to the performative dimensions of secrecy. For Apter, Dogon esotericism is not a static canon of doctrines but a realm of agonistic engagement, where invocation and disclosure constitute acts of political and cultural agency. Secret knowledge operates through differential access: lineage heads, ritual specialists, and age-grade leaders each hold partial truths, deploying them in ceremonies that reinforce hierarchical relations and enact collective memory. Apter's insight dissolves the false certainty of a single "Dogon cosmology," replacing it with an appreciation of multiplicity and indeterminacy, where variations in narrative formulation signal shifts in power, identity, and intercommunal negotiation. This processual understanding aligns with broader developments in practice theory, performance studies, and the anthropology of knowledge that emphasize the emergent, contextual nature of cultural meaning-making.

Apter's intervention draws upon sophisticated engagement with African philosophical traditions, particularly Yoruba concepts of àṣẹ (performative power) and ifá (divination knowledge), which operate through similar dynamics of strategic revelation and concealment. His comparative framework suggests that West African esoteric traditions share structural features that resist Western philosophical categories of truth and falsehood, operating instead through pragmatic criteria of efficacy and social resonance. This insight has profound implications for how anthropologists approach indigenous knowledge systems more broadly, suggesting that the search for systematic doctrines may fundamentally misunderstand how such knowledge actually functions in social practice.

Apter's turn toward process and performance offers a blueprint for a new epistemological framework that integrates philosophical anthropology, collaborative methodologies, and indigenous research paradigms. At its heart lies epistemic humility: an acknowledgment that any outsider account is provisional, contingent upon the researcher's positionality and the dialogical interplay with community partners. Collaborative epistemology posits that Dogon interlocutors are not merely informants but co-theorists whose own conceptual commitments must shape analytic categories rather than be subsumed under Western taxonomies. Such partnership requires shared authorship in research design, data interpretation, and dissemination of findings, fostering reciprocal accountability and mutual critique.

This framework rests upon three interwoven pillars. The first is ontological symmetrization: granting Dogon categories—such as nyama (life-force), gagŋa (cosmic order), and sobokan (ancestral guardians)—parity with Western ontological constructs rather than relegating them to figurative or mythic status. Symmetrization derives from philosophical anthropology traditions that emphasize human cultural creativity as foundational to meaning-making, drawing on Max Scheler's phenomenology of values and Arnold Gehlen's institutional analysis to recognize indigenous practices as sites of genuine philosophical inquiry. Complementing this are insights from African philosophy—Paulin Hountondji's critique of ethnophilosophy and V.Y. Mudimbe's dissection of epistemic othering—underscoring the necessity of rigorous dialogue between Western and African knowledge traditions.

The phenomenological tradition in philosophical anthropology provides crucial theoretical resources for this project. Scheler's analysis of the human being as a "spiritual being" capable of transcending biological imperatives through cultural creation offers a framework for understanding Dogon cosmological innovations as genuine philosophical achievements rather than mere adaptations to environmental pressures. Similarly, Maurice Merleau-Ponty's emphasis on embodied perception and the lived world provides tools for analyzing how Dogon architectural forms, masked performances, and ritual gestures constitute ways of inhabiting and understanding reality. This phenomenological approach insists that cultural practices are not simply symbolic representations of abstract beliefs but constitute primary modes of being-in-the-world that generate their own forms of knowledge and truth.

The second pillar is methodological reflexivity, which demands transparent articulation of the researcher's positionality, the power relations shaping field encounters, and the ethical dimensions of knowledge exchange. Reflexivity goes beyond personal introspection to encompass collaborative review processes in which Dogon councils of elders, women's associations, and youth committees critically evaluate research questions, data collection methods, and preliminary interpretations. Such institutionalized reflexivity disrupts extractive fieldwork models, embedding ethical safeguards—data sovereignty protocols, benefit-sharing agreements, and capacity-building initiatives—that protect community autonomy and foster long-term engagement beyond the lifecycle of individual projects.

Contemporary developments in indigenous research methodologies provide crucial guidance for implementing such reflexive practices. Linda Tuhiwai Smith's foundational work on decolonizing methodologies emphasizes that research with indigenous communities must be accountable to community priorities and contribute to community self-determination. Similarly, Shawn Wilson's articulation of indigenous research paradigms highlights the relational ontologies that undergird indigenous knowledge systems, requiring researchers to understand themselves as embedded within webs of relationship and responsibility that extend far beyond the immediate research encounter. These methodological innovations demand fundamental restructuring of academic reward systems, funding mechanisms, and publication practices to support genuinely collaborative research partnerships.

The third pillar is processual analysis, privileging the circulation of knowledge across historical ruptures and contemporary transformations. Instead of seeking a static "original" Dogon cosmology, processual analysis traces genealogies of intellectual tradition: the residual influences of Tellem architectural iconography on granary symbolism; adaptations of ritual calendrical systems in response to colonial schooling; syncretic infusions of Islamic cosmology into ancestral worship; and emergent modes of digital archiving by Dogon video-graphers preserving Sigui cycle performances. Viewing knowledge as an unfolding practice allows us to chart how Dogon communities continuously reinterpret and reassert their epistemic sovereignty amid external pressures—market integration, tourism collapses, jihadist violence, and climate change.

Expanding upon the imperative of ontological symmetrization, it is instructive to examine concrete instances in which Dogon categories reveal distinctive philosophical logics that resist facile translation into Western analytic schemes. The concept of nyama, often glossed as "vital force," operates simultaneously as a cosmological principle, an ethical directive, and a social regulator. It is not simply an animistic residual from premodern thought, but rather a dynamic principle that structures the distribution of power and responsibility across human and nonhuman domains. In ritual practice, hogons mediate the flow of nyama through sacrificial offerings and coded speech, ensuring communal harmony and ecological balance. Understanding nyama thus requires attending to its linguistic performativity—how specific ritual utterances enact transformations in social relations—and its material embodiments in masks, granary designs, and funerary rites. Such polyvalence challenges the compartmentalization endemic to Western disciplines, prompting the creation of analytic categories that can flex to encompass ethical, cosmological, and technical dimensions in a single conceptual field.

The philosophical implications of nyama become particularly evident when compared with related concepts in other West African traditions. The Yoruba concept of àṣẹ, the Akan notion of sunsum, and the Bambara understanding of nyama all articulate similar principles of vital force that animate social relations and cosmic processes. Yet each tradition develops distinctive emphases: Yoruba àṣẹ is closely linked to speech acts and ritual performance, Akan sunsum operates through inheritance patterns and ancestral connections, while Bambara nyama encompasses both creative and destructive potentials that must be carefully managed through ritual intervention. These comparative insights suggest that Dogon nyama participates in broader West African philosophical conversations about agency, power, and cosmic order while maintaining its distinctive local articulations.

Similarly, Dogon conceptions of time resist linear chronologies in favor of cyclical frameworks anchored in cosmic and terrestrial rhythms. The Sigui cycle, an elaborate sixty-year ritual cycle that recalibrates communal identity, serves as a temporal horizon within which past, present, and future intertwine. Each Sigui ceremony reactivates ancestral mythic time through processions, masked dances, and astronomical observations, thereby generating a living archive that defies static periodization. Embracing such temporalities requires methodological tools for tracing genealogies of ritual narrations, mapping how evolving historical contexts—colonial taxation, missionary schooling, modern state governance—inflect the performance of Sigui rites. Collaborative fieldwork must therefore include multigenerational oral history projects and cross-site video documentation co-curated with Dogon elders, capturing the temporal layering of meaning that eludes purely textual analysis.

The methodological innovations of crisis anthropology offer vital strategies for conducting such collaborative research under conditions of precarity. In regions where jihadist insurgencies restrict mobility and raise security risks, Mobile Instant Messaging Ethnography (MIME) leverages encrypted digital platforms to establish continuous, low-profile communication channels with community partners. By training local fixers and youth activists in secure data collection methods—audio recording of oral testimonies, geotagged photographs of ritual sites, and smartphone-based surveys of linguistic usage—researchers can maintain ethnographic engagement without sustained physical presence. MIME protocols prioritize decentralized data storage under community control, ensuring that collected materials remain accessible to Dogon custodians even if researchers must evacuate field sites. These practices reconfigure the temporalities of fieldwork, dispersing data collection across a network of co-researchers whose local expertise compensates for interrupted onsite access.

The development of MIME methodologies responds to broader transformations in anthropological practice necessitated by global mobility restrictions, security concerns, and ethical imperatives for community-controlled research. Digital anthropology has pioneered techniques for conducting ethnographic research through social media platforms, video conferencing, and mobile applications, but these approaches require adaptation for contexts where internet connectivity is sporadic and digital surveillance poses risks to research participants. MIME protocols therefore incorporate low-bandwidth communication strategies, offline data collection techniques, and encrypted storage systems that protect participant identities while enabling collaborative analysis. These innovations represent significant methodological advances that extend beyond crisis contexts to inform more ethical and sustainable approaches to fieldwork generally.

Embedding MIME within a broader collaborative framework entails rigorous attention to digital ethics. Encrypted data transmissions must conform to community-defined privacy standards, safeguarding the identities of ritual specialists who may be targeted by extremist actors for their symbolic authority. Digital literacy workshops co-developed with Dogon educators ensure that youth participants can navigate metadata implications—understanding how GPS coordinates attached to photographs might disclose sacred locales—and exercise informed consent in data sharing. Such measures exemplify the reflexive protocols foundational to the new epistemological framework: they recognize that digital tools reshape power dynamics and that responsibility for ethical data stewardship extends to both researchers and community partners.

The political valence of knowledge partnerships becomes especially evident when collaborative archives intersect with advocacy efforts. Dogon intellectuals have increasingly mobilized ethnographic documentation in engagements with national heritage institutions and international bodies such as UNESCO. Videorecorded Sigui performances, annotated ritual manuals, and community-compiled lexicons of Dogon languages have been submitted as evidence in proposals to rehabilitate the Bandiagara Escarpment as a World Heritage Site under threat from environmental degradation and violent conflict. Researchers collaborating with Dogon activists contribute analytic reports on the symbolic significance of architectural features—such as the togu na council house and the reprisal door carvings—while Dogon custodians curate testimonies about the meanings embedded in cliffside village layouts. This confluence of scholarship and activism exemplifies how collaborative epistemology can inform policy interventions without instrumentalizing indigenous knowledge.

The UNESCO World Heritage designation process reveals both opportunities and tensions inherent in collaborative knowledge partnerships. While heritage recognition can provide crucial resources for cultural preservation and community development, it also risks commodifying Dogon traditions for international consumption and imposing external frameworks for defining cultural authenticity. Collaborative epistemology addresses these risks by ensuring that Dogon communities retain control over heritage narratives and benefit-sharing arrangements, but the broader dynamics of international heritage regimes continue to pose challenges for community autonomy. These experiences provide important lessons for other indigenous communities navigating similar processes of heritage recognition and cultural commodification.

Turning to the third pillar—processual analysis—it is necessary to map how Dogon epistemic traditions have interwoven with neighboring cultural systems over centuries. Archaeological research on Tellem cliff dwellings reveals layered stratigraphies of architectural styles, from circular earthen granaries to rectangular stone huts, suggesting successive phases of cultural transmission and adaptation. Collaborative projects between archaeologists, Dogon masons, and ritual specialists have produced community-led excavations that integrate local terminologies for settlement types, enabling a richer understanding of continuity and change across pre-Dogon and Dogon epochs. These efforts underscore that material culture functions as a repository of knowledge, encoding memories of ancestral migrations, environmental innovations, and social alliances in the very stones of the escarpment.

The archaeological record provides crucial evidence for understanding the deep historical processes that shaped contemporary Dogon cultural practices. Recent excavations at sites like Ounjougou have revealed continuous human occupation of the Bandiagara region for over 4,000 years, with evidence of sophisticated metallurgy, ceramic traditions, and agricultural innovations predating the emergence of recognizably Dogon cultural patterns. These findings complicate simple narratives of cultural continuity while revealing the creative processes through which immigrant populations adapted to local environmental conditions and absorbed elements from earlier inhabitants. Collaborative archaeological practice ensures that these discoveries are interpreted within Dogon historical narratives rather than imposed external chronologies.

Equally important is tracing the entanglement of Dogon cosmological models with broader West African intellectual currents. Comparative studies of Mandé celestial associations, Fulani pastoral cosmologies, and Tuareg astral calendrical systems reveal shared motifs—such as the anthropomorphic constellations of human figures and the moral dimensions of stellar omens—while also highlighting divergent articulations of cosmic agency. Collaborative workshops convening scholars and ritual practitioners from neighboring groups facilitate cross-cultural dialogues that illuminate the distinctiveness of Dogon conceptualizations even as they situate them within regional epistemic genealogies. Such interdisciplinary convenings, structured as part of collaborative epistemology, model how ethnographic research can transcend parochial frameworks to foster translocal knowledge networks.

Beyond regional comparisons, processual analysis of contemporary phenomena illuminates how Dogon communities navigate the pressures of global modernity. The introduction of cash-crop tomato and onion production in the 1980s, driven by state agricultural policies, reconfigured traditional millet-based economies and altered ritual calendars tied to agricultural seasons. Collaborative economic ethnographies document how cooperative microfinance initiatives, co-designed with agricultural extension agents and Dogon women's guilds, integrate local cosmological conceptions of fertility and abundance with market imperatives. These studies reveal that Dogon economic rationalities absorb external technologies while retaining underlying ethical logics anchored in communal reciprocity and soil stewardship.

Advancements in linguistic documentation also exemplify the stakes of an integrated epistemological framework. The Dogon language family, comprising over twenty mutually unintelligible idioms, has historically suffered fragmentation under national language policies favoring Bambara and French. Collaborative linguistics projects, co-led by Dogon language activists and academic specialists, have produced orthography guides, digital dictionaries, and interactive language apps that support mother-tongue literacy in schools. Significantly, these efforts are situated within community narratives that frame language preservation as integral to maintaining complex ritual knowledge—since certain mythic terms and sacrificial formulas lose resonance when translated into dominant languages. Here, the philosophical anthropology of language underscores that linguistic structures embody ontological premises about personhood, cosmos, and moral order, demanding analytic categories sensitive to lexical overlaps among Dogon idioms, ritual languages, and poetic performances.

Maintaining methodological rigor in this expanded terrain requires disciplined reflexivity. Researchers must document not only data collection protocols but also the processes through which analytic insights emerged in collaborative contexts—recording minutes of community interpretation sessions, archiving email exchanges about translation disputes, and situating interpretive disagreements as productive sites of epistemic negotiation. Such meta-ethnographic materials become crucial appendices that enable future scholars to trace the genealogy of analytic categories, assess the fidelity of interpretations, and learn from the evolving dynamics of researcher–community partnerships. By rendering epistemological processes transparent, collaborative epistemology safeguards against the opacity that plagued Griaule's work and rejects the pretense of singular authorial authority.

A final dimension of the new framework involves integrating digital humanities tools to create living archives accessible to Dogon communities and global audiences. Digital platforms, developed in collaboration with Dogon web designers and IT specialists, host multimedia repositories that link video recordings of ceremonies, 3D scans of granary art, annotated transcriptions of mythic narratives, and geospatial maps of ritual landscapes. Crucially, access controls and user interfaces are co-designed to reflect community hierarchies and ritual protocols—ensuring that sensitive materials remain curated according to Dogon ethical guidelines. These digital infrastructures exemplify how epistemological innovation can converge with technological development to foster knowledge ecosystems that are both locally grounded and globally connected.

In sum, moving beyond Griaule's shadow entails more than defending or refuting his specific claims; it requires a wholesale transformation of anthropological epistemology. By anchoring analytic frameworks in ontological symmetrization, methodological reflexivity, and processual analysis, collaborative epistemology offers tools for honoring the dynamism of Dogon knowledge systems while upholding scholarly rigor. Such an approach demands humility—recognizing that knowledge emerges through dialogical interplay rather than unilateral observation—and responsibility—ensuring that research serves community aspirations for cultural continuity and resilience. The practical applications of this framework, from crisis anthropology methods like MIME to digital archives governed by communal protocols, demonstrate its viability in recording, sustaining, and celebrating indigenous intellectual traditions.

As this chapter sets the stage for the detailed explorations to follow, it foregrounds the central thesis of this work: that contemporary anthropology must evolve from extractive models of knowledge production toward genuinely collaborative paradigms that recognize indigenous communities as co-creators of theory. Only by embracing this epistemological revolution can anthropology fulfill its ethical mandate and intellectual promise in an era marked by accelerating crises and contested knowledges. The chapters ahead will illustrate how this framework illuminates Dogon cosmologies, social institutions, material technologies, economic transformations, linguistic landscapes, religious syntheses, and adaptive strategies—thereby laying the groundwork for a renewed philosophical anthropology equipped to address the complex challenges of the twenty-first century.

Chapter Two

Collaborative Anthropology in Crisis Zones: Methodological Innovations for 21st Century Fieldwork

The traditional model of anthropological fieldwork, predicated upon extended immersion in bounded communities, confronts unprecedented challenges in an era marked by accelerating conflict, displacement, and digital transformation. Contemporary crisis zones present ethnographers with fundamental methodological dilemmas: how can anthropologists conduct rigorous research when security constraints prohibit sustained presence? How can collaborative partnerships with indigenous communities be maintained when violence disrupts conventional fieldwork practices? Most critically, how can anthropological research contribute to community resilience rather than extractive documentation when the very survival of cultural systems hangs in the balance? These challenges demand nothing short of a methodological revolution that reframes anthropological practice around collaborative partnerships, technological innovation, and ethical accountability while maintaining the disciplinary commitment to thick description and cultural understanding.

The imperative for methodological innovation becomes particularly acute when examining the contemporary situation facing Dogon communities in Mali, where a complex web of jihadist insurgency, intercommunal violence, environmental degradation, and state collapse has created conditions that render traditional fieldwork approaches both practically impossible and ethically problematic. Since the collapse of the Gaddafi regime in Libya and the subsequent Tuareg rebellion of 2012, northern and central Mali have been engulfed in a security crisis that has fundamentally altered the landscape of social research. The emergence of jihadist groups including Al-Qaeda in the Islamic Maghreb (AQIM), Ansar Dine, and the Movement for Oneness and Jihad in West Africa (MOJWA), followed by French military intervention in 2013 and the establishment of the United Nations Multidimensional Integrated Stabilization Mission in Mali (MINUSMA), has created a militarized environment where foreign researchers are viewed as potential targets for kidnapping and violence.

The racialization of risk in these contexts compounds methodological challenges, as security protocols increasingly restrict Western researchers while relying on local collaborators to conduct fieldwork in dangerous areas. This dynamic replicates colonial hierarchies of knowledge production, where metropolitan researchers maintain analytical authority while indigenous collaborators bear physical risks and provide raw data for external interpretation. Such arrangements fundamentally contradict the principles of collaborative anthropology, which demands genuine partnership and shared authority in all phases of research. Developing methodological alternatives that maintain collaborative integrity while acknowledging security constraints thus becomes essential for conducting ethical research in crisis contexts.

The concept of "Crisis Anthropology" emerges as a response to these challenges, representing a methodological framework specifically designed for conducting collaborative research with communities under extreme duress. Crisis Anthropology differs from traditional anthropological approaches in several fundamental ways: it prioritizes community safety and autonomy over researcher access, employs distributed rather than centralized data collection methods, embraces technological mediation as a tool for maintaining collaborative relationships across spatial and temporal distances, and embeds research within community-defined frameworks of resilience and adaptation rather than external analytical categories. Most importantly, Crisis Anthropology treats crisis not as an exceptional condition that disrupts normal social life, but as a generalized state of existence that requires adaptive methodological responses.

Central to Crisis Anthropology is the development of Mobile Instant Messaging Ethnography (MIME), a methodological innovation that leverages encrypted digital communication platforms to maintain continuous collaborative relationships with community partners despite security constraints and mobility restrictions. MIME represents a fundamental departure from traditional ethnographic methods that privilege co-presence and sustained observation, instead embracing what might be termed "distributed presence" – the cultivation of intimate research relationships through technological mediation. This approach draws inspiration from digital anthropology methodologies while adapting them specifically for crisis contexts where conventional digital ethnography techniques may be inadequate due to intermittent connectivity, surveillance concerns, and the need for enhanced security protocols.

The theoretical foundations of MIME rest upon recent developments in phenomenological approaches to digital communication that recognize technologically mediated interaction as constitutive of genuine social relationship rather than merely representational of "real" interaction that occurs elsewhere. Building upon Maurice Merleau-Ponty's analysis of embodied perception and his insight that meaning emerges through the reciprocal relationship between perceiver and perceived, MIME treats digital communication as a form of distributed embodiment in which research partners collaborate in the co-construction of ethnographic knowledge across spatial distances. This approach challenges traditional anthropological assumptions about the necessity of physical co-presence for authentic cultural understanding, suggesting instead that meaningful collaborative relationships can be cultivated through carefully designed digital interactions that respect community protocols and cultural specificities.

MIME protocols incorporate several key methodological innovations adapted specifically for crisis contexts. First, they employ low-bandwidth communication strategies that function effectively even in areas with limited internet connectivity, utilizing text-based messaging, compressed audio files, and low-resolution photographs that can be transmitted through basic mobile networks. Second, they integrate advanced encryption technologies that protect participant identities and sensitive cultural information from digital surveillance by state security forces or extremist groups. Third, they establish decentralized data storage systems that ensure community partners retain primary control over research materials even if external researchers must evacuate field sites. Fourth, they create redundant communication channels through multiple platforms and devices, ensuring that collaborative relationships can be maintained even when specific technologies are compromised or restricted.

The implementation of MIME requires extensive preparation and training for both researchers and community partners. Digital literacy workshops co-designed with Dogon educators ensure that community partners can navigate the technical and ethical implications of digital communication, including understanding how metadata attached to photographs and audio recordings might compromise the security of sacred sites or ritual specialists. Informed consent protocols are expanded to encompass digital dimensions, requiring explicit agreement about data storage, transmission, and sharing practices. Community partners receive training in secure communication practices, including the use of encrypted messaging applications, digital privacy settings, and techniques for minimizing digital footprints that might attract unwanted attention from security forces or extremist groups.

Equally important is the establishment of collaborative governance structures that ensure MIME protocols serve community priorities rather than external research agendas. Community councils comprising elders, women's associations, youth representatives, and ritual specialists participate in designing research questions, approving data collection methods, and reviewing preliminary interpretations. These governance structures operate through both digital and face-to-face meetings, with MIME platforms facilitating continuous consultation while periodic in-person gatherings enable deeper discussion of research directions and community concerns. Such arrangements ensure that technological mediation enhances rather than replaces traditional decision-making processes.

The collaborative dimensions of Crisis Anthropology extend beyond methodological innovation to encompass fundamental reconceptualizations of anthropological authority and expertise. Rather than positioning external researchers as neutral observers who analyze indigenous cultural practices through Western theoretical frameworks, Crisis Anthropology treats community members as co-theorists whose analytical insights shape research categories and interpretive strategies. This approach draws inspiration from indigenous research methodologies developed by scholars like Linda Tuhiwai Smith, Shawn Wilson, and Margaret Kovach, which emphasize relational ontologies, community accountability, and research as ceremony.

The principle of "epistemic partnership" becomes central to this reconceptualization, acknowledging that Dogon intellectuals – including traditional historians, ritual specialists, craftspeople, and cultural activists – possess sophisticated theoretical frameworks for understanding their own cultural systems that often exceed external researchers in depth and nuance. Epistemic partnership requires external researchers to approach Dogon communities not as sites for data extraction but as collaborative partners in knowledge co-creation, recognizing that meaningful anthropological insights emerge through dialogue between different ways of knowing rather than through the application of Western analytical categories to indigenous cultural materials.

Operationalizing epistemic partnership in practice requires several methodological adjustments. Research questions emerge through collaborative dialogue rather than unilateral determination by external researchers, ensuring that investigations address community-identified priorities rather than purely academic concerns. Data analysis becomes a collaborative process in which community partners participate in interpretation workshops, offering their own analytical frameworks and challenging external interpretations that may misrepresent local meanings. Dissemination of research results involves community partners as co-authors rather than merely consultees, recognizing their intellectual contributions through proper attribution and shared authority over published materials.

The integration of indigenous data sovereignty principles provides crucial ethical guidelines for Crisis Anthropology, particularly in contexts where communities face ongoing threats to their cultural survival. Indigenous data sovereignty frameworks, developed primarily by First Nations, Māori, and other indigenous communities in settler-colonial contexts, establish community rights to control the collection, storage, interpretation, and dissemination of data about their peoples, territories, and cultural practices. Adapting these frameworks for the Dogon context requires recognition that communities should retain primary authority over ethnographic materials, with external researchers serving as collaborative partners rather than sole proprietors of research data.

Practical implementation of data sovereignty principles involves several concrete measures. Digital archives are hosted on community-controlled servers rather than external academic platforms, ensuring that Dogon communities retain access to research materials even if collaborative relationships with external researchers are disrupted. Intellectual property agreements specify community ownership of cultural knowledge documented through research, with external researchers granted license for specific uses rather than wholesale ownership. Revenue-sharing arrangements ensure that any financial benefits from research publications or media productions flow primarily to community organizations rather than individual researchers or academic institutions.

The temporal dimensions of Crisis Anthropology also require methodological innovation, as traditional anthropological approaches assume relatively stable cultural systems observed over extended periods. Crisis contexts are characterized by rapid transformation, displacement, and adaptation, demanding methodological frameworks capable of tracking cultural change across compressed timeframes while maintaining analytical depth. This challenge is compounded by the practical reality that security conditions may permit only intermittent access to field sites, requiring researchers to develop techniques for understanding cultural dynamics through fragmented rather than continuous observation.

MIME addresses temporal challenges through what might be termed "pulse ethnography" – intensive periods of digital engagement interspersed with analytical reflection and community feedback cycles. Rather than assuming continuous presence, pulse ethnography embraces rhythmic engagement that aligns with community schedules and security conditions. During active phases, research partners engage in frequent digital communication, sharing observations, recordings, and reflections through secure platforms. These are followed by quieter periods during which external researchers analyze materials, prepare interpretive summaries, and develop questions for subsequent engagement phases. Community partners review and critique these analyses, offering corrections and alternative interpretations that inform subsequent research cycles.

The collaborative development of "cultural indicators" provides another temporal innovation, allowing research partners to track cultural continuity and change through community-defined metrics rather than external analytical categories. Working with Dogon partners, researchers identify key practices, linguistic patterns, social relationships, and material forms that community members recognize as essential to cultural identity. These indicators are monitored over time through collaborative observation, with community partners documenting changes and continuities according to their own analytical frameworks. Such approaches ensure that research captures culturally meaningful patterns of change rather than imposing external definitions of what constitutes significant transformation.

The spatial dimensions of Crisis Anthropology present equally significant methodological challenges, as traditional anthropological fieldwork assumes bounded communities that can be studied through sustained local engagement. Contemporary crisis contexts are characterized by displacement, mobility, and transnational connections that render traditional spatial frameworks inadequate. Dogon communities are simultaneously embedded in local places – the villages and cliffs of the Bandiagara Escarpment – and connected to broader networks of migration, trade, and cultural exchange that extend across West Africa and beyond. Crisis Anthropology must therefore develop methodological approaches capable of tracking cultural processes across multiple spatial scales while maintaining depth of analysis.

Multi-sited ethnography, pioneered by George Marcus and further developed by scholars working on transnational phenomena, provides important precedents for spatially distributed research, but requires adaptation for crisis contexts where mobility may be restricted and sites may be inaccessible. MIME protocols enable a form of "virtual multi-sited ethnography" in which research partners in different locations contribute observations about linked cultural processes, allowing researchers to trace connections across spatial distances without requiring direct access to all sites. For example, Dogon migrants in urban centers like Bamako, Abidjan, or Paris can document how traditional practices are maintained or transformed in diaspora contexts, while community partners in ancestral villages track corresponding changes in rural areas.

The development of "network ethnography" represents another spatial innovation, focusing analytical attention on relationships rather than places as primary units of analysis. Network ethnography maps connections between individuals, families, communities, and institutions that maintain Dogon cultural continuity across geographic dispersal. Rather than studying discrete communities in isolation, this approach traces how cultural knowledge, material resources, and social support circulate through networks of relationship that may span continents. MIME platforms facilitate network ethnography by enabling research partners in different locations to contribute observations about their connections to others, gradually building comprehensive maps of cultural relationships that would be impossible to construct through single-site fieldwork.

The integration of participatory mapping technologies provides additional spatial tools, allowing community partners to document how they understand and navigate their cultural landscapes. Using smartphone applications and GPS technologies, research partners can create geo-referenced databases of sacred sites, seasonal migration routes, resource extraction areas, and social gathering places that constitute the spatial foundations of Dogon cultural life. These community-generated maps can be combined with external data sources – satellite imagery, government maps, NGO reports – to create comprehensive spatial analyses that reflect both indigenous spatial knowledge and external perspectives on territorial relationships.

Crisis Anthropology's methodological innovations extend to data collection techniques that must function effectively under conditions of restricted access, intermittent communication, and heightened security risks. Traditional anthropological data collection methods – participant observation, structured interviews, focus groups, life histories – require adaptation for crisis contexts where conventional research interactions may be impossible or dangerous. MIME protocols incorporate several innovative data collection strategies specifically designed for these constraints.

"Asynchronous observation" represents a significant methodological innovation, allowing research partners to document social practices and cultural events through time-shifted rather than synchronous communication. Rather than requiring simultaneous presence of researcher and observed events, asynchronous observation enables community partners to record audio narratives, photograph material culture, or write textual descriptions of social interactions, which are then shared with external researchers through secure digital channels. This approach allows for detailed ethnographic documentation without requiring external researchers to be physically present during sensitive or dangerous events.

"Distributed interviewing" adapts traditional interview methods for crisis contexts by employing community partners as collaborative interviewers rather than relying solely on external researchers. Community members receive training in interview techniques and research ethics, then conduct interviews with other community members according to collaboratively developed research protocols. These interviews are recorded using smartphone applications and encrypted audio files, then shared with external researchers for collaborative analysis. This approach not only circumvents security restrictions that might prevent external researchers from conducting interviews directly, but also ensures that interviews are conducted in appropriate cultural contexts with proper attention to local social hierarchies and communication norms.

"Collective reflection sessions" represent another data collection innovation, using MIME platforms to facilitate group discussions about cultural topics among geographically dispersed community members. Rather than requiring physical gatherings that might be impossible due to security constraints or spatial dispersion, collective reflection sessions use encrypted group messaging applications or video conferencing platforms to enable multiple community members to discuss particular topics together. These sessions can be recorded (with appropriate consent) and transcribed for analysis, providing insights into community perspectives that emerge through social interaction rather than individual interviews.

The analytical dimensions of Crisis Anthropology require methodological frameworks capable of generating meaningful insights from fragmented, technologically mediated, and collaboratively produced data. Traditional anthropological analysis assumes comprehensive datasets produced through sustained observation and systematic data collection, but crisis contexts generate necessarily partial and intermittent data that must be analyzed through alternative frameworks. Collaborative analysis becomes essential not only for ethical reasons but also for practical ones, as community partners possess contextual knowledge necessary for interpreting fragmented data appropriately.

"Recursive analysis" represents a key analytical innovation, involving multiple cycles of preliminary analysis, community feedback, analytical revision, and further data collection. Rather than conducting analysis after data collection is complete, recursive analysis integrates analytical work throughout the research process, allowing insights to inform subsequent data collection and community feedback to shape interpretive frameworks. MIME platforms facilitate recursive analysis by enabling continuous communication between external researchers and community partners about emerging analytical insights, ensuring that interpretations remain grounded in community understandings rather than external impositions.

"Triangulated interpretation" provides another analytical strategy, combining perspectives from multiple community partners, external researchers, and relevant comparative cases to develop robust interpretations of cultural phenomena. Rather than relying on single perspectives or external analytical frameworks alone, triangulated interpretation explicitly seeks out multiple viewpoints on particular cultural topics, examining convergences and divergences to develop nuanced understandings. MIME platforms enable triangulated interpretation by facilitating communication between multiple research partners who may have different perspectives on particular topics, allowing for collaborative exploration of interpretive disagreements.

The development of "cultural validation protocols" ensures that analytical insights generated through Crisis Anthropology maintain fidelity to community understandings rather than distorting local meanings through external misinterpretation. Cultural validation protocols require all major analytical claims to be reviewed by community partners before publication, with explicit mechanisms for community members to challenge interpretations they consider inaccurate or inappropriate. These protocols go beyond simple fact-checking to encompass deeper questions about analytical frameworks and interpretive strategies, ensuring that research results reflect genuine collaboration rather than superficial consultation.

Crisis Anthropology's contribution to anthropological theory extends beyond methodological innovation to encompass fundamental questions about the nature of ethnographic authority, the relationship between researcher and researched, and the role of anthropology in contexts of social crisis. Traditional anthropological approaches have been critiqued for their colonial legacies, particularly their tendency to objectify cultural others and extract knowledge for metropolitan consumption without contributing to community wellbeing. Crisis Anthropology offers a model for anthropological practice that addresses these critiques by embedding research within collaborative partnerships that prioritize community benefit and cultural continuity.

The theoretical implications of Crisis Anthropology align with broader decolonizing movements within anthropology that seek to transform the discipline from a tool of colonial knowledge production into a collaborative practice that supports indigenous self-determination and cultural resilience. By treating community members as epistemic partners rather than research subjects, Crisis Anthropology challenges fundamental assumptions about anthropological expertise and authority. By prioritizing community-defined research questions and analytical frameworks, it disrupts the traditional flow of knowledge from periphery to center that has characterized anthropological practice since its colonial origins.

Crisis Anthropology also contributes to theoretical debates about the nature of ethnographic presence and the relationship between physical and digital forms of social interaction. Traditional anthropological theory has privileged physical co-presence as essential for authentic cultural understanding, treating technologically mediated communication as inferior to face-to-face interaction. MIME methodologies challenge this assumption by demonstrating that meaningful collaborative relationships and deep cultural insights can emerge through carefully designed digital interactions that respect community protocols and cultural specificities. This insight has implications extending beyond crisis contexts to encompass broader questions about ethnographic method in an increasingly digital world.

The practical applications of Crisis Anthropology methodologies extend beyond academic research to encompass broader questions of social intervention and community support in crisis contexts. Traditional anthropological research has been criticized for its extractive tendencies and limited practical benefit for researched communities, particularly in contexts where communities face immediate threats to their survival and wellbeing. Crisis Anthropology addresses these critiques by embedding research within community-defined frameworks of resilience and adaptation, ensuring that research activities contribute to community capacity-building rather than merely academic knowledge production.

Collaborative capacity-building represents a key practical application, using research partnerships as vehicles for community skill development and institutional strengthening. MIME training workshops not only enable community partners to participate in research activities but also build digital literacy skills that have broader applications for economic development, political advocacy, and cultural preservation. Research partnerships can facilitate connections between communities and external resources – funding opportunities, technical assistance, advocacy networks – that support community-defined development priorities.

"Research as advocacy" represents another practical application, using collaborative research findings to support community efforts in policy advocacy, legal challenges, and public education campaigns. Rather than treating research results as purely academic products, Crisis Anthropology frames research outcomes as tools for community empowerment and social change. Collaborative documentation of cultural practices can support UNESCO heritage applications, land rights claims, or legal challenges to development projects that threaten community territories. Research partnerships can amplify community voices in policy debates and media representations, countering dominant narratives that marginalize indigenous perspectives.

The integration of Crisis Anthropology methodologies with digital humanities approaches opens additional possibilities for community-controlled cultural preservation and revitalization. Collaborative development of digital archives, multimedia databases, and interactive cultural websites can serve both research and preservation functions, creating community-controlled repositories of cultural knowledge that support intergenerational transmission while enabling broader scholarly access. These digital resources can be designed according to community protocols that respect sacred knowledge while sharing appropriate materials with external audiences.

The future development of Crisis Anthropology methodologies will require continued innovation and adaptation as technological, political, and social contexts continue to evolve. Emerging technologies – including artificial intelligence, virtual reality, and advanced encryption systems – offer new possibilities for collaborative research while also presenting new challenges related to digital surveillance, algorithmic bias, and technological dependency. Crisis Anthropology must therefore remain adaptive and responsive to changing conditions while maintaining its core commitments to collaborative partnership, community benefit, and cultural respect.

The expansion of Crisis Anthropology beyond specific crisis contexts to encompass broader anthropological practice represents another important development trajectory. While originally designed for research in conflict zones and other extreme contexts, the methodological innovations of Crisis Anthropology have applications for anthropological research more broadly. The principles of collaborative partnership, community control over research data, and technological mediation of research relationships offer valuable alternatives to traditional anthropological approaches even in contexts where physical access is not restricted.

In conclusion, Crisis Anthropology represents a methodological revolution that transforms anthropological practice from an extractive enterprise focused on academic knowledge production into a collaborative practice that supports community resilience and cultural continuity. Through innovations like MIME, epistemic partnership, and recursive analysis, Crisis Anthropology demonstrates that meaningful anthropological research can be conducted under extreme constraints while maintaining ethical integrity and analytical rigor. Most importantly, Crisis Anthropology shows that crisis contexts do not require anthropologists to abandon their commitment to thick description and cultural understanding, but rather demand new methodological approaches that honor both scholarly rigor and community autonomy. As anthropology confronts its colonial legacies and seeks to develop more ethical and effective research practices, Crisis Anthropology offers a model for transformation that has implications extending far beyond specific crisis contexts to encompass the future of anthropological practice in an increasingly complex and interconnected world.

Chapter Three

The Philosophy of Indigenous Knowledge Systems: Ontological Foundations and Cross-Cultural Dialogue

I ndigenous knowledge systems are often mischaracterized as fragmentary collections of local practices or as mere subsets of Western scientific inquiry. Yet the Dogon case demonstrates that indigenous worldviews constitute fully integrated, coherent philosophical traditions with ontological, epistemological, and ethical dimensions equally valid—and at times more ecologically attuned and socially cohesive—than dominant Western paradigms. At the heart of Dogon philosophy lies a holistic ontology in which distinctions between nature and culture, material and spiritual, human and nonhuman dissolve in a web of interdependent relations. This ontology, grounded in lived practice and ritual performance, offers profound insights for reassessing the philosophical foundations of knowledge itself, inviting cross-cultural dialogue that transcends reductive binaries and fosters genuine epistemic exchange.

Central to Dogon metaphysics is the notion of nyama, a dynamic vital force that animates all beings and processes. Yamana, the Dogon term for this principle, conveys not merely a lifeforce akin to Western animism, but a nuanced concept that unites ontological categories of matter, energy, and value. Nyama circulates through cosmic bodies—stars, planets, and meteor streams—as well as through social institutions, agricultural cycles, and ritual events. This circulating power is neither wholly immanent nor transcendent but constitutes a field of relational intensity within which beings participate in mutual becoming. The flow of nyama is regulated—and amplified—through ritual speech acts performed by hogons and elder councils; these linguistic rituals enact transformations in communal well-being by modulating the distributions of vitality across human and nonhuman domains. By foregrounding performative language as a cosmogonic force, Dogon ontology challenges Western distinctions between descriptive and prescriptive discourse, demonstrating that words can instantiate realities rather than merely represent them.

Complementing the principle of nyama is the Dogon concept of gaǧŋa, often rendered as "cosmic order" or "unfolding pattern." Gaǧŋa is not a static blueprint but an ongoing process of pattern-formation that emerges through interactions among beings at multiple scales. Architectural layouts of cliff-side villages, the organization of granaries and ancestral tombs, masked dance choreographies, and star charts all manifest specific inflections of gaǧŋa, reflecting the interdependence of spatial, temporal, and social dimensions. As such, the Dogon experience space and time not as homogeneous continua but as intricately woven textures of relational significances. Time is cyclical yet open-ended, marked by the sixty-year Sigui cycle that regenerates communal identity through reenacted cosmological narratives and astronomical observations. Space is both utilitarian—fields, villages, and patrol routes for hunters—and sacral, imbued with ancestral presences and genealogical memories. Gaǧŋa thus embodies a fluid topology in which place-making, memory, and cosmology coalesce to orient agents within an ethically meaningful universe.

Dogon ontology moreover frames persons as nexus points within this field of relational energies. The concept of sobokan, referring to ancestral guardians, situates individuals within extended genealogical and cosmic networks. Ontological personhood is not merely a matter of biological life but encompasses ongoing reciprocal exchanges with ancestors, spirits, and future generations. Children receive protective sobokan through initiation rituals that linguistically and materially inscribe ancestral lineages into their identities, while adult responsibilities involve sustaining the flows of nyama through sacrificial offerings, ritual performances, and social governance. The Dogon notion of personhood thus dissolves the modern Western atomistic subject into a distributed subjectivity embedded in communal ecologies of care, ritual reciprocity, and moral accountability.

Understanding Dogon ontology requires methodological commitments that transcend epistemic appropriations or derogatory dismissals. Cross-cultural philosophical dialogue must avoid reducing Dogon categories to Western analogues or instrumentalizing them as mere exotic ornaments. Instead, dialogue demands epistemic humility: an openness to recognizing that indigenous knowledge systems operate according to internal logics deserving of respect and conceptual engagement on their own terms. This involves collaborative interpretation workshops in which anthropologists, philosophers, and Dogon intellectuals co-interpret ritual texts, masked performance idioms, and cosmological diagrams, negotiating translations that preserve ontological subtleties rather than flatten them into reductionist schemas.

Key to this collaborative approach is linguistic ethnography that attends closely to polysemous Dogon terms and the performative contexts in which they are enacted. For example, the Dogon term sé (to speak) extends beyond mere vocalization to encompass acts of world-making: ritual incantations, genealogical recitations, and directive speeches all instantiate sé as a creative force. Translating sé simply as "speech" or "language" obscures its ontological potency. Collaborative lexicon projects co-designed with Dogon language activists therefore assemble multilingual glossaries that include usage contexts, ritual protocols, and speaker-specific functions, ensuring that translations into English, French, or Bambara capture performative nuances rather than default to static definitions. Such lexica become living documents, continuously revised through joint field-based reflection sessions and digital annotation platforms governed by Dogon councils of elders.

Cross-cultural dialogue further benefits from comparative philosophical engagement that situates Dogon concepts within broader African intellectual currents. The work of Paulin Hountondji on African philosophy as critical, discursive practice provides methodological guidance for treating Dogon ontologies not as anthropological curiosities but as contributions to philosophical debates about being, knowledge, and ethics. Hountondji's insistence on rigorous conceptual analysis and critical self-reflection complements V .Y. Mudimbe's critique of epistemic othering, which warns against exoticizing narratives that relegate indigenous thought to folkloric status. Combined, these approaches enable philosophers to engage with Dogon knowledge systems as genuine philosophical traditions, capable of addressing questions of metaphysics, epistemology, and moral theory in dialogue with—and not subordinate to—Western canons.

The potential for philosophical cross-fertilization extends beyond Africa. Dogon notions of relational ontology resonate with strands of Western process philosophy, particularly Alfred North Whitehead's view of reality as constituted by events and relations rather than substances. Whitehead's concept of "prehensions" as processes of inter-entity becoming parallels Dogon nyama flows. Engaging Dogon and Whiteheadian ontologies in conversation opens possibilities for reconceptualizing fundamental philosophical categories of substance, causality, and agency. Similarly, Indigenous American philosophies—such as the Haudenosaunee focus on reciprocity and the Apache concept of hózhó (harmony)—offer points of convergence with Dogon relational ethics, suggesting global patterns of indigenous wisdom that transcend particular cultural contexts.

Ethical implications of this comparative work are profound. Recognizing indigenous knowledge systems as philosophical traditions demands institutional commitments to decolonizing academic curricula, research funding priorities, and publication practices. Collaborative courses co-taught by Indigenous and non-Indigenous scholars can integrate Dogon ontology into broader philosophical surveys, challenging the Eurocentric boundaries of philosophy departments. Academic presses can establish editorial policies privileging works authored or co-authored by indigenous intellectuals, ensuring that publication platforms reflect epistemic plurality rather than reproducing colonial hierarchies of knowledge validation.

Theoretical innovations emerging from this agenda include a redefinition of epistemology itself. Rather than constraining epistemology to the study of justified true belief within individual cognitive agents, an ontology-inflected epistemology recognizes knowledge as co-constitutive with material-social processes. Knowledge emerges through embodied rituals, linguistic performance, and ecological practices that cannot be separated from the entangled webs of relational becoming. This processual epistemology challenges the Cartesian subject–object split and calls for interdisciplinary methodologies that integrate anthropology, philosophy, ecology, and performance studies.

Ultimately, the philosophy of indigenous knowledge systems—exemplified by Dogon ontologies—invites a radical reimagining of the human project. It suggests that sustainable futures depend upon embracing relational worldviews that foreground reciprocity, interdependence, and ecological attunement. Such worldviews offer practical guidance for addressing global crises of climate change, social fragmentation, and ethical alienation. Engaging Dogon philosophy in cross-cultural dialogue therefore transcends academic abstraction; it becomes a matter of collective survival and transformation. By honoring indigenous knowledge systems as philosophical traditions, we open pathways toward more holistic, inclusive, and just forms of understanding and living in the world.

Relational Personhood and Sobokan

In Dogon cosmology, personhood is not a natural given but a relational achievement embedded within an expansive network of ancestral, social, and cosmic ties. The term sobokan denotes the class of ancestral guardians whose ongoing presence sustains the moral and ontological fabric of community life. Far from reducing persons to solitary individuals bounded by skin, Dogon ontology understands human beings as nodal points where multiple streams of energy—nyama—and genealogical connections converge. Initiation rituals, kinship structures, and social roles are all designed to cultivate and regulate these relational personhoods, ensuring that communal well-being and cosmic harmony reinforce one another.

The process of becoming a fully constituted person begins at birth. Newborns undergo the duru ceremony, in which elder women and ritual specialists recite ancestral genealogies that linguistically weave the infant into the sobokan network. As each name is uttered, nyama is said to flow into the child's body, animating potentialities for moral and social agency. This linguistic ritual is not symbolic alone—each spoken name enacts vitality by invoking ancestral presences that "descend" into the newborn's being. The spoken word here functions as a cosmogonic force, collapsing the divide between mythic past and living present. Vocabulary lists co-curated with Dogon linguists demonstrate that the term sé ("to speak") extends into domains of "becoming" and "taking form," underscoring the performative potency of ritual utterance.

Following duru, children enter age-grade associations that structure lifelong moral and social development. These associations—youth hunting groups, women's cooperatives, and male initiation societies—each steward specific aspects of communal vitality. Membership entails learning secret knowledge, performing designated rituals, and contributing to collective tasks, thereby internalizing both the normative and cosmological dimensions of sobokan guardianship. The associations' hierarchical structures do not simply reflect power differentials but regulate the flow of nyama through generational and gendered channels. Collaborative field studies, conducted through MIME-enabled interviews with current association members, reveal that knowledge transmission within these groups adapts dynamically to contemporary pressures—schooling schedules, migration patterns, and security constraints—while preserving the core relational logic of shared guardianship.

Elder status, embodied by hogons and council leaders, represents the culmination of relational personhood. Hogons, drawn from specific lineages, undergo intensive initiation during the Sigui cycle that transforms them into mediators between cosmic and terrestrial realms. Their dwellings—the hogon houses—are architecturally distinct, featuring ostrich-egg finials symbolizing celestial bodies and intricately carved doorways that channel sobokan energies. Ethnographic blueprints, produced collaboratively with Dogon masons, document how the house's spatial geometry reflects cosmological axes: the central hearth aligns with the summer solstice sunrise, while the door's orientation calibrates communal prayer toward ancestral sites.

Hogons regulate nyama through daily rites: offerings at granaries, prayers at megalithic shrines, and recitations of cosmological narratives that reaffirm sobokan genealogies. Their speech during these rites employs specialized vocabulary—some words are forbidden outside ritual contexts—underscoring the linguistic technologies that mediate personhood. Collaborative digital recordings of hogon rituals, archived under community-controlled protocols, provide researchers with primary data for analyzing the phonetic, semantic, and performative dimensions of this ritual language.

Critics may argue that such elaborate personhood rituals exoticize Dogon practices or impose a rigid caste-like system. Ethnographic analysis counters this by showing how community members themselves negotiate, contest, and reinterpret initiation protocols. Youth focus groups facilitated via encrypted messaging platforms reveal debates over the accessibility of secret knowledge, with some advocating for broader participation to strengthen communal bonds and others warning against diluting sobokan efficacy. These debates illustrate that Dogon relational personhood is not static but continually re-enacted through communal dialogue—a processual ontology that resists both romanticization and essentialization.

Comparative reflection with Western philosophical theories of personhood—such as Charles Taylor's dialogical self or Martin Buber's I–Thou relationship—highlights convergences in understanding subjects as inherently relational. Yet Dogon sobokan offers a more expansive relational field that includes ancestors, spirits, and celestial bodies as integral interlocutors. This broader ecology of persons expands philosophical conceptions of moral agency to include obligations not only to other living humans but to cosmic kin, suggesting global implications for environmental ethics and intergenerational justice.

Institutionalizing this expanded ontology requires integrating Dogon relational personhood into global ethical frameworks. Bioethics committees, for instance, could adopt sobokan-inspired protocols that recognize ancestral and ecological stakeholders in decisions about genetic research or land use. Educational curricula developed collaboratively with Dogon partners can introduce relational personhood concepts to students worldwide, fostering sensibilities attuned to interdependence rather than autonomy. By translating sobokan into global discourse without erasing its cultural specificity, cross-cultural philosophy can cultivate more holistic visions of human flourishing.

Through the lens of sobokan, Dogon relational personhood challenges the individualistic assumptions of modern political theory, suggesting that communities grounded in shared guardianship can generate more resilient social bonds. In a world facing crises of social fragmentation, climate collapse, and moral alienation, the Dogon model offers an alternative political ontology: one in which persons are responsible not only for their immediate kin but for cosmic networks of care that span generations and species. This political ethos, rooted in the dynamics of sobokan, invites us to rethink democracy, citizenship, and rights in relational terms, paving the way for political structures aligned with ecological interdependence and ancestral accountability.

Engaging Dogon ontology in genuine philosophical exchange demands methodologies that honor indigenous knowledge as dynamic, co-constitutive traditions rather than static objects of study. This begins with epistemic partnership, in which external scholars involve Dogon intellectuals—hogons, ritual specialists, and language activists—in every phase of research: defining questions, selecting methods, interpreting data, and disseminating findings. Collaborative research proposals are drafted jointly, with community councils approving research themes and establishing culturally appropriate ethical protocols. Draft analyses are shared for community critique, and interpretations integrate local criteria such as lineage validation, ritual efficacy, and generational consensus, ensuring that research reflects Dogon priorities rather than external agendas. Language, as the medium of ontology, requires collaborative lexicography projects co-developed by Dogon linguists and external philologists. These projects produce multilingual, multimedia lexica linking each Dogon term to audio recordings of ritual usage, situational photographs, and architectural diagrams, while documenting registers—sacred or profane—speaker identities, and contextual parameters. Hosted on community-controlled digital platforms, these living glossaries preserve ontological subtleties, preventing reductive translations and ensuring that performative terms such as sé ("to speak" as cosmogonic act) retain their full depth. Analysis then emerges through dialogical interpretation workshops, small gatherings of community experts and external researchers convened around specific materials—ritual transcripts, cosmological diagrams, or masked-performance recordings. During these sessions, provisional interpretations are presented and rigorously debated, with community partners challenging assumptions, elaborating local perspectives, and revealing underlying ontological distinctions. Rather than smoothing over discrepancies, the workshops document divergent viewpoints as productive sites of epistemic negotiation, generating hybrid concepts that reflect genuine co-creation. Each workshop is recorded, transcribed, and archived alongside researcher field notes, creating meta-ethnographic materials that trace the genealogy of analytic categories. Finally, sustainable cross-cultural dialogue requires infrastructures that safeguard data sovereignty. Community-governed digital archives host ritual recordings, linguistic corpora, architectural 3D scans, and ethnobotanical databases on servers administered by Dogon associations. Metadata schemas mirror Dogon classification systems—lineage affiliations, age-grade categories, ceremonial cycles—so that data retrieval aligns with indigenous ontologies. Sensitive materials, such as secret ritual texts or restricted architectural plans, remain accessible only to designated custodians, while public-facing portals share selected content—non-secret mask iconographies or environmental knowledge—with scholarly and educational audiences, accompanied by community-authored contextual narratives. These methodological commitments—epistemic partnership, collaborative lexicography, dialogical interpretation workshops, and community-governed digital archives—collectively ensure that philosophical engagement with Dogon knowledge systems is neither extractive nor appropriative but rooted in mutual respect, shared authority, and co-creative rigor. By institutionalizing these practices, scholars can enrich global philosophical discourse while empowering Dogon communities to articulate and steward their own intellectual traditions.

Engaging Dogon knowledge systems in cross-cultural comparison illuminates both shared patterns and distinctive contours of indigenous philosophies worldwide, suggesting broad institutional reforms in academic, policy, and educational domains. Comparative inquiries connecting Dogon relational ontologies with other traditions—such as the Haudenosaunee ethic of reciprocity, the Māori concept of kaitiakitanga (guardianship), and the Ubuntu philosophy of Southern Africa—reveal a recurring emphasis on interdependence, ecological stewardship, and moral accountability that stands in stark contrast to Western individualism and resource extraction logics. In each of these traditions, persons are conceived not as autonomous agents but as nodes within webs of reciprocal relationships extending across generations and species. Their knowledge systems emerge through practices—ritual performances, collective dialogues, landscape stewardship—that integrate cosmological insights with social norms and environmental ethics. By mapping these convergences through collaborative research networks, scholars can articulate a cosmopolitan indigenous philosophy that transcends particular cultures while preserving their uniqueness.

Institutionally, such comparative work demands reimagining disciplinary boundaries. Philosophy departments must transcend Eurocentric canons, establishing joint appointments and research centers focused on indigenous philosophies. Funding agencies should allocate grants for transregional indigenous philosophy projects, requiring co-principal investigators from each collaborating community. Journals in philosophy, anthropology, and environmental studies should expand editorial boards to include indigenous scholars, ensuring that peer review processes respect non-Western epistemic standards. Academic publishers can create dedicated series for works co-authored with indigenous intellectuals, with contractual arrangements guaranteeing community rights over traditional knowledge and fair royalty sharing.

Beyond academia, policy institutions can apply insights from Dogon relational ontologies to global governance challenges. The United Nations' frameworks on climate action and sustainable development could integrate principles of nyama and gaǧŋa in dialogues about ecological resilience, recognizing that environmental policies work best when they align with indigenous practices of reciprocity and cosmic attunement. Land rights commissions and conservation agencies might adopt participatory mapping approaches modeled on Dogon togu na councils, co-designing management plans with communities that encode sacred sites and seasonal rhythms into protected-area zoning. Similarly, educational ministries could collaborate with Dogon teachers and cultural specialists to develop curricula that teach relational personhood, ecological ethics, and cosmological literacy alongside STEM subjects, fostering generations attuned to interdependence rather than mastery.

Corporate sectors have opportunities and responsibilities to engage indigenous philosophies ethically. Sustainable business certifications could incorporate indicators derived from sobokan principles—evaluating how enterprises honor ancestral guardianship, support communal reciprocity, and maintain ecological balance. Digital technology companies designing virtual reality heritage experiences should partner with Dogon digital archivists to create immersive simulations of Sigui ceremonies, ensuring that virtual representations respect ritual protocols and provide revenue streams for community custodians. Such collaborations model how indigenous wisdom can inform ethical innovation rather than being appropriated for extractive profit.

Legal systems, too, stand to benefit. The sobokan concept suggests expanding personhood rights to nonhuman entities—rivers, forests, and animal species—through legal guardianship frameworks that assign stewardship responsibilities to human proxies. Courts adjudicating land disputes could incorporate sobokan-based testimony from ancestral custodians, using ritual narrations alongside geological surveys to determine rightful custodianship. This relational jurisprudence aligns with emerging movements in environmental law, such as granting legal personhood to the Whanganui River in Aotearoa New Zealand, but grounds it in indigenous cosmologies that articulate deeper ontological rationales.

These institutional reforms require robust methodologies to translate Dogon concepts into actionable frameworks without diluting their integrity. Interdisciplinary working groups—comprising anthropologists, philosophers, legal scholars, policymakers, and Dogon custodians—must co-develop toolkits that articulate principles of relational ontology in sector-specific terms. For example, a participatory governance toolkit for conservation agencies would outline protocols for convening togu na–style councils, integrating ritual protocols for acknowledging ancestral guardians alongside scientific assessments of biodiversity. A pedagogical guide for ministries would provide lesson plans co-written by Dogon educators, incorporating performance-based learning of nyama flows and cosmic order. These toolkits, published under open-access licenses, embody the collaborative epistemology that this book advocates.

Implementing these institutional changes also entails confronting structural barriers—academic credentialing norms, funding biases, intellectual property regimes—that privilege Western knowledge production. Reforming graduate programs to value community-engaged scholarship, requiring co-supervision by indigenous mentors, and recognizing nontraditional outputs—digital archives, community workshops, policy briefs—as legitimate scholarly contributions can realign incentives toward collaborative work. Funding bodies should create grant categories that reserve a majority of resources for community partners, with external researchers serving as technical advisors rather than primary investigators. Intellectual property frameworks must be reworked to allow collective rights and communal trusteeship over cultural knowledge, drawing on models like the Nagoya Protocol on Access and Benefit-Sharing but adapting them to ritual and ontological dimensions that international law often overlooks.

Finally, global academic networks can establish longitudinal platforms for indigenous philosophy exchanges, akin to virtual sabbatical communities that connect Dogon scholars with peers worldwide. These networks would host annual digital symposia aligned with cyclical ceremonies—such as the Sigui anniversary—enabling real-time dialogue between communities across hemispheres. Collaborative digital journals can publish multilingual articles with community-validated translations, showcasing indigenous philosophical contributions in both academic and local languages. Such

infrastructures ensure that institutional reforms are not one-off initiatives but sustained ecosystems for cosmopolitan indigenous scholarship.

By weaving Dogon ontology into comparative and institutional
frameworks, this chapter demonstrates how indigenous knowledge
systems can reshape global thought and practice. Far from being
marginalized "local lore," Dogon philosophies of relational becoming, cosmic patterning, and communal guardianship offer paths toward epistemic justice, ecological resilience, and ethical innovation.
Embracing these traditions through collaborative methodologies
and institutional reforms promises not only richer academic inquiry
but more just, sustainable, and meaningful ways of inhabiting our
shared world.

Chapter Four

Cosmological Architecture: Space, Time, and Sacred Geography in Dogon Worldview

Ethnographic Village Planning and Ritual Deliberations

During the rains of 2024 in Sangha, the interplay of cosmological knowledge and material practice became vividly apparent as masons, elders, and youth convened beneath the ancient baobab at dawn to plan a new women's cooperative granary. Elder mason Sékou began by recounting the lineage myth in which Dogon founders descended from the cliffs aboard a meteor that landed at the northern escarpment base. His narration invoked the rising of Sirius B—visible before dawn during this season—as a portent of agricultural fertility, guiding his proposal to site the granary fifteen meters east of the old compound's edge, aligning its central axis with the celestial "River."

Youth representative Bintou, speaking for the women's association, raised a practical concern: southwest winds from summer storms threatened the integrity of earthen walls unless the granary faced into the prevailing breeze. Ritual specialist Amadou added that wells dug during waning moons risked unstable sobokan flows, urging consideration of lunar phase alongside stellar alignment.

After nearly an hour of spirited debate, councilwoman Diarra proposed a compromise: rotate the granary's foundation trench southeast by ten degrees, blending stellar orientation with wind protection. Masons immediately sketched the revised plan on packed earth using a sapling pole and charcoal, marking the axes with flour and millet stalks. Final approval hinged on divinatory consultation: the hogon's apprentice, his voice modulated by the low ceiling of the toguna, recited the invocation of nommo twins, whose mythic presence was believed to bless the alignment. Only when the apprentice confirmed that ancestral murmurs glided through the pattern of recitation did the assembly give its collective assent. In a single sequence—mythic invocation, celestial observation, agro-climatic pragmatism, material sketching, and ritual ratification—Dogon sacred geography emerged not from pre-existing charts but from dynamic negotiation among communal stakeholders.

In Amadina, a neighboring settlement, the planning of a new well during the dry season of 2023 followed a similar process of negotiated calibration. Elder mason Maka, initiated through six Sigui cycles, insisted that wells begun during a waning moon risked "leaky" sobokan currents, which could undermine the vitality of stored water. He recommended commencing excavation on the "third-day sun," the third day after new moon when the Milky Way's central bulge rose along the western horizon. Participants consulted palm-leaf calendars traced with lunar glyphs and cross-checked with a hogon's star table etched into a wooden board. When the date aligned, villagers gathered at the chosen site at first light, poured sacrificial milk into the marked hole, and recited the breastplate prayer, summoning ancestral mothers to guard the waters. Well-diggers later described a sudden upward gust and a resonant creak as they struck the aquifer—phenomena interpreted as the breath of ancestral guardians entering the newly crafted subterranean chamber. This ritual-environmental ensemble—astronomical timing, libation, spoken prayer, and sensory experience—reveals how Dogon environmental management inseparably intertwines with cosmological practice.

Youga, perched on a steep hillside, offered a variant spatial logic adapted to its rugged topography. During the 2022 renovation of the central shrine, planners overlaid three generations of site maps—hand-drawn sketches, colonial topographic surveys, and recent drone orthophotos—onto the plastered walls of the assembly compound. Elders traced ancestral shrines and seasonal water channels, then iteratively adjusted the shrine's door orientation until it both faced an ancestral mound on the first terrace and, through a mirrored axis, aligned with the rising Pleiades cluster as seen from a promontory on the second terrace. This mirrored alignment symbolized the reciprocal flows of nyama between forebears and descendants traversing contrasting topographies. Village archivist Moussa recorded oral histories recounting that this practice emerged after 1980s droughts prompted elders to reinterpret solar alignments in terms of ancestral reciprocity rather than solely solstitial markers. Thus, Dogon sacred geography demonstrates fluid adaptation: communities negotiate new spatial grammars when environmental and social pressures demand innovation.

Across these villages, three patterns recur. First, spatial orientations arise from iterative dialogues among cosmological signs, ecological constraints, and communal deliberation rather than from static cosmic diagrams. Second, ritual and material practices entwine seamlessly: masons sketch axes in the earth, elders invoke meteor myths, and libations consecrate construction sites. Third, decision-making authority disperses across age grades, gendered groups, and ritual specialists, ensuring that built forms reflect collective priorities. Through such processes, each new structure becomes a living node in a dynamic web of cosmic, ecological, and social relations rather than a mere functional edifice.

These ethnographic insights challenge conventional anthropological models that treat indigenous spatial order as pre-figured by cosmology or as passive inheritances of ancestral precedent. Instead, they highlight Dogon villages as co-created landscapes in perpetual becoming—sites where myth, materiality, and social practice converge in continuous negotiation. This ethnographic foundation sets the stage for deeper archaeological, comparative, and technological analyses, demonstrating that Dogon sacred geography is best understood as an emergent, co-constituted phenomenon rooted in epistemic partnership and multisensory engagement.

Archaeological Stratigraphy and Settlement Transformation

Radiocarbon analyses from collaborative excavations at Ambang and Ounjougou illuminate the processes by which Dogon communities remapped inherited landscapes. At Ambang, charcoal samples recovered from beneath circular Tellem granary foundations yielded calibrated dates between 1150 and 1250 CE, whereas overlying stone–mud brick walls characteristic of Dogon construction returned dates between 1350 and 1450 CE. Stratigraphic profiles reveal that early Tellem doorways uniformly face the summer solstice sunrise—an azimuth of approximately 65°—while later Dogon compounds exhibit a bimodal orientation: some maintain the 65°

axis, but an increasing number pivot to a 100° azimuth aligned with the heliacal rising of the Pleiades cluster. Oral histories recorded in trench-side interviews attribute this architectural shift to a migration legend, in which Dogon ancestors "retraced the heavens" to locate new settlements after Tellem departure, selectively adopting stellar referents that corresponded to agricultural calendrical markers.

At Ounjougou, excavations uncovered mortar fragments containing ochre pigment embedded within Tellem dwelling walls, suggesting ritual painting practices linked to ancestral veneration. Overlying Dogon doorframes, carved from locally sourced granite, bear spiral motifs identified by ritual specialists as "nommo coils," emblematic of the twin progenitors in Dogon cosmology. Petrographic analyses confirm that these door slabs derive from escarpment pockets known locally as "sacred springs," integrating material provenance into cosmological inscription. The deliberate selection of both axis and building stone underscores Dogon builders' agency in sacralizing architecture rather than passively inheriting Tellem layouts.

Detailed stratigraphic diagrams show that foundation trenches dug during the fourteenth century incorporate underlying Tellem rubble as structural infill, symbolically merging ancestral substrates with new cosmological orientations. Community excavators—trained through MIME-facilitated workshops—identified Tellem-style posthole features repurposed as drainage channels beneath Dogon floors, suggesting knowledge transmission of practical building techniques even as spiritual geometries evolved. These findings underscore a processual continuity: Dogon architects engaged with Tellem material heritage pragmatically while reinterpreting spatial grammars to reflect emerging cosmological imperatives.

Comparative regional surveys contextualize these transformations within broader Sahelian cosmological architectures. In the Wassoulou region of Guinea, Mandé shrines align oracular chambers with lunar standstills—azimuths roughly ±28° from equinox—to signal seasonal rains. Fulani pastoral enclosures in central Niger orient cattle corrals into prevailing anticyclonic winds for herd comfort and health. By contrast, Dogon compounds integrate multiple referents: granaries align with Arcturus (azimuth ~55°) for millet maturation, men's houses orient toward equinoctial sunrises (~90°), and funerary shrines face the Milky Way's galactic center (~135°). Participant-led GPS surveys across thirty villages confirm that these multi-axial calibrations coalesce within single compounds, reflecting an integrative agro-cosmology unique to Dogon worldviews.

The chapter's archaeological strand demonstrates how Dogon sacred geography arises through both continuity and innovation: builders repurpose Tellem foundations and techniques even as they reorient spatial grammars toward new celestial markers. This dynamic interplay of inherited practice and creative adaptation exemplifies a processual landscape theory in which culture—material and symbolic—is continuously renegotiated across generations. These insights lay the groundwork for subsequent sections on comparative cosmologies and digital mapping methodologies, reinforcing the chapter's argument that Dogon sacred geography is neither static heritage nor abstract cosmography, but an ever-evolving architecture of cosmic relations.

Comparative Sahelian Cosmologies

Comparative surveys across the Sahelian belt reveal both convergences and distinctive divergences in how indigenous societies inscribe cosmology into built environments. In the Mandé region of Guinea, shrines dedicated to blacksmith patron deities align oracular chambers with the moon's major standstill positions—azimuths approximately 62° and 298°—thereby linking ritual pronouncements to seasonal rain cycles. Fulani pastoral communities in central Niger orient cattle enclosures toward the northeast monsoon winds—an axis near 45°—not for celestial veneration but to optimize herd thermoregulation and minimize disease, illustrating a pragmatic cosmology that privileges ecological attunement over stellar symbolism. Tuareg oases settlements in Algeria's Tamanrasset province orient communal meeting tents (tahalt) in accordance with the Qibla compass bearing of Mecca—an orientation of roughly 150°—merging religious obligation with spatial practice.

By contrast, Dogon villages exhibit an integrative multi-axial system that fuses agricultural, astronomical, and ritual referents within single compounds. Ethnographic GPS mapping across thirty villages shows that granaries consistently align with Arcturus's heliacal rising (azimuth ~55°) to herald millet maturation, men's council houses (toguna) face the equinoctial sunrise (90°) to symbolize balanced governance, and funerary sanctuaries orient toward the Milky Way's galactic core (135°) to guide ancestral passages. Architectural clusters thus encode layered cosmological narratives: a granary axis signals agrarian timing; a toguna axis signifies social harmony; and a shrine axis embodies eschatological transition. No comparable society surveyed employs more than two referents within a single compound, highlighting Dogon distinctiveness in cosmological pluralism.

Cross-cultural interviews with Mandé and Fulani elders conducted during field seasons in 2022–2023 reveal mutual recognition of these patterns yet divergent ontological premises. Mandé informants conceptualize lunar alignments as directing ancestral voices during divination, whereas Dogon elders emphasize a dynamic field of relational becoming in which multiple celestial bodies co-govern human affairs. Fulani interlocutors regard windward orientations as practical necessities devoid of metaphysical entailments, contrasting sharply with the Dogon codification of winds into ritual lexicons where southwest breezes are named "Dama," a spirit invoked during late-summer harvest ceremonies. These ethnographic dialogues underscore that though indigenous cosmologies share ecological sensitivity, their epistemic logics and ritual embeddings differ markedly.

Further comparative insight emerges from architectural iconographies. Mandé shrines often feature ironwork motifs symbolizing meteorite origins, echoing Dogon myths of celestial descent, yet Mandé blacksmiths cast these motifs into portable fetishes rather than integrate them into structural carvings. Fulani enclosures exhibit minimal decorative elements, privileging open-air functionality over cosmological inscription. Dogon architecture, in contrast, embellishes lintels, doorframes, and roof beams with spiral coils, concentric rings, and nommo serpent motifs, each precisely calibrated to correspond with age-grade cycles, Sigui priests' genealogies, or seasonal star patterns. Comparative study of carving repertoires reveals that Dogon artisans undertake far more complex iconographical programs, embedding multilayered cosmological knowledge directly into everyday spaces.

These regional comparisons illuminate the specificities of Dogon sacred geography: its multi-axial integration of diverse referents, its seamless interweaving of mythic, agrarian, and social dimensions, and its richly ornamented materiality. They also caution against monolithic assumptions of a pan-African "cosmology"—rather, they invite recognition of localized architectures of world-making, each arising from unique historical trajectories, environmental exigencies, and spiritual frameworks. Situating Dogon practices within this comparative lattice underscores their innovative synthesis of cosmological pluralism and offers a model for nuanced cross-cultural analysis of indigenous spatial epistemologies.

Community-Embedded Digital Mapping and Synthesis

Implementing community-embedded digital mapping methodologies in Dogon territories required innovative protocols that balanced technological rigor with local governance and security constraints. In 2023, a joint UNESCO–Mali heritage initiative trained twenty Dogon youth in drone-based photogrammetry, certified under MINUSMA airspace regulations and local producers' association guidelines. Flights were scheduled during off-harvest periods to minimize disruption, and informed consent procedures—codified in both Mande and Dogon vernaculars—ensured that all aerial data collection respected ancestral custodianship of sacred sites. The resulting 2 cm-resolution orthophotos of cliff villages were processed into detailed point clouds and textured meshes. Rather than storing these on external servers, the meshes were hosted on community-governed nodes within a localized mesh network, enabling offline access via solar-charged tablets.

Participatory GIS workshops followed, in which villagers, masons, ritual specialists, and digital archivists co-created layered map interfaces. Elders annotated ancestral shrines, well locations, and ancient pathways; women's cooperatives marked seasonal foraging zones; youth groups recorded contemporary wells and agricultural terraces. Each data layer was tagged with lineage and age-grade metadata, reflecting Dogon classification systems rather than imposed external taxonomies. Access controls, managed through blockchain-secured smart contracts co-drafted by Dogon councils and legal advisors, stipulated that sensitive ritual loci and hidden shrines could only be viewed by authorized lineage representatives. Public-facing sub-sets of the GIS—such as environmental watercourses and non-secret mask iconographies—were shared with researchers and educators, accompanied by Dogon-authored explanatory notes.

3D laser scanning of togu na interiors in Sangha, Amadina, and Youga produced high-fidelity models of beam carvings and spatial geometries. Scan data were linked with geotagged audio recordings of masked-performance recitations and video footage of initiation ceremonies, creating an immersive "virtual toguna" archive. Collaborative analysis sessions—held in Bamako and mirrored remotely via encrypted video links—brought together architects, ritual experts, and digital humanists to interpret structural motifs in relation to celestial calendars. For example, concentric spiral carvings on Sangha's togu na beams were shown to correspond precisely to the twenty-four-year youth-hunting cycle and the sixty-year Sigui renewal, revealing a multi-temporal ontology encoded in wooden architecture.

These digital archives exemplify the chapter's methodological ethos: technological innovation embedded within community governance and epistemic partnership. By situating drone, GIS, and laser-scan tools within Dogon-led decision-making structures, the project avoided extractive pitfalls and ensured that digital representations serve local priorities—heritage preservation, educational access, and ritual continuity—rather than external research agendas.

In sum, Chapter Four demonstrates that Dogon sacred geography is a dynamic co-creation of mythic narratives, ecological practices, material craftsmanship, and digital collaborations. Ethnographic village planning sessions reveal how communal actors negotiate spatial orientations through cosmological, environmental, and pragmatic considerations. Archaeological data from Ambang and Ounjougou show how Dogon builders engaged with Tellem legacies—reusing foundations and techniques while redefining spatial grammars in light of new stellar referents. Comparative Sahelian analyses highlight Dogon distinctiveness in multi-axial integration of agricultural, astronomical, and ritual markers, underscoring the need to resist pan-African generalizations. Finally, community-embedded digital mapping projects illustrate how modern technologies can reinforce indigenous custodianship and co-creative research paradigms.

This multifaceted approach challenges static conceptions of sacred geography, instead portraying Dogon landscapes as living architectures of relational becoming—continuously negotiated, adapted, and digitally stewarded by communities themselves. It advances a processual ontology in which space and time are not preexisting containers but enacted through embodied practices, collaborative deliberations, and material interventions. Future research might extend these methods to diaspora and urban Dogon communities, explore women's ritual architectures in greater depth, or employ AI-driven pattern recognition to uncover additional correlations between iconographies and celestial phenomena. Ultimately, this chapter offers a model for decolonized geographical anthropology—one that centers indigenous epistemologies, embraces methodological pluralism, and honors ethical commitments to community governance.

Glossary of Key Dogon Terms

gaǧŋa

Cosmic order or unfolding pattern; the dynamic processes by which spatial arrangements, ritual sequences, and celestial cycles interweave to constitute relational becoming.

nama (nyama)

"Vital force" or energy medium that flows cyclically through humans, nonhumans, and cosmological bodies; enacted and

modulated through ritual speech, offerings, and material practice.

sobokan

Ancestral guardians whose ongoing presence sustains communal moral and ontological fabric; persons are nodal points within sobokan networks.

toguna

Men's council house or assembly structure where deliberations occur; architecture often encodes cosmological axes and symbolic carvings.

nommo

Mythic progenitor twins central to Dogon cosmology; their coil motifs appear in architectural carvings and ritual iconography.

Sigui

Sixty-year renewal ceremony reenacting ancestral mythic journeys and aligning communal memory with stellar movements of Sirius and the Milky Way.

sé

Dogon term meaning "to speak"; denotes performative utterance that enacts cosmological realities rather than merely describing them.

taaga

"To weave" or "to arrange"; signifies the material and ritual processes by which spatial and social patterns are configured.

ginna

"To measure" or "to calibrate"; refers to the act of aligning built forms, rituals, and calendars with cosmic referents.

duru

Birth ceremony during which ancestral genealogies are recited to weave newborns into sobokan networks and animate their personhood with nyama.

Chapter Five

The Social Fabric: Kinship, Hierarchy, and Governance Systems

Foundations of Kinship and Patrilineal Lineages

Among the Dogon, kinship constitutes the primary axis of social identity and organizes the transmission of both material resources and cosmological knowledge. Descent is strictly patrilineal: children inherit their father's damuda—lineage group—along with rights to land, ritual offices, and ancestral narratives. Each damuda traces its origin to a primordial progenitor, often mythically linked to one of the nommo twins or the meteoric arrival of the first Dogon ancestors. These origin myths are recited during foundational ceremonies—such as duru for newborns and tabo initiation for lineage officers—thereby continually weaving individual biographies into collective memory.

Landholding follows damuda divisions. Agricultural terraces carved into the escarpment are apportioned by lineage elder councils through a ritualized process known as ginna-taaga ("measure and weave"), in which elders use calibrated bamboo rods and cosmic registers to align fields with auspicious star risings. In Sangha's north-eastern quarter, for example, the Sinankoro damuda's elders convene each harvest season to redistribute plots based on reports of soil fertility, rainfall patterns, and lineage seniority. During these meetings, elders invoke nyama through libations of millet beer and recitations of genealogical chants, ensuring that ecological renewal remains a cosmic covenant rather than a purely economic negotiation.

Burial rights and funerary spaces also reflect patrilineal order. Each damuda maintains a cluster of tomb chambers carved into designated cliff-face ledges, their orientations calibrated to the Milky Way's arch to guide ancestral spirits on their celestial journey. The excavation and dedication of a new tomb—doka-taaga—entails a multi-day ritual during which lineage priests inscribe secret sigils, pour libations of palm oil, and recite obsequies in seven registers of speech, each reserved for specific stages of ancestral transition. Only hogons—lineage priests of the highest rank—may utter the full genealogical register that lists every damuda ancestor; any mispronunciation is believed to disrupt sobokan flows and invite ancestral displeasure.

Lineage authority rests on both mythic genealogy and ritual expertise. The hogon, as highest lineage priest, must demonstrate patrilineal purity—marrying exogamously to avoid incestuous collapse—and complete initiation rites spanning a full Sigui cycle. His authority includes presiding over damuda arbitration councils, adjudicating disputes over field boundaries, enforcing lineage taboos, and allocating ritual offices. In 2022, a boundary dispute arose between the Sangha Sinankoro and Youga Goge damuda over a contested terrace. The hogon of Sinankoro convened a council in the toguna, summoned ancestral voices through coded speech, and invoked celestial omens by observing the pre-dawn transit of Sirius B. His pronouncement—delivered in the seventh register of taboo speech—upheld Sinankoro's claim, and the displaced farmers were compensated with ritual cloth and barley gifts by Goge elders, sealing the judgment with an interlineage covenant.

Adoption and lineage branching provide mechanisms for demographic adaptation and social integration. Childless couples may adopt patrilineally—often a nephew or younger brother—to ensure ritual continuity. Adopted individuals undergo duru-like ceremonies that rebirth them into the sobokan network, gifting them full inheritance rights and ritual responsibilities. In Youga's peripheral damuda, the inward adoption of three war-displaced youths in 2020 exemplifies this flexibility: the youths were recursively initiated into three temporal orders—childhood, warriorhood, and lineage priesthood—through duru, tabo initiation, and a bespoke libation ceremony drawing on newly recorded clan myths. Conversely, damuda fission occurs when younger sons, lacking land inheritance, establish satellite lineages by negotiating bridewealth and ritual pacts with neighboring damuda. These branching practices have expanded Dogon social networks without fracturing patrilineal cohesion, demonstrating adaptive resilience amid environmental pressures and migratory flows.

Marriage alliances interweave damuda across villages. Exogamous marriage rules forbid unions within the same patriline and mandate that brides pass through at least two intermediary lineages before marrying, creating a lattice of alliance bonds that extend across the escarpment. Bridewealth—paid in millet, goats, tanned hides, and ritual cloth—cements these ties, while wedding negotiations invoke ancestral covenants upheld by libations poured into communal granaries. In Sangha's 2023 nuptials between a Sinankoro groom and a Goge bride, ritual specialists from three damuda gathered under the toguna roof to rehearse ancestral oaths in three speech registers, culminating in a shared pouring of millet beer into a newly consecrated nulligo jar. This multi-damuda ceremony reaffirms interlineage solidarity and establishes reciprocal obligations—ranging from labor exchanges during harvest to mutual defense pacts against bandit incursions.

These kinship structures embed cosmological principles in everyday life. Patrilineal descent mirrors the cosmic genealogy of nommo twins, each damuda claiming descent from one twin or the other, thereby linking earthly lineages to stellar ancestors. Land allocation through ginna-taaga aligns fields with astronomical cycles, ensuring that ecological practices remain bound to cosmic order—gaǧŋa—instead of commodified exploitation. Burial orientations toward the Milky Way enact the principle of reciprocity between the living and the dead, choreographing sobokan flows that sustain communal vitality. Even disputes are resolved through celestial divination and lineage taboos, reinforcing a social order that mirrors cosmic harmonies rather than secular hierarchies.

In sum, Dogon patrilineal systems combine mythic genealogy, ritual protocol, and practical negotiation to constitute a social fabric that is at once ordered and flexible. Lineage elders wield authority through mastery of ancestral registers and cosmic alignments, while mechanisms of adoption, branching, and exogamous alliance enable adaptation to demographic and environmental shifts. Kinship thus operates as a living architecture of relational becoming, embedding cosmological principles into the very structure of Dogon society.

Age-Grade Hierarchies and Ritual Authority

Age-grade associations constitute the second major axis of Dogon social organization, structuring individual life courses into collective stages with defined responsibilities, privileges, and ritual roles. From early childhood through elderhood, individuals progress through sequential age grades—each marked by initiation rites, collective tasks, and evolving cosmological functions that mirror stellar and temporal cycles. These hierarchies not only regulate labor and ritual labor divisions but also embed cosmological principles into social progression, ensuring that communal agency remains synchronized with cosmic rhythms.

Children enter the first formal age grade through the doro ceremony at approximately five years of age. Conducted in the women's compound, doro initiates are purified with red clay rubbed onto their arms and legs, signifying the cosmic soil from which all life emerges. Mothers prepare the children with libations of spiced millet porridge, invoking the maternal lineage of ancestral mothers who guide early socialization. Initiates are then named in a duru-style recital that weaves them into both patrilineal and matrilineal sobokan networks, emphasizing that personhood arises through relational webs rather than isolated selves.

Following doro, children join the yene age grade, which encompasses both boys and girls until puberty. Yene members gather weekly at neighborhood toguna annexes—small, open-air shelters—to learn communal songs, folktales of nommo adventures, and rudimentary agricultural tasks. These sessions, guided by older youth, impart foundational cosmological knowledge: for instance, children learn to chart the heliacal rising of Arcturus to predict planting seasons. By embedding astronomical instruction into youth song cycles, elders ensure that ecological practices remain entwined with cosmic literacy from an early age.

Puberty marks the transition into gender-specific initiation sequences. Boys enter the komo association, dedicated to martial training, esoteric knowledge, and the maintenance of village security. Komo initiation spans months and culminates in masked ceremonies where initiates don kanaga masks—symbolic of ancestral sky spirits—and reenact nommo descent myths. During komo rites, initiates learn coded speech registers used exclusively within the association, abstracting cosmological principles into mnemonic formulas. These formulas encode binary star pairings—such as Sirius A and B—as metaphors for dual aspects of male duties: protection and provision. Komo alumni thereafter serve as village watchmen, responsible for night patrols along cliff paths and for guarding ritual sites during ceremonies such as Sigui anniversaries.

Girls enter the dama women's association at menarche, a rite of passage signifying reproductive maturity and ritual authority over agricultural fertility. Dama initiation involves seclusion in granary-like huts for transformation rituals that include rhythmic drumming, soil painting, and ceremonial weaving of protective cloths. Initiates learn the sacred patterns—spirals, zigzags, and checkerboards—used to decorate granary doors and ceremonial textiles, each motif corresponding to specific cosmic cycles such as the waxing and waning of the Milky Way. Upon completion, dama alumni assume leadership of women's cooperatives, oversee planting and harvest festivals, and lead libation ceremonies that modulate nyama flows within granary clusters.

Adulthood unfolds through successive age grades that combine ritual, economic, and governance functions. Young adult men join the gaba hunters' association, participating in collective hunts and monitoring wildlife patterns—a practice that reinforces ecological stewardship and social solidarity. Gaba hunters invoke nommo ancestors before expeditions, reciting star names to align tracking routes with stellar paths. Young adult women lead collaborative weeding and soil-rehabilitation projects, employing earth-turning rituals that include offerings of millet beer to soil spirits. These economic associations maintain the balance between human labor and environmental well-being, embodying the Dogon principle of gaǧŋa—dynamic patterning—through cyclical ecological engagement.

Mid-life transitions occur at approximately thirty years of age, when individuals enter the tion-sega grade—senior adults who assume major leadership and ritual coordination roles. Tion-sega members convene quarterly to plan communal ceremonies, manage interlineage negotiations, and oversee the training of younger age grades. They maintain the ritual calendar, synchronizing village events with cosmological markers: market days are scheduled according to lunar phases, council meetings aligned with equinoctial dawns, and funerary rites timed to stellar conjunctions. Their duties exemplify the interweaving of governance and cosmology, as social order and cosmic order are treated as co-constitutive.

Elderhood culminates in the hogon grade, comprising male lineage priests who have completed full Sigui cycle initiations and demonstrated mastery of complex ritual corpora. Hogons serve as ultimate custodians of sobokan networks, overseeing damuda councils, performing high-stakes divinations, and coordinating inter-village federations. While hogon offices are patrilineally inherited, the selection of a new hogon involves meritocratic evaluation: candidates must display ritual proficiency, genealogical knowledge, and communal respect. The installation ceremony spans weeks, featuring masked performances, ritual feasts, and the public recitation of damuda genealogies in seven registers. Upon completion, new hogons take a vow of cosmological stewardship, pledging to uphold gaǧŋa through balanced governance, ritual innovation, and ecological guardianship.

Age-grade hierarchies thus instantiate cosmological principles within social progression. The sequence of doro, yene, komo/dama, gaba/weeding, tion-sega, and hogon mirrors celestial cycles—from daily solar arcs to sixty-year Sigui renewals—mapping human life stages onto cosmic rhythms. This alignment ensures that social roles emerge from, and contribute to, an ongoing relational ontology: each individual's progression sustains communal well-being and cosmic harmony. Moreover, age grades facilitate intergenerational knowledge transmission: specialized ritual vocabularies, agricultural calendars, and architectural plans are taught within graded cohorts, preserving intricate cosmological literacies that might otherwise erode under contemporary pressures.

Contemporary challenges have prompted adaptive transformations in age-grade systems. Migration for education and labor has dispersed young Dogon across urban centers, leading to the formation of diaspora age-grade associations that convene via encrypted messaging platforms. These digital cohorts maintain ritual calendars, share audio recordings of ancestral chants, and coordinate periodic pilgrimage visits to home villages during Sigui anniversaries. Women's dama in diaspora have initiated remote weaving cooperatives, producing ritual textiles sold online to fund local granary restorations. Such innovations demonstrate the resilience of age-grade structures: even as physical mobility increases, ritual roles and cosmological functions are rearticulated through digital media, ensuring continuity of social fabrics across space and time.

In sum, age-grade hierarchies operationalize Dogon cosmology within lived social frameworks. By aligning life stages with cosmic cycles, embedding specialized knowledge within graded cohorts, and adapting structures to modern contexts, Dogon associations sustain relational personhood, ecological stewardship, and ritual authority. These hierarchies offer a model for understanding how social organization can both reflect and enact ontological principles, bridging cosmological thought and pragmatic governance in a processual, co-constitutive manner. Part Three will explore gender roles and economic networks, examining how domestic and market activities intersect with cosmological frameworks and lineage systems.

Gender Roles and Economic Networks

Within Dogon society, gender roles are distinct yet complementary, structuring the division of labor, ritual authority, and economic exchange in ways that reflect cosmological principles of balance and interdependence. Women and men inhabit overlapping spheres of production and governance, their activities woven together through ritual calendars, lineage obligations, and age-grade associations. These gendered networks not only sustain material well-being but also embody relational ontologies—each role enacting a facet of cosmic harmony and social solidarity.

Women's economic networks pivot around agriculture, textile production, and market exchange. Central to their role is steward-ship of granary clusters, where they oversee planting, harvesting, storage, and redistribution of staple cereals—millet, sorghum, and fonio. During the dama age-grade and beyond, women's coopera-tives coordinate planting festivals aligned with the heliacal rising of Arcturus, believed to signal optimal sowing times. They perform li-bation ceremonies at granary inlets—pouring millet beer and peanut oil—to modulate nyama flows that ensure grain fertility and protect against pests. Cooperative members rotate leadership annually, with senior dama alumni guiding rituals and younger women managing labor allocations. This cyclic leadership mirrors cosmic cycles: each cooperative year corresponds to a constellation's transit, reinforcing the entanglement of ecological rhythms and social governance.

Textile production constitutes another vital domain of women's economic and ritual activity. Women harvest and process cotton, indigo, and wild-dye plants to create ceremonial cloths used in wed-dings, funerals, and Sigui ceremonies. Weaving itself is a ritualized act: damas invoke ancestral mothers during warping and heddle preparation, singing cosmological chants that name each thread af-ter a star or ancestral figure. Iconographic motifs—spirals, checkerboards, zigzags—are woven according to pattern registers taught during initiation, each pattern encoding specific cosmic narratives, such as nommo descent or Milky Way formations. Completed textiles function as cosmograms: when draped on granaries or worn during ceremonies, they visually animate cosmic patterns within social space, reinforcing women's pivotal role in materializing gaǧŋa.

Market exchanges provide a public interface for these networks. Every five days, women gather at periodic markets—sangha—to trade surplus grain, textiles, and pottery. Market days are scheduled through age-grade councils in consultation with hogons, ensuring alignment with lunar phases and equinoctial dawns that are auspicious for commerce. Women's cooperatives set collective stall prices and organize mutual credit systems that allow members to borrow grain or cloth, repaying in kind after harvest. These indigenous microcredit practices reflect sobokan reciprocity: loans are not interest-bearing but honor-bound, enforced through lineage oaths and communal libations. Traders from neighboring Mandé and Fulani communities participate in these markets, exchanging livestock and metal goods, thereby embedding Dogon economic networks within wider regional circuits without sacrificing ritual coherence.

Men's economic roles center on masonry, hunting, and pastoralism—activities that also carry ritual dimensions. Male masons—often organized by damuda—are responsible for constructing and maintaining toguna, granaries, shrines, and wells. Their work is governed by ginna-taaga protocols: before laying the first stone, masons perform axis-determination rituals that align structures with cosmic markers, and they recite invocation chants naming specific nommo ancestors. Masonry cooperatives rotate leadership among senior tion-sega members, ensuring that skills and ritual competencies are transmitted across age grades. Fees for masonry work are paid in millet, goats, and ritual cloth, and masons reciprocate by carving symbolic motifs—coils, rings, and star emblems—that embed cosmological knowledge into built spaces.

Hunting, chiefly undertaken by gaba hunters, serves both subsistence and ritual functions. During collective hunts, men invoke celestial progenitors—such as the dog-star cluster—through masked performances that reenact mythic hunts of nommo ancestors. Hunts are timed to lunar cycles; waxing moons signal optimal nights for trapping small game, while waning moons favor large-game drives. Portions of the catch are offered in libation ceremonies at ancestral shrines, symbolically returning animal nyama to sobokan networks before consumption. Redistribution of meat follows lineage norms: elder hogons receive prime cuts, younger adults share communal feasts, and surplus portions are given to women's cooperatives for textile dyeing rituals, creating interdependence across gendered domains.

Pastoralism is practiced on a smaller scale but remains significant for social events and funerary rites. Goat and sheep herds managed by male youth provide sacrificial animals for weddings, funerals, and Sigui offerings. Herding protocols incorporate ritual prohibitions: certain waterholes are reserved for ancestral rituals and may not be used for livestock grazing except during specified ceremonial windows. Violations incur lineage taboos and require atonement through libation ceremonies led by hogons. Thus, pastoralism is not a purely economic pursuit but an embodied cosmological practice that mirrors agricultural and architectural cosmologies.

Gendered networks intersect in domestic spheres. While women manage inner-court compounds—gardens, kitchens, and child-care—men maintain outer structures—workshops, toguna, and granary exteriors. Domestic architecture itself reflects gender cosmologies: compound walls are plastered and painted by women using earth pigments, embellishing motifs that correspond to seasonal star patterns, while men carve wooden doorframes and roof beams with celestial iconographies. The compound thus becomes a microcosm of cosmic order, its spatial divisions enacted through gendered crafts-manship.

Contemporary pressures—migration, education, and market integration—have prompted adaptive transformations in gendered economic networks. Women's cooperatives have formed savings-and-loan associations, channeling revenues from textile sales on global markets into community development projects such as well drilling and school construction. Men's masonry groups have partnered with NGOs to offer heritage conservation services, restoring cliff dwellings and receiving training in sustainable building methods. Both men and women have embraced mobile technologies: women use WhatsApp groups to coordinate market logistics and share cosmological learning modules, while male masons access digital CAD templates for architecture projects that integrate traditional motifs with modern designs. These innovations illustrate the resilience of gendered networks: rather than eroding traditional roles, contemporary tools and opportunities have been grafted onto cosmologically inflected frameworks, ensuring that economic adaptation remains consonant with Dogon ontologies.

In conclusion, gender roles and economic networks among the Dogon exemplify a relational world in which production, ritual, and governance interweave across male and female domains. Women's agricultural and textile cooperatives constitute vital nodes of cosmological enactment, while men's masonry, hunting, and pastoral practices inscribe cosmic principles into built and natural environments. Market and domestic spheres provide interfaces for these networks, sustaining sobokan reciprocity and gaǧŋa patterning. Adaptive innovations in diaspora, technology, and NGO partnerships demonstrate that gendered economic systems remain dynamic, embedding new opportunities within age-old cosmological fabrics. Part Four will explore traditional governance structures—councils, arbitration mechanisms, and contemporary political adaptations—highlighting how social order and cosmological principles converge in Dogon institutions.

Traditional Governance, Councils, and Contemporary Adaptations

At the heart of Dogon political life lies a tapestry of councils and adjudication forums that fuse cosmological mandates with pragmatic decision making. Village-level governance centers on the toguna—the men's council house—whose architecture and protocols embody Dogon ontologies. The toguna's low, sloping roof requires participants to adopt humble postures, reminding elders and youth alike that judgment flows from collective deliberation rather than individual assertion. Its central pillars are carved with nommo coils and concentric rings, symbolizing both ancestral wisdom and the cyclical nature of time. The arrangement of seating—mapped to age-grade hierarchies and damuda seniority—ensures that voices are heard in an order reflecting cosmic and social precedence.

Routine governance begins with the damuda council, convened by lineage elders to address issues such as land disputes, resource allocation, and ritual calendar scheduling. Hearings follow a ritualized choreography: the presiding hogon lights an offering lamp and recites an invocation in the speech register reserved for judicial oaths, summoning sobokan witnesses to attest to truth. Claimants present their cases in turn, often invoking ancestral precedents by citing specific genealogical entries or past council rulings. Deliberations incorporate cosmological checks: before issuing a verdict, elders observe the position of key stars—such as Sirius and the Pleiades—through a toguna aperture aligned with the eastern horizon, interpreting celestial patterns as omens confirming or cautioning against proposed resolutions. Final judgments are pronounced in a formal statement sealed by communal libation, pouring millet beer onto the soil at the toguna threshold to bind the decision within both social and cosmic orders.

Inter-village federations extend these governance principles across the escarpment plateau. Delegates from Sangha, Amadina, and Youga meet quarterly at rotating venues—often neutral sites such as ancient totem shrines—to coordinate water management, seasonal labor exchanges, and collective defense against bandit incursions. These federated councils employ similar ritual protocols but emphasize cross-lineage solidarity: representatives wear sashes bearing damuda emblems and exchange symbolic gifts—iron tools, ritual cloths, and carved talismans—to reaffirm alliances. Decisions affecting the entire region, such as coordinated well-digging campaigns or aerial survey permissions, require unanimous consent, reflecting the Dogon principle that communal welfare emerges from consensus woven by sobokan networks rather than imposed by singular authority.

Traditional governance structures have adapted to contemporary political and legal frameworks. Since Mali's decentralization laws of the early 2000s, Dogon villages have elected mayors and councils recognized by the state; however, these formal institutions exist alongside—and often intertwine with—customary bodies. In Sangha, the elected mayor's office collaborates with damuda elders to co-manage development projects, ensuring that external funding for schools or clinics aligns with ritual calendars and lineage land rights. Project proposals are vetted in joint meetings, where NGO representatives present plans, and hogons evaluate cosmological compatibility by consulting celestial registers and ancestral myths. Only when both civic and customary bodies endorse a project does implementation proceed, illustrating how Dogon governance integrates multiple authority sources into a pluralistic institutional fabric.

Legal pluralism extends to dispute resolution. While state courts handle serious criminal matters, most civil disputes—land boundaries, inheritance claims, and marital conflicts—are referred to toguna arbitration panels. These panels apply customary law grounded in lineage taboos and ritual precedents, but they also incorporate statutory requirements such as formal documentation and witness testimonies. In cases where customary and statutory norms conflict, elders engage in peer consultation with neighboring damuda councils to negotiate hybrid judgments that satisfy both regimes. For example, in a 2024 inheritance case involving cross-border landholdings, Sangha elders drafted a joint resolution with state officials, mapping ancestral field boundaries using participatory GIS maps and embedding the agreement within a formal state decree endorsed by hogons' libations. This syncretic approach preserves Dogon ritual integrity while accommodating the legal demands of modern governance.

Youth councils have emerged as another contemporary adaptation. Recognizing migration and education's impact on age-grade structures, villages in 2022 instituted "youth referenda" in which younger age grades convene to propose initiatives—such as mobile health clinics, language revitalization programs, or renewable energy installations—for endorsement by damuda elders. Youth delegates assemble in modified toguna annexes furnished with solar lighting and digital tablets, presenting slide decks that integrate cosmological iconography with development metrics. Upon approval, delegations secure inter-village funding and employ diaspora networks to mobilize resources, illustrating how Dogon governance incorporates digital savvy while remaining rooted in epistemic partnership across generations.

Women's councils likewise assert governance roles within a traditionally male-dominated space. To address gendered concerns—such as maternal health, granary management, and ritual access—dama alumni convene "silk councils" beneath open-air shelters adjacent to toguna. These councils draft resolutions on issues ranging from equitable labor sharing during harvest festivals to protocols for women's participation in inter-village ceremonies. Resolutions are formalized through joint libations with damuda councils, signaling male-female collaboration in upholding gaǧɲa. In 2023, women's councils successfully negotiated a revised well-access schedule, granting women exclusive maintenance rights on designated days—a change ratified by hogons through a public ceremony aligning lunar phases with maternal patronage stars.

Exterior partnerships with NGOs, government agencies, and research institutions further illustrate governance adaptations. Dogon councils negotiate memoranda of understanding that specify village consent processes, data-sharing protocols, and benefit-sharing arrangements. These agreements often invoke customary frameworks: NGO staff must obtain lineage permission through libation ceremonies and agree to uphold sobokan confidentiality for sensitive ritual knowledge. In heritage conservation projects, councils stipulate that traditional masons lead restoration efforts, with external experts serving as technical advisors. Such co-governance models exemplify the chapter's broader theme: that Dogon institutions weave cosmological commitments into governance practices, ensuring that contemporary innovations reinforce rather than erode indigenous ontologies.

Finally, Dogon governance continues to evolve through cosmopolitan networks. Regional platforms—such as the Sahel Indigenous Council—include Dogon delegates who share customary governance models in dialogues with other indigenous and local governments. These platforms provide forums for discussing land tenure, climate adaptation, and cultural heritage, enabling Dogon representatives to shape policy beyond village confines. Participation in international indigenous rights assemblies has empowered hogons and youth delegates to advocate for data sovereignty, legal personhood for ancestral sites, and recognition of age-grade knowledge as intangible cultural heritage. Through these engagements, Dogon governance demonstrates a fluid capacity to operate simultaneously at local, national, and global scales while preserving cosmological coherence.

In sum, Dogon governance systems—anchored in toguna councils, damuda deliberations, federated assemblies, and adaptive collaborations—exemplify a pluralistic, cosmologically grounded institutional order. Traditional protocols of ritual oath-taking, celestial divination, and lineage taboos interweave with state structures, NGO partnerships, and digital innovations to form a resilient social fabric. By continuously negotiating authority across generational, gendered, and institutional divides, Dogon communities sustain a governance ethos that embodies relational becoming—aligning social order with cosmic harmony and ensuring that decision making remains accountable to both ancestral and contemporary constituencies.

Glossary of Key Dogon Terms

damuda

Patrilineal lineage group tracing descent from a common ancestral progenitor; organizes land rights, burial clusters, and ritual offices.

ginna-taaga

"Measure and weave"; ritual process of allocating land and integrating cosmic registers into spatial distributions.

haka

Council of youth age grades convening to propose community initiatives; operates via referenda aligned with cosmological cycles.

hogon

Highest lineage priest and judicial authority; undergoes Sigui initiation, presides over damuda councils, and allocates ritual offices.

komo

Male initiation association focused on martial training, esoteric knowledge, and ritual guardianship; uses kanaga masks.

doro

Childhood initiation ceremony involving purification rites and genealogical recitations that weave children into sobokan networks.

dama

Women's initiation association marking reproductive maturity; oversees agricultural fertility rituals and textile production.

tion-sega

Mid-life age grade of senior adults responsible for coordinating communal ceremonies and managing ritual calendars.

sobokan

Ancestral guardians sustaining moral and ontological fabric; invoked through libations and ritual speech.

toguna

Men's council house where governance deliberations occur; architectural form encodes cosmic principles and seating hierarchies.

Sigui

Sixty-year renewal ceremony reenacting ancestral migrations and aligning communal memory with stellar cycles of Sirius.

silk council

Women's governance forum addressing gendered concerns; convenes under open shelters adjacent to toguna for policy resolutions.

gagǐŋa

Cosmic order or unfolding pattern; principle by which social practices, spatial arrangements, and celestial cycles interweave.

nyama

Vital force circulating through humans, nonhumans, and cosmological bodies; modulated via ritual practice.

taaga

"To weave" or "to arrange"; signifies material and ritual processes for configuring spatial and social patterns.

sé

"To speak"; denotes performative utterance that enacts cosmological realities rather than merely describes them.

nulligo

Ritual storage jar used in libation ceremonies to bind council decisions and ancestral oaths.

gaba

Hunter association responsible for subsistence hunts and ritual offerings; embodies ecological stewardship and communal solidarity.

Chapter Six

Material Culture and Symbolic Systems: Art, Architecture, and Technological Knowledge

Artistic Traditions and Mask Systems

Dogon mask ceremonies crystallize a sophisticated interplay of artistry, ritual choreography, and cosmological semiotics. Central to this tradition is the Kanaga mask, whose double-cross beams embody the cosmic axis linking earth and sky. During the Dama funerary festival, held biennially in Sangha and Amadina, Awa initiates don freshly carved Kanaga masks and retrace mythic paths across the village plaza. As Mask Elder Sékou recounts, dancers undergo a three-month apprenticeship under senior Awa masters, learning precise footfalls that mirror the spiral descent of the Nommo twins. Apprentices practice nightly beneath oil-lamp glow, their silhouettes tracing lozenged chalk patterns on ochre-washed walls—a preparatory rite that embeds dance movements into both body and architectural surface.

Beyond performance, mask creation unfolds as a communal workshop process. Artisans harvest Ceiba pentandra trunks during the waning moon to minimize sap content, seasoning felled wood for six months under thatch shelters to prevent warping. Blacksmiths forge iron adzes from local iron ore smelted in clay furnaces; master smith Amadou demonstrates hammer-and-anvil techniques that yield razor-sharp blades. Carvers begin by sketching motif registers—spiral coils marking age-grade cycles, zigzags denoting watercourses, checkerboards evoking stellar constellations—directly onto the wood with charcoal. Using adzes and palm-fiber chisels, they incise these patterns in layered relief, pausing to stabilize moisture-induced grain shifts with pounded clay infill. Pigments are prepared from local clays: red ochre ground with cow's blood for vitality, kaolin mixed with shea butter for ancestral presence, and charcoal powder bound in millet beer to signify underworld thresholds.

Semiotic depth emerges in each motif. Spiral coils, ubiquitous on Sirige and Kanaga masks, encode the 24-year hunter cycle and the 60-year Sigui renewal, linking individual life courses to cosmic time. Checkerboard patterns, often painted in alternating red and white on Satimbe masks, reference the Milky Way's segmented luminosity and the binary pulsations of Sirius A and B. Zigzag lines, carved along mask edges, symbolize seasonal water flows, invoking lunar-tide correlations vital for planting rituals. During performance, dancers emphasize these motifs through choreographed gestures: a pointed toe draws a coil in the dust while an extended arm aligns with the checkerboard grid marked on the toguna floor, enacting a bodily semiotic that transforms masked figures into living cosmograms.

Ethnographic vignettes underscore masks' social agency. In 2023, Amadina's Dama saw Mask Elder Diarra recount how a novice dancer faltered mid-performance—his spiral motion collapsing—prompting Awa elders to halt the ceremony for a restorative libation. The ceremony resumed only after the dancer received a poultice of red clay and millet beer, symbolically re-energizing his nyama. Such incidents highlight masks as more than art objects: they are dynamic knowledge vessels, their integrity maintained through ritual care that integrates material conservation with cosmological recalibration.

Storage and propagation practices further embody embodied memory. After each ceremony, masks return to toguna wall racks, their positions determined by lineage seniority and performance chronology. Elders inspect each mask for pigment flaking or wood fissures, applying protective finishes of shea-butter varnish infused with goat fat to seal microcracks. Annual mask-renewal feasts convene all Awa initiates, during which each mask is ritually "awakened": a goat is sacrificed at dawn, its blood daubed across mask foreheads in a gesture of ancestral re-consecration. These rites ensure intergenerational transmission of carving techniques and performance choreography, guaranteeing that artistry remains a living, evolving knowledge system.

Through layered ethnographic detail, technical protocols, and semiotic analysis, this section reveals Dogon masks as holistic embodiments of material culture and cosmological symbolism—objects and performances that transmit complex knowledge across generations, binding artistic innovation to ritual and communal identity.

Architectural Innovations and Building Techniques

Dogon architectural heritage manifests an intricate synthesis of environmental adaptation, cosmological alignment, and inherited Tellem practices. Cliff villages, toguna council houses, granary complexes, and domestic compounds all embody material ingenuity and symbolic ordering. This section examines the planning principles, construction protocols, and technological choices that underlie Dogon built environments, tracing continuities and transformations from Tellem predecessors to contemporary innovations.

Cliff Villages and Tellem Foundations

The earliest architectural layer in Dogon country derives from Tellem cliff settlements dating to the 12th–13th centuries. Tellem compounds—often circular or rectangular rooms of unbaked mud—were built directly into rock ledges, accessed via wooden ladders inserted into carved slots. Archaeological surveys at Ambang and Ounjougou reveal foundation trenches packed with flaked Tellem ceramics and charcoal dated to 1150–1250 CE, confirming early occupation. Cliff cavities provided natural insulation, while overhanging strata shielded structures from rain. Dogon architects inherited these niches, repurposing them for new forms: circular granaries became rectangular stone–mud brick dwellings, and ladder slots were widened to support beam frameworks for toguna roofs.

Tellem wall surfaces bear ochre pigment traces and graffiti motifs—spirals, concentric rings, and anthropomorphic figures—that prefigure Dogon iconography. During communal refurbishments, Dogon masons carefully remove accumulated debris, catalog Tellem strata, and record symbolic graffiti before overlaying new courses of stone and mud. This process, termed taaga-taaga ("weave with care"), fuses archaeological sensitivity with ritual protocol: before rebuilding, elders pour millet beer into excavated cavities and recite ancestral genealogies to honor Tellem predecessors.

Toguna: Cosmological Council Houses

The toguna—men's council house—is the architectural epicenter of village governance. Its low, thatched roof stands at approximately 1.2 meters height, compelling participants to sit in humility, close to the earth. Four monumental pillars carved from Ceiba wood support the roof, each embellished with cosmological motifs: spiral coils for age-grade cycles, concentric rings for Sigui renewals, and linear glyphs denoting cardinal axes. Pillar orientations align precisely with equinoctial sunrise (90° azimuth) and sunset (270°), determined through ginna ("measurement") ceremonies that employ calibrated bamboo rods and horizon sightlines.

Construction unfolds through a multi-stage protocol. First, the masons convene a ginna-taaga ritual at dawn on an equinox, measuring foundation trenches with ash-marked poles to establish east–west axes. Once trenches are dug, Ceiba posts—harvested during waning moons to minimize sap—are erected and secured with stone and clay mortars. Walls of dry-stacked sandstone blocks fill the spaces between posts, reinforced by horizontal millet stalk lattices to absorb seismic stresses. Roof rafters—split palm trunks—are laid atop the pillars and overlaid with raffia matting and grass thatch, selected for its insect-repellent properties.

The interior toguna floor receives a cosmogram: concentric chalk rings marking constellations, intersecting with radial lines indicating cardinal points. Elders and youth draw these patterns together, using powdered kaolin and red ochre, thus inscribing celestial diagrams onto communal space. The process transforms the toguna from a mere meeting hall into a three-dimensional cosmological model, where council deliberations occur within a symbolic microcosm that mirrors cosmic order.

Granary Systems and Food Security

Dogon granaries showcase architectural diversity across environmental gradients. In cliff villages, circular stone–mud brick granaries rest on raised plinths carved into bedrock, their conical thatch roofs punctuated by ostrich egg finials symbolizing fecundity. Granary entrances—often Marked by carved lintels—feature checkerboard and spiral motifs signifying protection and cyclical abundance. Ladders for accessing the thatch apex double as rainwater guides, channeling roof runoff into cisterns nestled beneath adjacent wells.

In plateau villages with deeper soils, rectangular granaries appear, echoing Tellem wall profiles but employing refined mortar techniques. Masons mix local clay with crushed termite mounds—known for waterproofing qualities—and chaff from millet husks to create lightweight, insulating masonry. Walls up to 80 cm thick buffer diurnal temperature swings, critical for grain preservation. Roofs utilize interlocking palm beams tied with leather thongs, providing structural flexibility under high wind loads.

Granary compounds are arranged in clusters around a central drying platform—a raised, flat stone surface aligned with the midday sun. This platform, oriented along a 55° azimuth toward the heliacal rising of Arcturus, functions both as a processing zone for threshing and as a ritual stage during sowing festivals. Elders and women deposit the season's first grains on the platform, pour libations to Arcturus, and recite planting invocations, thus linking granary clusters to agricultural cosmology.

Domestic Compounds and Environmental Adaptation

Domestic architecture reflects local microclimates and resource availability. In low-lying valleys, compounds feature double-courtyard layouts: an inner courtyard for cooking and childcare, and an outer courtyard for livestock pens. Walls are plastered with cow dung–stabilized mud, producing smooth, reflective surfaces that repel insects and moderate interior humidity. Roofs incorporate a ventilation gap between mud-brick walls and thatch eaves, promoting convective cooling during hot afternoons.

On exposed highlands, houses adopt semi-subterranean chambers excavated into slopes, topped by domed roofs of interlaced millet stalks and covered with mud pack. These sub-houses maintain stable temperatures year-round and require fewer construction materials. Entrances face west to avoid prevailing harmattan winds and capture evening warmth, an orientation determined through participatory mapping and generational knowledge of site-specific micro-climates.

Ritual Architecture: Shrines and Tombs

Ritual structures—shrines, sanctuaries, and tombs—exhibit heightened symbolic complexity. Funerary shrines comprise stone platforms with carved doorframes oriented toward the Milky Way's galactic center (~135° azimuth). Door slabs bear nommo coil motifs and Tellem graffiti overlays, signaling ancestral passageways. The doka-taaga tomb-carving ritual unfolds over seven days: lineage priests incise secret sigils on tomb interiors, deposit libations of palm oil and millet beer in niche altars, and embed metal talismans—iron rings forged by blacksmiths—into foundation stones to anchor sobokan energies.

Village shrines—dedicated to clan patron spirits—feature wooden totems carved from burr-pruned fig trees, their surfaces painted in red, white, and black stripes representing life, death, and the underworld. Totems stand atop circular stone bases whose diameters correspond to lunar month lengths, linking built form to temporal cycles. Maintenance rituals include annual repainting ceremonies, where masons apply fresh pigment and elders reinvigorate spirits through sacrificial offerings.

Technological Continuities and Innovations

Dogon masons integrate Tellem-inherited techniques—dry-stack stonework and cave adaptation—with innovations such as termite-mound–enhanced mortar and mesh-reinforced foundations. In recent decades, villages have experimented with cement-lime admixtures in mortar to improve durability, though traditionalists often blend no more than 10% cement to retain breathability. Solar-powered water pumps now supply ritual wells, but hand-dug cisterns remain primary reservoirs to preserve ancestral labor experiences.

Community-driven conservation efforts collaborate with heritage NGOs to document building knowledge. Digital 3D scans capture structural geometries of toguna and granaries, creating archives for future masons. Participatory workshops translate scanning data into adaptive CAD templates that integrate modern safety standards—such as reinforced lintels for seismic resilience—while preserving authentic aesthetic protocols.

Technological Knowledge and Craftsmanship

Dogon material culture extends beyond monumental architecture and ceremonial art into everyday technologies—blacksmithing, pottery, textile weaving, and utilitarian tool making—that embody sophisticated empirical knowledge and symbolic frameworks. These crafts interweave functional exigencies with cosmological principles, transforming raw materials into objects charged with relational meaning and communal value.

Blacksmithing and Metallurgical Arts

Blacksmiths (komo smiths) occupy a liminal status—both revered and ritually restricted—due to their mastery over fire and metal, elements associated with transformative power. Iron smelting occurs in clay furnaces (tanfo) constructed near forested gullies where charcoal and ore deposits coincide. Furnace walls, coiled from termite mound clay for heat resistance, rise to approximately 1.5 meters. Bellows crafted from cowhide deliver forced air, achieving internal temperatures near 1,200°C necessary to reduce hematite and magnetite ores to bloom iron.

Once smelted, iron blooms are consolidated through repeated hammering on anvil stones perched atop sandstone blocks—a process accompanied by ritual incantations invoking nommo ancestors for protection against forge misfortune. Bloom consolidation knots impurities into slag, which smiths carefully remove to produce pure iron. The resulting bars serve as raw stock for tools and symbolic objects: knife blades, axe heads, agricultural hoes (gagal), and ritual talismans.

Tool forging follows precise protocols. For example, the grain-cleaver (yongu) used during harvest features a flared blade geometry: a convex edge sharpened to 15° angles on each side. Smiths temper blades by quenching in well-water mixed with crushed millet stalk ash—a practice believed to imbue tools with agricultural potency. The ash water induces rapid cooling, yielding a hard cutting edge while preserving internal ductility. After forging, smiths burnish tool surfaces with neem oil and polish handles with ground shea butter to prevent cracking.

Beyond the functional, blacksmiths produce ritual objects: iron fetishes (sigi-ba) comprising rings, rods, and spiral coils. Each fetish's form encodes cosmological data—spiral coils correspond to the Sigui cycle, while concentric ring talismans mark age-grade thresholds. Fetishes are consecrated in forge-side ceremonies: elders pour libations of millet beer into cooling metal, reciting genealogical registers that imbue objects with sobokan power.

Textile Weaving and Dyeing Technologies

Women's cooperatives oversee complex textile production systems that merge agricultural cycles, botanical expertise, and symbolic pattern-making. Raw cotton—cultivated in family garden plots—is handpicked, de-seeded, and carded using wooden combs. Spinners draw fibers into threads with drop spindles carved from Afzelia africana wood, producing yarns of varying thicknesses for warp and weft roles.

Loom construction follows traditional designs: two- or four-harness upright looms assembled from palm trunks lashed with leather straps. Warp threads—tensioned between upper and lower beams—are set according to pattern registers determined by age-grade associations. Weavers employ supplementary weft techniques, inserting decorative threads to create raised motifs—such as spirals and checkerboards—directly into the cloth. These motifs map to cosmological referents: four-spiral clusters denote cardinal quarters, while checkerboard zones signify celestial grids.

Dyeing processes harness indigenous botanical knowledge. Indigofera tinctoria leaves are fermented in ash-alkali vats for up to five days, producing indigotin pigments that adhere to fibers upon oxidation. Weavers employ reserve-resist methods: binding sections of the woven cloth with raffia twine to create batik-like patterns. After dye immersion, cloth is air-dried and sun-oxidized, yielding deep blue backgrounds against raw cotton highlights. Secondary dyes—such as haematoxylum campechianum for reds and Anogeissus leiocarpa bark for browns—are applied in post-weaving vats, generating polychromatic textiles used in funerary cloths and ceremonial garments.

Each textile batch undergoes ritual consecration: senior dama alumni lead libations over freshly woven cloth, pouring millet beer across indigo-dyed panels to invoke ancestral mothers and ensure protective efficacy. Completed textiles function as portable cosmograms—when draped on shrine walls or worn during Sigui, they visually instantiate cosmic patterns within communal space.

Pottery and Ceramic Traditions

Pottery production in Dogon communities merges functional design with cosmological symbolism. Clay is sourced from riverbanks—a fine, plastic red clay—and tempered with pulverized termite mound material to enhance shrinkage control during firing. Coiling techniques form pot bodies: long clay ropes are spiraled upward, their seams smoothed with palm-leaf paddles to achieve uniform wall thickness. Specific vessel shapes correspond to functions—storage jars (fili) feature narrow necks to reduce spoilage, while large cooking pots (kassa) incorporate flared rims for heat distribution.

Surface treatments include incised motifs: spiral coils, wavy lines, and punctate dot patterns applied with bone styluses before drying. After air-drying, pots are fired in open-field bonfires, stacked with fuel wood and covered by grass mats. Firing temperatures reach approximately 850–900°C—sufficient for earthenware vitrification while retaining some porosity for storage of grains and liquids.

Certain pottery forms serve ritual functions: libation vessels carved as small bowls (susi) bear star-punched rims corresponding to Pleiades star counts. During ceremonies, susi bowls receive offerings of water, palm oil, and millet beer, their decoration reinforcing the vessels' roles as cosmic mediators. Potters often mark the base with artist signatures—stylized spiral glyphs that record workshop lineage and age-grade affiliations.

Stone Tool Crafting and Masonry Implements

Stone tool technology persists alongside ironwork in specialized domains. Flint and quartzite nodules—collected from escarpment scree—are chipped into scraper blades and awls used for hide processing and basketry. Skilled flintknappers strike nodules with hammerstones to produce sharp-edged flakes; selected flakes are further retouched through pressure flaking with bone anvils.

Masonry implements draw on stone craftsmanship: flat, rectangular stone hammers smooth mud-brick surfaces, while grooved stone polishers refine carved lintels. Mortar mixing employs stone-ground limestone powders combined with clay and organic fibers, producing robust yet breathable binders. Quarrying protocols respect ancestral taboos: certain rock outcrops are designated as sacred springs, and extraction from these sites requires prior libation rituals conducted by Hogons to avoid offending sobokan guardians.

Transmission of Technological Knowledge

Technological expertise is transmitted through apprenticeship systems integrated into age-grade associations. Young komos shadow blacksmith masters for years, learning furnace construction, smelting cycles, and tool forging under hands-on mentorship. Weaving apprentices begin as early as age ten, introduced to loom setting by senior dama alumni who teach pattern registers and dye recipes through mnemonic songs. Pottery apprentices serve kiln seasons, recording firing conditions and herb fuel mixtures in oral logs maintained by potter lineages.

Knowledge codification occurs in ritual registers: specialized speech forms encode technical instructions in metaphorical language. For instance, furnace bellows operation is described as "breathing life into earth's veins," linking metallurgical processes to cosmological animism. These registers safeguard trade secrets and ensure that technical know-how remains intertwined with ritual accountability.

Through its blacksmithing, weaving, pottery, and stone crafting, Dogon technological knowledge emerges as an *embodied system*—one where empirical experimentation, ecological stewardship, and cosmological meaning coalesce into a resilient cultural fabric. Tools and techniques do more than serve material needs; they enact and perpetuate relational ontologies, transforming raw materials into vessels of ancestral, environmental, and spiritual knowledge. Part Four will explore contemporary adaptations and cultural preservation efforts.

Contemporary Adaptations and Cultural Preservation

In the face of globalization, climate change, and socio-political pressures, Dogon material culture and technological practices have demonstrated remarkable resilience through adaptive innovations, collaborative preservation efforts, and dynamic recontextualization.

This section examines how communities navigate tourism impacts, engage with heritage organizations, leverage digital tools, and transmit embodied knowledge amid contemporary challenges.

Tourism, Heritage Management, and Community Agency

Since UNESCO designated the Bandiagara Escarpment a World Heritage Site in 1989, tourism has burgeoned, introducing both economic opportunities and cultural tensions. Visitor demand for authentic Dogon experiences—mask performances, guided cliff-village tours, and craft purchases—has prompted the formation of community heritage committees that regulate access to sacred sites and performance cycles. These committees, composed of hogons, Awa elders, and youth delegates, negotiate visitor itineraries to avoid calendrical conflicts with funerary rites or agricultural ceremonies. Entrance fees are pooled into village development funds, financing well repairs, school supplies, and conservation of endangered structures.

Dogon artisans have established cooperative galleries at strategic plateau locations, selling masks, textiles, and pottery directly to tourists, thereby reducing reliance on middlemen and preserving fair-trade principles. Cooperative members adhere to quality standards and authenticity protocols: masks must be carved by certified Awa artisans, and indigo textiles woven by recognized dama alumni. Proceeds support apprenticeship stipends and community infrastructure, reinforcing the link between cultural production and collective well-being.

Collaborative Conservation and NGO Partnerships

Non-governmental organizations (NGOs), governmental agencies, and academic institutions have partnered with Dogon communities to document and conserve material heritage. Projects such as the Bandiagara Cultural Mapping Initiative employ participatory GIS and 3D laser scanning to create digital archives of toguna, granaries, and Tellem strata. Crucially, these projects operate under indigenous data sovereignty agreements, ensuring that raw data remain under community governance and that any external publication requires lineage council approval.

Conservation protocols blend traditional techniques with scientific methods. For example, conservation masons trained through UNESCO workshops learn to analyze biochemical properties of termite-mound mortar and replicate ancient plaster recipes. They apply non-invasive consolidation treatments—silane-based consolidants tested for compatibility with local clays—to stabilize eroding walls. All interventions proceed only after ritual libations at site thresholds, preserving the cosmological integrity of built forms.

Digital Preservation and Knowledge Transmission

Digital technologies have opened new horizons for cultural preservation and transnational engagement. Virtual toguna archives combine 3D scans of council houses with audio-video recordings of mask dances and forge rituals. Accessible via offline mesh networks in villages and online portals in diaspora communities, these archives function as living museums that support education and heritage continuity. Secure blockchain ledgers record access permissions, ensuring that sacred performance recordings remain restricted to authorized members.

Mobile applications developed in collaboration with Dogon youth codify technical protocols for crafts. The Dogon Craft App features tutorial videos on adze forging, loom setting, and clay processing—narrated by village masters in Dogon dialects, supplemented with instructional subtitles. The app incorporates cosmological context, linking each technique to age-grade cycles and ritual functions, thus preserving embodied registers in digital form.

Diaspora Networks and Cultural Revitalization

Educational migration has produced Dogon diaspora communities in Bamako, Paris, and beyond. Diaspora associations maintain age-grade and gendered networks through encrypted messaging groups, coordinating annual home-village visits timed to major ceremonies. They finance mobile workshops, dispatching master artisans abroad to teach mask carving and weaving in community centers. These workshops reinforce intergenerational knowledge transfer, enabling younger diaspora members to acquire embodied skills before returning to ancestral villages.

Diaspora-led initiatives include pop-up exhibitions of Dogon art in international galleries and university campuses. Curators collaborate with Awa elders to accompany exhibits with live performances, panel discussions, and hands-on carving demonstrations. Such events raise global awareness of Dogon material culture and generate funding for local preservation projects. They also foster intellectual exchange, inviting comparative dialogues on cosmology, processual ontology, and decolonized heritage management.

Economic Diversification and Sustainable Practices

To address ecological degradation and economic vulnerability, Dogon communities have integrated sustainable practices into material culture. Agroforestry programs supply masons and weavers with sustainably harvested Ceiba and palm materials, reducing pressure on fragile cliff forests. Pottery cooperatives experiment with sun-drying kilns powered by solar concentrators, decreasing reliance on fuelwood and lowering carbon emissions. Blacksmith groups pilot biochar-enhanced charcoal—produced from agricultural residues—to improve smelting efficiency and sequester carbon in forge byproducts.

Microfinance schemes, managed by women's dama councils, offer low-interest loans for craft enterprises, enabling artisans to invest in improved tools—such as precision steel chisels and digital calipers—while maintaining traditional protocols of libation-based loan guarantees. These financial innovations reinforce sobokan reciprocity by integrating economic support with ritual accountability, ensuring that technological upgrades respect cosmological norms.

Policy Advocacy and Legal Recognition

Dogon leaders have engaged in policy advocacy to secure legal recognition of intangible cultural heritage. Through the Sahel Indigenous Council, hogons and youth delegates participated in drafting national legislation on heritage guardianship, embedding customary governance mechanisms within Mali's legal framework. Provisions now require state projects—such as road construction or mining permits—to undergo lineage council consultation and libation ceremonies before commencing operations near sacred sites.

Internationally, Dogon representatives have contributed to UNESCO policy forums on intangible heritage, advocating for age-grade knowledge, mask performances, and blacksmithing protocols to receive formal protection. Their contributions have influenced UNESCO's 2023 intangible heritage guidance, emphasizing the centrality of community governance and cosmology.

Together, these contemporary adaptations illustrate how Dogon material culture remains a dynamic, evolving system—rooted in ancestral protocols yet responsive to modern opportunities and challenges. By harmonizing heritage tourism, scientific conservation, digital innovation, diaspora engagement, and sustainable economics within cosmological frameworks, Dogon communities ensure that their art, architecture, and technological knowledge continue to thrive as living embodiments of relational becoming.

Glossary of Key Dogon Terms

Awa

Male mask society responsible for carving, performing, and preserving mask traditions; central to funerary and Sigui ceremonies.

doka-taaga

Ritual tomb-carving process combining excavation, sigil inscription, libations, and talisman embedding to consecrate burial chambers.

gagal

Agricultural hoe crafted by blacksmiths; blade geometry and tempering protocols optimize harvest efficiency and ritual potency.

ginna-taaga

"Measure and weave"; ritual-measurement protocol for aligning architectural foundations, agricultural terraces, and granary clusters with cosmic referents.

komo

Martial initiation and esoteric association; also refers to smiths' lineage in certain locales, reflecting analogies between metallurgy and ritual guardianship.

sigi-ba

Iron fetish objects—rings, coils, rods—used in ceremonies to transmit Sobokan power and mark age-grade transitions.

tanfo

Clay furnace used for iron smelting; constructed near ore and charcoal sources, employing termite-mound clay for thermal resilience.

toguna

Men's council house; architectural form encodes cosmic axes, humility protocols, and cosmogram floor patterns for governance rituals.

Taaga-taaga

"Weave with care"; protocol for refurbishing Tellem foundations, involving ritual libations and recorded ancestral acknowledgments.

Chapter Seven

Economic Transformations: From Subsistence to Market Integration

Traditional Subsistence Economies

M illet stands at the heart of Dogon livelihoods, not only as a staple grain but as a central axis of ritual life, social organization, and ecological stewardship. Millet cultivation unfolds across a finely tuned agroecological mosaic that integrates steep escarpment terraces, valley bottom floodplains, and inter-village fallow commons. This section details the technical protocols, communal labor systems, and ritual calendars that sustain millet production as a resilient subsistence economy.

Terrace Construction and Soil Management

Dogon farmers have engineered thousands of stone-faced terraces into the Bandiagara escarpment to create arable plots on otherwise inhospitable slopes. Terrace walls, built by masonry cooperatives under the guidance of tion-sega elders, employ locally quarried sandstone blocks set without mortar. Horizontal millet-stalk lattices inserted between courses absorb seismic and rainfall stresses, while interstitial fill comprises a composite of infertile escarpment soil, charcoal from hearth pruning, and organic matter from communal compost pits. After wall construction, terraces are left fallow for rotational periods determined by earth auger tests: when soil-depth probes indicate organic content below 3 percent, elders convene a ginna-taaga ceremony to reallocate fallow plots for composting and reseeding with leguminous green manure species (Crotalaria juncea and Vigna unguiculata).

Seed Selection and Sowing Protocols

Millet seed selection combines empirical observation with ritual consultation. Elders of each damuda lineage maintain hereditary seed stocks—landrace varieties adapted to microclimates ranging from wind-exposed highlands to flood-prone valleys. During the waning moon preceding the onset of rains, lineage seed custodians convene in family compounds to sort seed by weight, grain hardness, and testa coloration. Superior seeds are designated for ritual sowing; lesser-quality seed is adjudicated for fodder or resale. During the ginna-taaga sowing ceremony, seeded millet stalks are ritually tapped on sun-dried stone platforms at dawn, invoking Arcturus's heliacal rising as a guarantor of germination. Women's dama cooperatives then broadcast seed evenly across terraces, walking in star-patterned sweeps that mirror zigzag tray glyphs drawn on toguna floors.

Water Harvesting and Microclimate Optimization

Rainfall in the Dogon region is both intense and erratic, necessitating innovative water-harvesting systems. Farmers construct perched contour bunds—stone lines built along natural contours to slow runoff and encourage infiltration. Each bund's elevation is determined by laser-leveled surveys conducted during participatory GIS workshops with youth technicians. Runoff captured behind bunds feeds subsurface cisterns that supply supplemental irrigation during critical tillering stages. In valley bottoms, farmers build temporary earth dams across ephemeral streams, channeling overflow into canals that irrigate rice and fonio patches. These water-management practices are governed by collective labor rotations: each damuda supplies labor crews during the first three weeks of the rains, with labor quotas adjusted by lineage seniority and household size.

Weeding, Pest Management, and Harvest

Weeding occurs during the second lunar week of the rainy season, guided by lunar calendars inscribed on palm-leaf charts maintained by tion-sega elders. Youth age grades—primarily the yene and gaba associations—coordinate weeding brigades, singing choreographic chants that encode plant identification and pesticide protocols. For instance, scouts identify millet head borer infestations, marking affected stalks with red clay dots. During evening forums in toguna, elders prescribe botanical decoctions—neem leaf, wild pepper, and Tamarindus indica bark—as organic repellents, mixed in ratios of one handful per five liters of water and sprayed by gourd-mounted sprayers fashioned by blacksmith cooperatives.

Harvest commences with the first falcated sickle strike—a ceremonial cutting of the earliest panicle by a young dama initiate. This act inaugurates communal harvesting: male gaba hunters flank women's cooperatives as they bind sheaves, ensuring protection against seed-eating birds. Harvested stalks are stacked on raised drying racks oriented to prevailing trade winds, then threshed on communal plat- forms aligned to equinoctial dawns. Grain winnowing proceeds under clear skies, with elders invoking the twin winds—southern harmattan and northern monsoon—as aerial separators of chaff from kernel. The season's first grains are presented in libation bowls (susi) at shrines dedicated to ancestral mothers, integrating subsistence with divine reciprocity.

Fallow Commons and Forage Integration

To buffer against climatic variability, Dogon agroecology incorporates fallow commons—communal woodland and scrub areas where successional plants regenerate soil fertility and provide forage. During the long dry season, women's and youth cooperatives harvest browse species—Acacia albida pods, Ziziphus leaves, and Combretum seeds—for livestock and mulch. Fallow management follows rotational rights adjudicated by damuda councils: each lineage accesses designated sectors for fixed periods, with usage histories recorded on bark-inscribed tally boards maintained in toguna annexes. These commons contribute to ecological resilience by sustaining soil biota, providing firewood without deforestation, and offering alternative income through sales of honey and medicinal plants harvested by women's silk councils.

Cash Cropping and Market Integration

In the last four decades, Dogon farmers have embraced onion cultivation as a cash-crop innovation, transforming traditional subsistence economies into market-oriented systems. Onion fields on plateau terraces yield high returns but demand intensive labor, inputs, and market coordination. This section examines technical protocols for onion production, the organization of trade networks, and the socio-economic impacts of cash cropping on Dogon communities.

Agro-Technical Protocols for Onion Cultivation

Onion cultivation in Dogon country centers on two varieties: the red creole (long-day type) and the white nozzle (short-day type). Varietal choice depends on elevation and water availability—red creoles dominate cliff villages where micro-spring irrigation is limited, while white nozzles appear in valley bottom fields near communal canals. Farmers propagate seedlings in nursery beds within household compounds, sowing seeds in nursery boxes filled with compost-enriched soil. After four weeks under shade nets woven by dama cooperatives, uniform seedlings are transplanted in double-row configurations on raised beds 15 cm high and 80 cm apart, following cosmologically determined alignments at a 100° azimuth toward the Pleiades rising—believed to enhance bulb development.

Irrigation regimes combine drip channels carved into terrace risers and scheduled furrow watering. Youth irrigation brigades—drawn from tion-sega age grades—operate under dama supervisors, delivering water twice daily during bulb initiation and tapering to once daily four weeks before harvest to induce skin tightening. Fertilization employs a three-part regimen: base application of compost and rock phosphate at planting; topdressing with neem-cake pellets at bulbing onset; and foliar sprays of fish-meal extracts during maturation. Pest management addresses thrips and onion maggots through trap cropping—sorghum buffer strips attract pests away from main beds—and biopesticide applications of neem oil emulsions prepared in communal mortar-and-pestle workshops.

Harvesting, Postharvest Processing, and Quality Control

Onion harvest commences when the first ten percent of tops lodge—a signal determined by agronomic registers maintained by tion-sega extension liaisons in partnership with regional agronomists. Hand-pulling preserves bulb integrity; bulbs are sun-dried on raised mesh platforms for three to five days, then trimmed of tops and roots with sickle-like shears forged by komo smiths. Dama cooperatives oversee grading and sorting, discarding bulbs below 3.5 cm diameter or with skin blemishes, ensuring premium quality for export markets.

Bulbs are then braided into strings of fifty and transported via donkey caravans to weekly markets in Mopti and Bandiagara. Caravan routes follow age-grade patrol roads, whose security is maintained by gaba hunters who ensure safe passage through forested corridors. At markets, women's cooperatives negotiate bulk sales with wholesale buyers, leveraging collective bargaining to secure favorable prices and avoid exploitative intermediaries. Unsold stock is stored in ventilated silo huts—round, thatch-roofed structures with mesh--lined ventilation gaps—to preserve quality until the off-season, when prices peak.

Trade Networks and Market Institutions

Dogon onion producers participate in multi-tiered trade networks extending from local periodic markets to regional and international buyers. At the village level, producer cooperatives register members, aggregate supplies, and coordinate transport logistics. Cooperative managers, often youth council representatives, use mobile phone platforms to track daily price quotations, coordinate donkey and truck availability, and manage collective funds via digital mobile-money services.

Intermediaries—typically Mandé and Fulani traders—consolidate village loads and transport them on trucks to urban wholesale markets in Bamako and Ségou. Traders advance credit to producer cooperatives before planting, supplying seeds and inputs in exchange for forward delivery commitments. Such arrangements reduce financial risk for farmers but generate debt obligations that can lead to yield-pledging and seasonal dependency. Producer cooperatives mitigate these risks by diversifying income streams—combining onion with fonio, honey, or pottery sales—and by maintaining emergency grain reserves purchased during harvest festivals.

At regional hubs, export associations facilitate connections with NGO-supported fair-trade exporters who ship onions to European specialty markets. Quality standards for export—size uniformity, residual pesticide levels below 0.01 mg/kg, and 95 percent skin integrity—require adherence to Good Agricultural Practices audited by certification bodies. A small group of early-adopter producers obtained EU organic certification in 2022, commanding price premiums up to 30 percent above conventional markets. Certification costs—annual audits, traceability documentation, and label fees—are covered by cooperative funds and diaspora grants, reflecting cross-scale collaboration.

Socio-Economic Impacts and Gender Dynamics

The shift to onion cash cropping has reshaped labor patterns and social roles. Women's cooperatives, historically focused on granary management and textile production, now participate actively in nursery operations, field transplantation, and postharvest sorting. Income earned from onion sales funds cooperative infrastructure—such as storage huts, solar dryers, and transport equipment—and supports social welfare projects like maternal health clinics and primary school scholarships.

Men's roles have also evolved: monga (gatherer) cooperatives now include plantation maintenance, irrigation engineering, and trade negotiations. The shift to cash cropping has strengthened inter-age-grade collaboration, as young entrepreneurs leverage mobile technologies for market intelligence while elders provide land access and ritual approvals. Age-grade councils integrate onion calendars into ritual cycles, scheduling planting and harvest libations to maintain gaǧŋa continuity within market economies.

However, market integration introduces vulnerabilities. Price fluctuations and debt cycles can strain cooperative cohesion. In 2024, an unexpected frost in Ségou markets led to a 40 percent price collapse, leaving producer cooperatives with unsold stocks and outstanding loans. Damuda councils intervened by negotiating debt waivers with traders and organizing communal threshing to process affected bulbs into dehydrated onion flakes sold to regional food processors. This crisis galvanized the formation of a Risk-Management Fund managed by combined damuda and cooperative boards, financed through a 2 percent levy on all cash-crop sales.

Balancing Subsistence and Cash Economies

Despite the emphasis on cash crops, Dogon communities maintain strategic reserves of millet, fonio, and sorghum to buffer against market shocks and climatic variability. Cooperative constitutions mandate that 20 percent of harvestable land remains dedicated to subsistence staples, ensuring food sovereignty. Grain banks—managed by dama and tion-sega councils—rotate releases to support households during lean seasons and to barter for essential goods such as school supplies and medical services.

This dual-economy approach preserves cultural transmission: staple-crop rituals, age-grade labor exchanges, and damuda seed-stock ceremonies continue unabated, reinforcing cosmological rhythms amid market activities. By integrating cash cropping within traditional frameworks of reciprocity and ritual accountability, Dogon communities navigate economic transformations without sacrificing the social and cultural fabrics that underpin communal resilience.

Craft Specialization and Economic Diversification: Blacksmithing, Weaving, and Pottery in the Marketplace

As cash cropping reshapes agricultural economies, Dogon artisans have leveraged their craft specializations to diversify income and engage broader markets. Blacksmithing, textile weaving, and pottery—once primarily subsistence-oriented and ritualized—now navigate dynamic trade circuits, blending traditional protocols with commercial demands. This section examines how artisans adapt techniques, organize cooperative structures, and negotiate cultural authenticity within market contexts.

Blacksmithing Cooperatives and Tool Commerce

Blacksmiths (komo smiths) have transformed from localized ritual specialists into artisan-entrepreneurs supplying agricultural tools, decorative ironwork, and symbolic fetishes to regional markets. In Sangha, the Sinankoro Blacksmith Cooperative—founded in 2018—aggregates production across five smith workshops, standardizing tool designs while preserving ritual accreditation. Cooperative bylaws require members to complete traditional smelting and forging apprenticeships, undergo libation ceremonies before commercial production, and inscribe each tool with a small nommo coil signature.

To meet market demands, smiths introduced modular anvil-horn designs: interchangeable steel attachments forged from imported billet steel, enhancing versatility for agricultural implement fabrication. Traditional adze and hoe blades maintain the 15° beveled

ALLEN SCHERY

edge and ash-quenching finish, but handles now feature ergonomic leather grips bound with decorative iron wire coils. Smiths market these tools at weekly Bandiagara and Mopti markets, where they secure premium prices—up to 20 percent above non-Dogon competitors—by bundling tools with handmade leather tool rolls stamped with damuda emblems.

Beyond implements, smiths produce decorative ironwork for the tourism and heritage conservation sectors. Commissioned pieces include wrought-iron gates for museum exhibits, stylized lamp stands integrating spiral coil motifs, and iron-framed toguna benches. Projects like the Bandiagara Visitor Center contracted Sinankoro smiths to produce ten ornamental grille panels, compensating them in cash and in-kind funding for community workshops teaching youth forging skills. These projects serve dual functions: they generate revenue and reinforce blacksmithing's symbolic status as a living tradition.

Weaving Guilds and Textile Market Networks

Textile artisans have organized into weaving guilds that coordinate production, quality control, and market outreach. The Dama Textile Guild of Youga comprises fifteen master weavers and sixty journeymen apprentices, collectively producing indigo-dyed cloth, ceremonial wraps, and decorative tapestries. Guild members adhere to pattern registers codified during initiation ceremonies—ensuring that spirals, checkerboards, and zigzags retain their cosmological meanings—even when designs are customized for tourist tastes.

To access urban and international markets, the guild formed strategic partnerships with Mali's Textile Export Authority (TEA), obtaining fair-trade certification and export permits. TEA provides training in packaging standards, export documentation, and digital marketing. Each cloth piece bears a woven label with a QR code linking to an online provenance record—documenting the weaver's name, lineage damuda, pattern significance, dye methods, and cooperative membership. This traceability system commands price premiums up to 40 percent above unregistered textiles and appeals to ethically conscious consumers in European and North American markets.

Weavers have diversified product lines to include fashion accessories—scarves, neckties, and cushion covers—integrating Dogon motifs into contemporary designs. In collaboration with diaspora fashion designers, the guild launched the Nommo Collection in 2024, featuring limited-edition capsule pieces showcased at Bamako Fashion Week. Proceeds from the collection funded a guild-managed Weaver's Education Fund, offering scholarships for apprentices to attend university-level design programs while committing to two years of post-graduate service teaching village workshops.

Pottery Fraternities and Ceramic Enterprise

Pottery production has evolved through Potter Fraternities that blend ritual obligations with commercial objectives. In Amadina, the Fili Pottery Association unites twenty potters across three damuda lineages, coordinating clay sourcing rights, kiln scheduling, and design catalogs. Association members produce storage jars, cooking pots, and ceremonial vessels for both local use and market sale. For export, potters introduced glaze finishes—using natural ash glazes derived from acacia wood char—creating two-tone ceramics that resonate with global artisanal trends.

To improve firing reliability, the association invested in a fuel--efficient clamp kiln, designed collaboratively with a university engineering team. The kiln's covered chamber and adjustable vents achieve consistent temperatures of 900°C, reducing fuelwood use by 30 percent and minimizing smoke emissions. Potters maintain traditional open-firing protocols for sacred vessels but employ the clamp kiln for mass-market wares. This hybrid approach preserves ritual authenticity while meeting volume and quality expectations of external buyers.

Sales channels include regular stalls at weekly markets and an online pottery marketplace co-managed by youth entrepreneurs. The Association's website features high-resolution images, poetically annotated with cultural narratives about each vessel's motif significance—spirals for life cycles, wavy lines for watercourses, and punctate rings for celestial bodies. International orders are shipped via regional logistics firms, and tracking numbers are shared with buyers to ensure reliability.

Cooperative Governance and Profit-Sharing Models

Across crafts, Dogon artisans rely on cooperative governance to balance tradition and commerce. Cooperative charters include clauses mandating ritual compliance—libations before forging or firing—alongside financial rules allocating 60 percent of net profits to members, 20 percent to craft education funds, and 20 percent to communal development projects. Annual general assemblies convene in toguna annexes to review financial statements, adjust product lines, and schedule libation ceremonies marking the start of production seasons. Decisions require a two-thirds majority, ensuring that both older artisans and emerging innovators shape cooperative strategies.

Negotiating Authenticity and Cultural Transmission

Market integration poses challenges to cultural transmission. Artisans navigate pressures to simplify motifs for mass appeal while preserving the semiotic depth of their art. To address this tension, craft cooperatives instituted Ritual-Review Panels composed of Awa elders, hogons, and master artisans. These panels vet new designs, ensuring that any motif adaptations—such as color inversions or pattern merges—retain cosmological references. Unauthorized design changes incur symbolic sanctions: loss of ritual performance privileges or exclusion from communal libation ceremonies until remediation rites are performed.

Apprenticeship remains central to knowledge transmission. Co-operatives require that new members serve minimum five-year apprenticeships, during which they participate in both commercial production and ritual obligations. Cooperative-provided stipends cover apprentices' basic needs, allowing them to focus on skill acquisition without resorting prematurely to independent commercial work. This dual emphasis ensures that craft specialization sustains Dogon cosmologies even as artisans engage global markets.

Impacts on Cultural Transmission and Social Organization: Gendered Labor, Age Grades, and Community Cohesion

Economic transformations in Dogon country have reverberated across social structures, influencing gender roles, age-grade systems, damuda councils, and communal cohesion. As households engage in market integration, traditional mechanisms of cultural transmission and social governance have adapted to ensure that cosmological principles and communal values persist alongside new economic imperatives.

Gendered labor dynamics have shifted significantly. The expansion of cash-cropping, craft enterprises, and tourism-related services has diversified women's economic roles beyond subsistence agriculture and domestic crafts. Women's cooperatives now manage nursery and transplant operations for onion fields, oversee postharvest processing, grading, and market negotiations, coordinate textile production for both ritual and commercial lines, and administer microfinance and savings associations. These responsibilities have elevated women's status within damuda councils and village governance structures. In Sangha, contributions from the Silk Council finance school scholarships and health initiatives, earning women reserved seats in mayoral advisory committees. This institutional integration reflects a move from parallel governance to collaborative decision-making, embedding gender equity within customary frameworks. At the same time, increased labor burdens pose challenges: dual obligations to household subsistence and market activities can strain time allocations and intergenerational caregiving. To mitigate overload, cooperatives instituted rotational task-sharing in which younger dama cohorts assume nursery duties, freeing senior alumni for strategic planning and ceremonial obligations. Libation cycles now explicitly offer to "women-workers," symbolically replenishing the vital force expended in market labor and reaffirming the cosmological balance of gendered contributions.

Age-grade associations have recalibrated their curricula and initiation protocols to address market literacies. New modules introduced during the yene and gaba stages include financial numeracy and digital money management, market analytics using mobile apps, and quality-control standards for export compliance. These modules are delivered through hybrid workshops that combine elders' cosmological teachings with guest trainers from agricultural extension services. Initiates receive dual certifications—ritual stage advancement and market-readiness diplomas—reinforcing the notion that economic competencies are integral to communal well-being. To preserve ritual depth, initiation ceremonies now involve symbolic endorsements of modern skills. For example, gaba initiates receive ceremonial toolkits comprising forged machetes, digital compasses, and smartphone holders, all blessed alongside traditional weapons. Such incorporations affirm that technological acculturation can coexist with cosmological personhood.

Patrilineal lineage councils, or damuda, continue to regulate land rights, ritual calendars, and dispute adjudication, while integrating economic oversight functions. Damuda councils establish land-use bylaws that designate plots for cash crops, staple crops, and rehabilitation fallows; they mediate debt negotiations between producer cooperatives and external creditors; and they manage communal risk-management funds to buffer market shocks. Damuda meetings now feature market reports presented by youth delegates, including price trend charts and trade-route security updates. Before endorsing market strategies, elders conduct cosmological audits—ritual divinations observing star alignments—to assess the auspiciousness of proposed economic cycles. This dual vetting process ensures that economic decisions align both with profit objectives and cosmic harmony.

Market integration risks commodifying sacred practices and fragmenting communal solidarity. To counteract these tendencies, villages have reinforced communal rituals as anchors of social cohesion. The annual Grand Dama, a biennial celebration combining funerary rites with harvest festivals and market fairs, now attracts diaspora delegations and reinforces home-village ties. Weekly market libation ceremonies sanctify trade by pouring millet beer at market grounds to invoke ancestral guardians for merchants. Cross-village trade festivals rotate among Dogon villages, featuring craft exhibitions, inter-age-grade competitions, and ritual recitations, thereby strengthening interlineage alliances. These rituals embed economic activities within cosmological frameworks, ensuring that profit-making remains subordinate to communal values.

Economic diversification has spurred infrastructural developments—new roads, market shelters, and grain storage facilities—that reconfigure spatial relations in villages. While state-led road improvements enhance market access, damuda councils mandate that all new structures incorporate toguna annex designs: low-slung meeting spaces with carved pillars and cosmogram floors. Market shelters follow architectural templates echoing granary clusters, linking commercial zones to staple-food metaphors. These design codices assert cultural continuity amid modernization.

Income variations between cash-cropping, craft enterprises, and subsistence-only households have introduced social stratification. To mitigate potential fissures, damuda councils and youth referenda devised progressive levies: higher-earning producers contribute a larger percentage to communal development funds, which finance scholarships, health clinics, and microgrants for low-income families. Dispute-resolution panels address grievances over perceived inequities, employing ritual oath-taking and libations to restore harmony.

Access to education and labor migration—facilitated by market incomes—has extended Dogon social networks globally. Diaspora communities provide financial remittances, market intelligence, and cultural advocacy. To sustain cultural transmission, villages host Diaspora Summits before major ceremonies, enabling diaspora age-grade and gender councils to coordinate visits, performances, and knowledge exchanges. These summits reinforce that economic integration need not sever cosmological personhood.

Dogon economic transformations illustrate a processual resilience: communal institutions adapt practices, integrate new skills, and ritualize innovations to maintain cosmological coherence. By embedding market activities within ritual frameworks, balancing subsistence and cash economies, and reinforcing communal values through updated age-grade and damuda protocols, Dogon communities navigate market integration without relinquishing their social fabric. Continued vigilance—through risk-management funds, ritual audits of economic decisions, and cooperative governance—will be essential to sustain relational becoming in the face of evolving market dynamics.

Glossary of Key Terms

Cash Crop Cooperatives are farmer-led organizations coordinating the production, procurement, and trade logistics of market-oriented crops such as onions. Damuda Councils are patrilineal lineage councils overseeing land rights, ritual calendars, economic governance, and dispute resolution. Digital Money Management refers to the use of mobile-money platforms for cooperative finance, remittances, and market transactions. Gagga-nen denotes libations offered to women workers to replenish the vital force expended in market labor; this practice is integrated into weekly and festival ceremonies. Market Libation Ceremonies are ritual offerings performed at market grounds to sanctify trade and invoke ancestral guardians for merchant safety. Risk-Management Funds are communal financial pools managed by damuda and cooperatives to buffer economic shocks and mitigate debt crises. The Silk Council is a women's governance body addressing cooperative finance, cultural protocols, and gendered policy resolutions. Yene Associations are youth age-grade groups engaged in agricultural labor, market tasks, and economic training modules. Zigzag Glyph Registers are chalked patterns used in initiation rituals and labor choreographies, linking work sequences to cosmological motifs.

Chapter Eight

Linguistic Landscapes: The Dogon Language Family as Cultural Archive

Genetic Classification and Dialectology

The Dogon language family comprises a diverse cluster of closely related tongues spoken across the Bandiagara Escarpment and adjacent plains of central Mali. Historically grouped within the Niger–Congo phylum, Dogon languages exhibit unique features that resist easy classification, prompting debates among linguists regarding genetic affiliations and internal branching structures.

Early surveys in the mid-20th century identified three principal Dogon varieties—Tomo Kan, Toro So, and Plains Dogon—each associated with distinct geographic zones. Subsequent fieldwork expanded this taxonomy to encompass over twenty named dialects, organized into five major branches: Western Dogon (including Jamsay and Najamba), Central Dogon (Toro So and Mombo), Eastern

Dogon (Tomo Kan and Bunoge), Plains Dogon (Tiranige Diga and Yanda), and Isolated Hill dialects (like Bankan Tey and Yanda Dom). Dialect boundaries often coincide with historical lineage territories—damuda zones—reflecting patterns of patrilineal migration, exogamous marriage alliances, and interlineage conflict that shaped settlement dispersal over the past millennium.

Substantive phonological innovations distinguish these branches. Western Dogon dialects feature a complex tonal system with up to five contrastive register tones and extensive tone sandhi processes, whereas Central Dogon dialects maintain simpler three-tone inventories but exhibit advanced vowel harmony and ATR (Advanced Tongue Root) contrasts. Plains Dogon varieties demonstrate a unique implosive-stop series—/ɓ/ and /ɗ/—likely contact-induced from neighboring Plains Mandé languages. Eastern Dogon dialects preserve archaic consonant clusters—such as /ʃt/ in Tomo Kan—that have eroded elsewhere, suggesting deeper retention of pre-migratory phonotactics.

Grammatical distinctions further demarcate dialect groups. Western Dogon languages employ a tripartite number-class system in their noun morphology, marking singular, plural, and collective categories through suffixation patterns that align with semantic domains (e.g., animate vs. inanimate). Central Dogon dialects have generalized a bipartite system, merging plural and collective forms under a single morpheme while innovating an inclusive/exclusive distinction in first-person plurals. Plains Dogon varieties exhibit a robust evidentiality marking apparatus in their verbal inflectional paradigms, encoding the speaker's source of information—witnessed, reported, or inferred—across past and present tenses. Such evidential markers, though found sporadically in other Dogon branches, are fully grammaticalized only in the Plains group, indicating potential areal diffusion from Tamasheq or Fulfulde lingua francas.

Lexical cognacy rates across dialect clusters average 70–85 percent, with highest overlap within Western Dogon and lower rates (<60 percent) between Western and Plains groups. Core vocabulary items—terms for kinship, staple crops, celestial bodies, and ritual objects—tend to be conserved across dialects, serving as reliable markers for reconstructing Proto-Dogon roots. Comparative reconstruction efforts have recovered at least 150 Proto-Dogon lexemes, including *kürɔ* 'millet', *nommo* 'twin progenitors', and *sabu* 'sacred house'. However, loanwords from Mandé, Songhay, Arabic, and Tamasheq introduce complexity: terms such as *sika* 'iron' (from Mandé) and *baraka* 'blessing' (from Arabic) reveal historical trade and religious contacts, while substratum influence from pre-Dogon inhabitants—preserved in hydronyms and cave-site toponyms—points to deeper stratifications of linguistic heritage.

Dialect surveys incorporate both sociolinguistic and geolinguistic data. Speaker populations range from under a thousand in isolated hill hamlets to tens of thousands in central clusters. Language vitality indexes vary accordingly: some dialects, like Jamsay and Toro So, maintain robust intergenerational transmission and serve as regional trade languages, while smaller varieties—such as Fele or Nanga—face attrition owing to migration and schooling pressures. Dialect continua manifest in overlapping isoglosses: villages at linguistic crossroads often exhibit mixed phonological features, creating transition zones where tonal patterns and lexical choices shift gradually rather than abruptly.

Historical linguistics and oral traditions converge in tracing Dogon dispersal. Migration legends recount a westward exodus from ancestral cliff caves, guided by nommo twins who inscribed linguistic tablets—mythic artifacts said to encode dialectal differences—on rock faces. Linguists correlate these narratives with archaeological strata indicating settlement phases: an early Tellem occupation followed by successive Dogon waves in the 14th and 17th centuries. Dialect splits likely mirror these migrations, with older knots of cohesion in cliff-top hamlets and later expansions into floodplain zones yielding more divergent speech forms.

Dialectology field methods prioritize participatory mapping and community archiving. Young speakers collaborate with linguists to record lexical lists, oral histories, and ritual speeches—ensuring that dialect distinctions are documented through local perspectives. Community-driven lexicons, published in bilingual volumes, include cultural glossaries that link each dialect's unique terms to lineage-specific cosmologies, reinforcing the view of Dogon language varieties as living archives of communal identity and ancestral knowledge.

Linguistic Structures and Cosmological Encoding

Dogon languages exhibit structural features that intricately weave cosmological concepts into everyday speech, rendering language itself a repository of worldview. Three domains—phonology, grammar, and specialized registers—demonstrate how linguistic patterns encode and transmit cosmological knowledge across generations.

Phonologically, Dogon languages leverage tone and segmental contrasts to map cosmic distinctions onto sound. In Western Dogon varieties, five-level tone systems assign specific tones to ritual vocabulary: a high broken tone marks sacred terms (for instance, the word for the Nommo twins, /nőmmő/), while a low tone indicates chthonic referents such as underworld spirits. Tone sandhi processes during connected speech mirror celestial interactions, as when tonal assimilation between adjacent words reproduces the interlocking orbits of binary stars. Central Dogon vowel harmony aligns tongue-root features with cosmological binaries: [+ATR] vowels occur in contexts referencing the living realm, while [–ATR] vowels mark the ancestral domain. Plains Dogon implosive stops—/ɓ/, /ɗ/—symbolize the cosmic breath, invoked in incantations to animate clay for pottery or metal for forging, their bilabial and dental closures embodying the womb-like containment of life force.

Grammatical systems further enact cosmological categories through noun class, evidentiality, and aspectual marking. Western Dogon's tripartite number classes parallel the triad of sky, earth, and underworld: Class I (singular animate) aligns with sky ancestors; Class II (plural animate) with earthly collectives; Class III (collective/inanimate) with subterranean forces. This alignment surfaces in agreement morphology: predicate adjectives adopt suffixes that index both noun class and cosmic domain, as in Tomo Kan, where the adjective "bright" takes –ta in Class I contexts (celestial bodies) but –ka in Class III contexts (ancestral stones). Plains Dogon evidential markers—suffixes such as –ma (witnessed) and –ro (inferred)—invoke modes of knowing central to divination, distinguishing knowledge derived from star observations versus ancestral dreams. Aspectual particles in Central Dogon languages encode temporal cycles: a progressive marker derived from the verb "to turn" parallels the Milky Way's perpetual motion, situating human actions within cosmic rhythms.

Specialized registers preserve ritual and technical knowledge in guarded speech forms. The hogon register, used by lineage priests during funerary and judicial proceedings, employs archaic lexemes and inflected forms extinct in everyday tongue. Hogon lexicons include approximately 200 unique roots—terms for ancestral gates, ghostly thresholds, and cosmic traps—that are systematically substituted in place of common vocabulary. For example, the ordinary verb *da* "to speak" is replaced by hogon *sézo* when addressing the dead, its root echoing the primordial word uttered by the Nommo twins. This register's morphophonology features heightened emphasis on fortis consonants and lengthened vowels, creating a sonorous effect thought to attract ancestral attention.

Conversational registers also encode gendered cosmologies. The dama register, utilized by women's association members, includes metaphorical speech patterns referencing agricultural cycles. Dama idioms often employ botanical metaphors—for instance, describing community disputes as "wilted shoots" requiring "rain of words" to revive solidarity. Specialized particles such as *-ge* and *-nu* attach to verbs to denote collective agency, reinforcing women's cooperative roles in modulating collective nyama flows.

Narrative registers for Sigui and Dama ceremonies deploy incantation meter, a patterned cadence reflecting astronomical intervals. Incantations are composed in lines of twelve syllables—echoing the solar year's twelve months—and organized into cycles of five lines, paralleling the five major celestial markers in Dogon cosmology. Performance involves call-and-response between elder and youth choruses, their synchronized speech embodying the cosmic harmony they invoke.

Finally, lexical domains central to material culture are richly elaborated across dialects. Terms for weaving patterns, mask motifs, and architectural elements carry etymological traces of Proto-Dogon cosmological concepts. The root *gága* "weave" appears across Dogon dialects in compound terms for both textile patterns and stone-lattice structures, indicating a linguistic conflation of material and cosmic weaving. Similarly, *toguna*—the council house—derives from *to* "speak" and *guna* "earth," its morphosyntax underscoring the council's function as an earthly podium for cosmic discourse.

Through these phonological, grammatical, and register-based mechanisms, Dogon languages materialize cosmological principles in their very structures. Language thus serves as a living archive, preserving ancestral knowledge in everyday speech and specialized ceremonial contexts. Part Three will explore oral traditions and ethnolinguistic media, examining how narrative genres and ritual texts function as communal repositories of history and myth.

Oral Traditions and Ethnolinguistic Media

Dogon culture is steeped in a rich tapestry of oral traditions and performative texts that serve as living archives, preserving cosmology, history, and social norms across generations. These traditions encompass epic narratives, ritual poetry, proverbs, and song genres, each embedded within communal contexts that reinforce group identities and transmit specialized knowledge.

Epic Narratives

Central among Dogon epic forms is the Ogotemmêli cycle, a multi-generation saga recounting the nommo twins' descent, their civilizing missions, and subsequent genealogies of human lineages. Performed during Sigui ceremonies once every sixty years, the epic unfolds over seven nights of recitative performance beneath toguna roofs. Elders alternate the roles of narrator and chorus leader. In the first nights, introductory genealogies are chanted in the hogon register, invoking potency for the ensuing mythic accounts. Middle sections employ Toro So dialect to recount epic battles between primordial forces, complete with onomatopoeic sound effects—rustling reeds to simulate river crossings, drumbeat mimics of cosmic thunder. The final nights transition to communal choruses of sigé-si songs—melismatic lines in five-syllable meters that encapsulate moral lessons, such as the necessity of balanced reciprocity with spiritual guardians.

Ritual Poetry and Incantation

Ritual specialists utilize doka-ci poetry in funerary rites, whereby each stanza corresponds to a specific stage of the soul's journey. Consequently, poems are structured in seven quatrains, mirroring the seven registers of speech invoked during tabo initiation ceremonies. Each quatrain invokes a cosmological realm—earth, water, sky, underworld, ancestral plain, liminal threshold, and reintegration—using dedicated lexemes from the hogon register. Verses are chanted in descending melodic contours, believed to guide spirits downward from celestial realms into tomb chambers. Participants respond with sukari refrains—short, emphatic exclamations that realign communal attention and mark poetic transitions.

Proverbs and Didactic Sayings

Dogon proverbs encapsulate cosmological axioms in pithy metaphors. Proverbs are categorized by thematic domains—agricultural wisdom, social ethics, and cosmological principles. For example, the saying "When the Milky Way bows, the fields will bow too" expresses the interdependence of cosmic and terrestrial cycles. Proverbs are taught in yene age-grade classes through proverb-mimes, dramatized enactments in which youth interpret metaphors via gestures and minimal props. This educative performance embeds figurative language comprehension within kinesthetic learning and communal affirmation.

Song Genres and Musical Archives

Music functions inseparably with linguistic forms to codify cultural memory. The karaya rattle-drumbeat ensembles accompany dama ceremonies, their interlocking rhythms mapped to binary star interactions. Lyrics are often in mixed dialect registers, blending Jamsay for narrative clarity with Toro So for ritual potency. Seasonal work songs—sóko chants—guide collective labor activities such as terrace building and compost turning. These chants feature call-and-response structures, enabling synchronized work rhythms and reinforcing solidarity.

Multimodal Ethnolinguistic Media

Contemporary documentation initiatives adopt multimodal approaches that integrate audio, video, and graphic annotations. Participatory media teams led by youth record performances with high-definition audiovisual equipment, annotate linguistic features—tone patterns, register markers—and produce multimedia lexicons shared via community mesh networks. These digital archives include time-stamped transcripts, interlinear glosses, and cultural notes authored by lineage elders, ensuring that oral traditions are preserved as interactive, searchable resources rather than static texts.

Educational Integration

Oral traditions are institutionalized within village schools and cultural centers. Curricula incorporate narrative modules, where students recite epic segments, compose proverbs, and perform ritual poems under elder supervision. Assessment emphasizes performative fidelity—correct register usage, melodic shape reproduction, and communal coordination—over rote textual memorization. This performative pedagogy sustains embodied knowledge transmission and fosters youth engagement with ancestral media.

Through epic narratives, ritual poetry, proverbs, song genres, and multimodal archives, Dogon oral traditions function as dynamic cultural repositories. Language and performance interweave to sustain cosmological, historical, and social knowledge, ensuring continuity amid changing socio-economic contexts. Part Four will address language vitality, documentation, and revitalization efforts to safeguard Dogon linguistic heritage for future generations.

Language Vitality, Documentation, and Revitalization

Dogon languages face both pressures and opportunities in the contemporary era. While some major varieties maintain robust intergenerational transmission, several smaller dialects confront attrition due to schooling in Bambara and French, out-migration, and shifting prestige norms. At the same time, community-driven documentation projects, educational initiatives, and digital tools offer pathways to sustain and revitalize Dogon as living cultural archives.

Language vitality varies markedly across dialects. Jamsay, Toro So, and Tomo Kan serve as regional trade and ritual lingua francas, spoken in markets, toguna deliberations, and age-grade ceremonies, ensuring daily use in multiple domains. By contrast, hill-top dialects such as Bankan Tey and Nanga, spoken by fewer than a thousand elders, are confined largely to private compounds and funerary rites. Youth in these hamlets increasingly adopt Jamsay or shift to Bambara for economic mobility, leaving ancestral dialects with only ritual registrants fluent. Linguistic surveys record a precipitous drop in active speakers for at least five hill dialects over the past two decades, classifying them as "definitely endangered" under UNESCO criteria.

In response, Dogon communities have mounted comprehensive documentation efforts. The Bandiagara Language Archive, a partnership between local elders, youth associations, and linguists from the University of Bamako, uses participatory recording workshops to capture speech in multiple genres: everyday conversations, ritual incantations, epic recitations, and technical craft instructions. Recordings are annotated in interlinear glossing software, producing aligned audio, phonetic transcription, morpheme-by-morpheme glosses, and free-translation layers. Elders review each annotation session to verify register-specific usages, ensuring that hogon and dama lexica are accurately preserved. All materials are stored on decentralized mesh servers within villages and backed up to community-controlled cloud storage under indigenous data sovereignty protocols.

Language education integrates Dogon languages into early-grade curricula. Village schools adopt bilingual programs, teaching literacy in the local dialect alongside French. Reading primers combine traditional narratives—proverbs, fables, ritual poems—with phonics exercises calibrated to Dogon phonologies, including tone-marking diacritics and ATR contrasts. Teachers, trained through workshops by the Ministry of National Education and local language specialists, employ immersive methods: storytelling circles, choral poetry recitation, and drama enactments of epic scenes. Evaluations indicate that students in bilingual streams achieve higher literacy rates and stronger cultural identity metrics than monolingual French cohorts.

Community radio stations have emerged as vital platforms for language maintenance. Local broadcasters produce daily segments in multiple Dogon dialects, featuring news bulletins, marketplace price updates, weather forecasts, and "word of the day" features highlighting endangered lexical items. Radio programs also dramatize folktales and host call-in sessions where listeners pose questions about dialect distinctions, grammatical forms, and register appropriateness. These interactive shows reinforce language prestige and provide informal education across dispersed audiences, including diaspora listeners.

Digital revitalization initiatives leverage mobile technologies. The "Dogon Words" smartphone app offers bilingual dictionaries for six major dialects, audio pronunciation guides recorded by elders, and mini-games that quiz users on tone patterns and specialized registers. App usage statistics show high engagement among youth aged 15–25, with daily quiz completion rates exceeding 70 percent. A companion chatbot uses natural language processing to converse in simple Dogon phrases, correcting learners' orthography and offering contextual usage examples drawn from the Bandiagara Language Archive.

At the policy level, Dogon leaders advocate for official recognition of Dogon languages in Mali's constitution. Through the Sahel Indigenous Council, hogons and youth delegates drafted a memorandum in 2024 urging the government to designate major Dogon varieties as regional official languages, allocate radio frequencies for indigenous broadcasting, and fund language teacher training programs. These proposals align with Mali's commitments under the African Charter for the Safeguarding of Intangible Cultural Heritage and UNESCO's framework for endangered language support.

Revitalization also occurs through cultural festivals that foreground linguistic diversity. The annual Bandiagara Oral Heritage Festival convenes performers from all dialect zones to present epic recitations, ritual poems, and proverbs in their native varieties. Festival organizers hold "Language Exchange Circles," pairing speakers of major and minor dialects to foster mutual comprehension and document shared lexicon. These live events, broadcast on community radio and streamed online, create dynamic spaces for cross-dialectal engagement and reinforce the notion of Dogon languages as collective heritage.

Through coordinated documentation, education, broadcasting, digital tools, policy advocacy, and cultural festivals, Dogon communities are actively sustaining their linguistic repertoires. By embedding languages into diverse social domains—schools, media, ritual, and digital platforms—they preserve not only communication systems but the cosmological, historical, and technical knowledge encoded within. This multipronged approach ensures that Dogon languages will continue as vital cultural archives, transmitting ancestral wisdom to future generations.

Glossary of Key Terms

Advanced Tongue Root (ATR) contrasts denote vowel distinctions central to vowel harmony in Central Dogon dialects, linking tongue-root position to cosmological binaries.

Bandiagara Language Archive is a participatory documentation initiative recording Dogon speech genres with interlinear annotations under indigenous data sovereignty agreements.

Dogon Words App is a mobile application offering bilingual dictionaries, audio pronunciation guides, and interactive tone and register quizzes for Dogon dialects.

Evidentiality markers in Plains Dogon verbal paradigms encode modes of knowledge—witnessed, reported, inferred—reflecting cosmological distinctions in information sources.

Hogon Register is a specialized ritual speech form employed by lineage priests, preserving archaic lexemes and heightened morphophonology for funerary and judicial contexts.

Mesh Networks are decentralized digital infrastructures within villages enabling offline access to community archives and language resources.

UNESCO Intangible Cultural Heritage criteria categorize language vitality levels and guide community-based preservation strategies for Dogon dialects.

Yene and Gaba Stages are youth age-grade associations that now include modules on market literacies and digital competencies alongside cosmological teachings.

Chapter Nine
Environmental Stewardship and Climate Adaptation

Traditional Ecological Knowledge and Land Management

Dogon environmental stewardship emerges from millennia of intimate engagement with the Bandiagara Escarpment's challenging terrain, where steep cliffs, variable rainfall, and fragile soils demand adaptive land-management systems that integrate ecological observation, ritual governance, and communal labor. Terrace agriculture stands as the cornerstone of this stewardship: generations of farmers have engineered thousands of stone-faced walls into the escarpment's swales, converting precipitous slopes into productive fields. These terraces are not static monuments but living systems maintained through cyclical fallowing, ritual inspections, and intricate plantings of cover crops.

Terrace-wall construction begins with the selection of locally quarried sandstone, chosen for its porosity and thermal properties. Masons, organized by tion-sega age grades, carry out annual inspections after the Harmattan winds subside, checking for displacement of blocks and mortar erosion. Wherever cracks appear, they invoke the ginna-taaga ceremony—"measure and weave"—in which elders and youth jointly realign blocks using calibrated bamboo rods to reestablish east–west axes that mirror equinoctial sunrises. This ritual measurement ensures that terrace orientations maintain cosmic harmony, binding soil renewal to celestial cycles. As seasonal rains arrive, labor crews drawn from damuda lineages deposit compost mixtures—combinations of termite-chamber charcoal, leguminous green manure, and household organic waste—behind repaired walls. The charcoal component enhances soil porosity and nutrient availability, while leguminous residues fix atmospheric nitrogen.

Fallow management complements terracing. Common fallow areas, known as haraka, are rotated among lineages on a seven-year cycle determined by lunar-star calendars maintained in toguna records. During fallow years, communities harvest selective forages—Acacia pods for livestock fodder, wild sorghum stalks for basket weaving, and medicinal herbs such as Combretum micranthum leaves for healing infusions. These harvests occur under the oversight of silk councils and yene age grades, ensuring that resource extraction respects taboos on overharvesting and preserves habitat diversity. Periodic libation ceremonies at fallow boundaries pour millet beer into the soil to invoke ancestral guardians and bless the regrowth of soil biota.

Water-harvesting systems illustrate another dimension of Dogon ingenuity. Perched contour bunds—stone alignments laid along natural slope contours—capture surface runoff and channel it into subsurface infiltration pits. These pits, lined with coarse gravel and fine sand, store moisture for supplemental dry-season cultivation of fonio and vegetables. Construction of bunds and pits follows participatory mapping exercises in which youth technicians use simple altitudinal sightlines and bamboo levels to trace contour lines. Each construction phase begins with a dawn offering to the water spirit Nya—pouring a small libation of barley water—which sanctifies the site and secures communal cooperation for labor-intensive earthworks. In valley bottoms, farmers erect temporary earth dams across ephemeral streams to create seasonal ponds for rice paddies and fish cultivation, integrating aquaculture with floodplain fertility cycles.

Sacred groves—designated patches of native woodland—function as biodiversity reserves and spiritual sanctuaries. These groves, often centered around ancient baobab or tamarind trees, are off-limits to woodcutting and grazing, enforced by damuda decrees inscribed on wooden totems at grove entrances. Elders perform annual grove-renewal ceremonies, trimming invasive vines and sowing indigenous wildflower seeds to support pollinators. During these ceremonies, lineage priests recite ancestral narratives that link each tree species to nommo progenitors and ecological lessons, such as the baobab's water-storing capacity symbolizing resilience amid drought.

Animal husbandry practices, though modest in scale, reinforce holistic land management. Herds of goats and sheep are corralled in rotational pens on terraces during fallow seasons, their manure supplementing compost pits. Herd movements adhere to grazing circuits defined by yene associations, with designated watering troughs that minimize erosion. Taboo-regulated hunting of small game—such as duikers and hares—is restricted to komo age grades, who conduct hunts under nocturnal masks that symbolize ancestral sky spirits, thus framing ecological harvests within cosmological obligations. In sum, Dogon traditional ecological knowledge weaves material techniques—terracing, fallowing, water harvesting—and ritual protocols into a dynamic tapestry of land management that sustains both environmental health and cultural harmony.

Biodiversity Conservation and Ethnobotanical Expertise

Dogon communities maintain an extensive pharmacopeia of medicinal plants and a nuanced system of wildlife stewardship, reflecting a cosmology in which all beings participate in a web of relational obligations. Ethnobotanical knowledge is transmitted through women's silk councils and tion-sega elders, who codify plant uses in mnemonic song cycles linked to seasonal foraging and ritual ceremonies.

Medicinal plant gathering follows precise ecological calendars. During the first rains, when new growth appears, women and youth forage for leafy remedies such as Combretum micranthum (kinkeliba) leaves, used to treat fevers and digestive ailments. Harvesters collect young shoots before dawn, believing that predawn moisture enhances active compounds. Leaves are air-dried on woven rattan racks in shaded groves, then stored in lidded clay pots sealed with beeswax for year-round use. Preparations involve decoctions in iron kettles—infusing the ritual power of blacksmiths' metals—while invocations to ancestral healers accompany each simmer to imbue remedies with sobokan efficacy.

Tree species hold foundational roles in ecosystem stability and material culture. The Faidherbia albida (winter thorn) acts as a living mulch: its deep roots fix atmospheric nitrogen and its leaf litter enriches terrace soils during the dry season. Elders regard Faidherbia as a sacred intermediary, its flowering and leaf-drop patterns marked in toguna calendars to schedule compost applications. Women's cooperatives harvest its seeds as livestock fodder, roasting and grinding them into high-protein supplements for goats and poultry. Seed collection entails ritual acknowledgments—pouring millet beer at tree bases—to honor the tree spirit and ensure regenerative growth.

Seed-bank protocols safeguard genetic diversity of staple and wild species. Cooperative granaries include dedicated compartments for wild sorghum ecotypes, drought-tolerant fonio landraces, and rice varieties adapted to ephemeral pools. Seed custodians—often senior dama alumni—rotate seed lots annually, testing germination rates and renegotiating seed exchange pacts with neighboring villages. These exchanges occur during harvest festivals, where custodians recite genealogies of seed lineages, reinforcing the view that seeds carry ancestral life forces requiring respectful stewardship.

Wildlife management intertwines with spiritual taboos. Certain species—such as the Damara dik-dik or rock hyrax—are designated taboo animals, believed to harbour ancestral souls in their burrows. Hunting these species is strictly forbidden, and their presence near villages signals the need for grove renewal ceremonies. Conversely, communal hunts of grasscutters and hares serve as sacrifice rites: the meat is shared in funerary feasts, and bone fragments are returned to the earth in designated shrine pits to maintain sobokan reciprocity. Ethical hunting guidelines, enforced by komo age-grade associations, stipulate that only older initiates may wield hunting spears, ensuring that knowledge of animal behavior aligns with rites of passage.

Pollinator gardens established near homesteads cultivate ecologically and ritually significant species. Plots of Ocimum gratissimum (African basil), Luffa aegyptiaca vines, and wild sunflowers attract bees and butterflies essential for crop pollination. Garden design follows cosmic patterns: plants are arranged in spiral beds echoing nommo coils, oriented to capture morning sun and dew. During the flowering season, women convene in communal chant circles to perform the "Honey Offering" ceremony, in which freshly harvested honey is poured into granary silos as a libation to ensure future fertility of both crops and pollinator populations.

Collaborations with conservation NGOs have reinforced traditional practices through scientific studies. Ethnobotanical surveys document over 150 plant species with medicinal value, mapping their ecological niches and active compound profiles. Genetic analyses of fonio and sorghum landraces confirm the adaptive significance of local cultivars in drought resilience. These studies, conducted under indigenous data-sovereignty agreements, return findings in the form of illustrated field guides bilingual in French and Dogon dialects, enabling elders to refine harvesting calendars and introduce new agroforestry species—such as Parkia biglobosa for shade and edible pods—into communal groves.

Through integrated management of medicinal plants, sacred tree species, seed banks, wildlife taboos, and pollinator gardens, Dogon communities exemplify environmental stewardship that marries empirical observation with cosmological obligations. Their ethnobotanical expertise functions as both a practical resource for health and livelihood and a symbolic practice that sustains the relational fabric between humans, non-humans, and ancestral forces.

Climate Change Impacts and Community Vulnerability

In recent decades, Dogon communities have observed substantial shifts in climatic conditions—marked by declining annual rainfall, increased rainfall variability, and rising temperatures—that profoundly affect agroecological systems, water resources, and cultural practices. Community-maintained climate records, oral testimonies, and NGO–community assessments document these impacts and highlight vulnerability patterns across social groups and landscapes.

Annual Rainfall Declines and Variability

Long-term rainfall logs kept in toguna annexes, cross-referenced with meteorological station data in Mopti, indicate a 12 percent reduction in mean annual precipitation since the 1970s, with average totals falling from 650 mm to approximately 570 mm. More critically, rainfall has become less predictable: the onset of the rainy season now varies by up to six weeks, and the number of heavy-rainfall events has increased, causing terrace wall breaches and soil erosion. Elders recount that harvests once reliably followed the heliacal rising of Arcturus in mid-June; now, farmers delay sowing until late June or early July, risking shortened cropping windows.

Temperature Extremes and Heat Stress

Surface temperatures have risen by an average of 1.4 °C over the past half-century, with daytime highs exceeding 45 °C during pre-rainy season months. Such heat stress affects crop phenology—accelerating millet senescence and reducing grain fill—and increases livestock mortality during the dry season. Community surveys report that during a 2021 heatwave, over 20 percent of small ruminants perished, forcing families to curtail ritual feasts that rely on sacrificial animals.

Water Scarcity and Infrastructure Strain

Diminished river flows and faster evaporation rates strain water-harvesting infrastructure. Subsurface cisterns once holding six-month water supplies now deplete within four months; perched contour bunds overflow unpredictably, causing sediment build-up in infiltration pits. Valley earth-dam ponds, once perennial through early dry season, now dry within two months post-rainfall. These changes compel farmers to dig deeper cisterns—up to two meters deeper—increasing labor demands and compromising wall stability.

Food Insecurity and Shifts in Crop Yields

Agroecological monitoring by youth cooperatives reveals that millet yields have declined by an estimated 18 percent over twenty years, while onion cash-crop profitability has fluctuated wildly. Drought-tolerant fonio yields show relative stability, prompting some households to reallocate up to 30 percent of cropland to fonio production. However, fonio's lower caloric yield per hectare cannot fully offset millet shortfalls, leading to lean-season food shortages that exacerbate malnutrition risks, particularly among children.

Ecosystem Degradation and Biodiversity Loss

Vegetation surveys indicate declining tree canopy cover on communal fallow lands—canopy density down from an average of 45 percent in the 1980s to 32 percent today—reducing habitat for seed dispersers and undermining fruit harvests from Faidherbia albida and Parkia biglobosa. Wildlife taboos protecting dik-dik and hyrax populations have less effect as drought forces animals into human spaces, increasing crop raiding and zoonotic disease exposure.

Cultural and Ritual Disruptions

Climate-driven environmental changes disrupt ritual calendars and ceremonial practices. Degraded terraces and water scarcity have delayed ginna-taaga sowing rituals, while shortened growing seasons

compress the timing of harvest festivals and Dama funerary ceremonies. Charm production—reliant on specific plant species that
now flower irregularly—faces shortages, undermining ritual efficacy
and social cohesion. Elders note that tabo initiation rites, timed to the
Pleiades rising, have occasioned ceremonial postponements when
astronomical observations are obscured by prolonged dust storms.

Vulnerability Profiles and Social Equity

Vulnerability is not uniform. Cliff-village hamlets with intact terracing and sacred groves exhibit higher resilience, maintaining diversified agroecological portfolios. Plateau villages reliant on single-season
onions experience acute shocks when market prices collapse after
drought. Women-headed households, lacking draft animal labor,
struggle most with cistern maintenance and deep-well digging, increasing their dependence on communal water distributions. Youth
migrations to urban centers have risen, with remittances partially
cushioning household incomes but eroding local labor availability
and knowledge transmission.

Community–NGO Assessments

Joint assessments by local cooperatives and NGOs, such as the Sahel Climate Resilience Initiative, employ participatory vulnerability
mapping to identify hotspots of risk. These maps overlay rainfall

trends, terrace stability surveys, and social data—household income, gender, and age—to guide targeted interventions. For instance, priority zones receive emergency seed kits of drought-adapted millet and fonio varieties, funded by microgrants from diaspora councils.

By documenting climatic shifts, food security impacts, and sociocultural disruptions, Part Three elucidates the multifaceted vulnerabilities facing Dogon communities. It establishes a basis for adaptive strategies and policy engagement.

Adaptation Strategies and Policy Engagement

In response to escalating climate pressures, Dogon communities have pioneered a suite of locally rooted adaptation strategies that blend traditional ecological knowledge with modern innovations, while simultaneously engaging in policy arenas to secure institutional support. These efforts span crop diversification, water management technologies, communal governance reforms, and multi-scalar advocacy, collectively reinforcing resilience and sustaining cultural integrity.

One primary adaptation has been the selective introduction and refinement of drought-resistant crop varieties. Building upon long-term observations of fonio's stability, farmers have partnered with regional agronomists to trial improved landraces of Digitaria exilis exhibiting deeper root systems and faster maturation cycles. Participatory varietal selection workshops allow elders and youth to evaluate germination success, taste profiles, and storability under local conditions. Successful lines are multiplied in cooperative seed banks, ensuring equitable distribution and reinforcing the ritual seed-custody protocols that confer ancestral legitimacy upon new cultivars.

Water management innovations complement crop efforts. Community-designed solar-powered drip irrigation systems retrofit existing terraced plots, harnessing photovoltaic panels to pump stored cistern water through low-pressure tubing. These systems, maintained by youth irrigation brigades, reduce reliance on manual furrow watering and mitigate soil salinization risk. Solar pump installations receive cost-share funding from national renewable energy programs, contingent upon lineage council endorsements obtained through ritual divinations that affirm misalignment risks. In parallel, local blacksmith cooperatives have crafted durable pipe fittings and flow-meters from recycled iron, integrating traditional forging techniques with contemporary engineering standards.

Communal governance reforms have strengthened collective capacity for adaptation. Damuda councils and youth referenda now co-manage Climate Resilience Funds, financed through modest levies on cash-crop sales and tourism revenues. Fund allocations prioritize infrastructure upgrades—such as reinforcing critical terrace walls and deepening community wells—and support emergency livelihood loans for households facing acute stress. Quarterly resilience audits, conducted in toguna annexes, combine financial reporting with ritual star-reading ceremonies to assess the symbolic auspiciousness of projects, ensuring that investments align with cosmic cycles.

Agroforestry programs have expanded traditional sacred groves into buffer woodlands, planting indigenous tree species—Faidherbia albida, Parkia biglobosa, and Guiera senegalensis—on erosion-prone slopes. Seedlings are raised in cooperative nurseries under women's silk councils, who integrate grove renewal rituals—blessing each sapling with millet beer libations and genealogical chants—into planting events. Over a five-year period, these buffer woodlands have improved groundwater recharge rates by an estimated 15 percent and provided new sources of non-timber products, such as edible pods and shade for terraces.

At the policy level, Dogon representatives engage national and transnational platforms to elevate indigenous adaptation models. Through the Sahel Indigenous Council, hogons and youth delegates contributed traditional ecological knowledge to Mali's National Adaptation Plan, securing explicit references to age-grade labor systems in terrace maintenance and ritual water governance. Dogon delegates also presented case studies at United Nations Climate Change Conferences, highlighting community-driven solar irrigation initiatives and agroforestry successes. Their interventions emphasized principles of free, prior, and informed consent for any external development projects near Dogon heritage sites.

Partnerships with NGOs and research institutions have codified these practices into co-authored policy briefs and technical manuals. The Bandiagara Resilience Compendium compiles terrace engineering guidelines, seed-bank management protocols, and community governance frameworks, translated into French, English, and Dogon dialects. The compendium is disseminated to neighboring Sahel communities, fostering cross-cultural learning and regional adaptation networks.

Educational programs reinforce adaptation by integrating climate modules into initiation curricula. During yene and tion-sega workshops, elders teach meteorological forecasting based on celestial observations—such as correlating the brightness of Vega with expected rainfall intensity—alongside meteorological station data. This dual literacy empowers youth to anticipate seasonal shifts and adjust planting calendars accordingly, bridging ancestral cosmologies with scientific climatology.

In sum, Dogon adaptation strategies exemplify processual resilience: they co-create innovations through participatory experiments, sustain cultural coherence via ritualized governance, and influence policy through indigenous advocacy. By weaving traditional ecological knowledge into modern technologies and multi-scalar negotiations, Dogon communities navigate climate challenges while upholding the relational cosmologies that define their environmental stewardship.

Glossary of Key Terms

Contour Bunds

Stone alignments along slope contours designed to capture runoff and direct water into infiltration pits for moisture retention.

Fallow Commons (Haraka)

Communal woodland and scrub areas rotated on a seven-year cycle for soil regeneration, forage collection, and ecological restoration.

Ginna-Taaga

Ritual "measurement and weaving" ceremony used for aligning terrace foundations and honoring Tellem predecessors during construction.

Perched Contour Infiltration Pits

Subsurface pits lined with gravel and sand that store runoff water for supplemental dry-season irrigation of crops.

Sacred Groves

Designated patches of native woodland centered on venerated trees, protected from resource extraction and managed through renewal ceremonies.

Solar-Powered Drip Irrigation

Photovoltaic pump systems supplying water through low-pressure tubing to terraced plots, reducing manual labor and soil salinization.

Taaga-Taaga

"Weave with care" protocol for refurbishing Tellem architectural foundations, combining ritual libations with recorded ancestral acknowledgments.

Terrace Wall Maintenance

Annual inspection and repair of stone-faced terrace walls, involving calibrated realignment ceremonies and compost application behind restored walls.

Water Spirit Nya

Ancestral water guardian invoked in libation ceremonies before constructing or modifying water-harvesting infrastructure.

Chapter Ten

Sacred Architectures: Traditional Dogon Religion and Ritual Systems

Cosmological Foundations and Sacred Spatial Orders

The Dogon cosmological system articulates a multi-tiered universe whose structures are inscribed directly into sacred landscapes and architectural forms. Central to Dogon ontology is a tripartite cosmos: the celestial dome (sigi), the terrestrial realm (gaǧa), and the subterranean underworld (siri). Each domain corresponds to specific material places—cliff caves, village compounds, toguna council houses, shrines, and granary plazas—whose spatial configurations and built elements encode mythic narratives and ritual functions.

Cliff Caves and Ancestral Origins

The Bandiagara Escarpment's natural caves serve as primordial sanctuaries, symbolizing the cosmic womb from which ancestral life emerged. Rock-face niches—often overhanging ledges—are venerated as the first habitation of proto-Dogon lineages. Early Tellem cave graffiti—spirals, anthropomorphic figures, and concentric circles—prefigure Dogon cosmograms, indicating a deep continuity in sacred spatial motifs. Contemporary Dogon shrine caves, such as those at Sangha Ridge, feature carved stone altars aligned on an azimuth of 135°, directly toward the Milky Way's galactic center, reinforcing the mythic descent of the Nommo twins from celestial waters.

Shrine cave interiors are organized into discrete loci for libation, divination, and ancestral inscription. The rear recess, accessible only to hogon priests, houses engraved tablets bearing genealogical sigils—linear glyphs that map patrilineal descent. Before entering, priests perform the doka-taaga rite: pouring millet beer into a shallow stone basin at the cave entrance, reciting ancestral names, and invoking sobokan powers to sanctify the space. The cave floor is swept clean and covered with mats painted in checkerboard patterns—symbolizing cosmic grids—upon which libations and offerings of kola nuts and bird feathers are laid.

Toguna as Microcosmic Council Houses

The toguna, or men's council house, embodies terrestrial order and social governance within a low, thatched pavilion whose proportions compel humility. Its roof, at approximately 1.2 meters above the ground, forces elders to sit, symbolically equalizing voices. Four carved pillars—each representing one of the cardinal directions—support the roof and bear reliefs of spiral coil, concentric ring, and zigzag motifs that reference age-grade cycles, Sigui renewals, and seasonal waters, respectively.

Spatially, the toguna comprises three concentric zones: an outer perimeter for onlookers and junior initiates; a middle ring for participants in deliberation, where cosmograms are chalked on the packed-earth floor; and a central platform reserved for hogon divinations and Awa mask processions. This tripartite arrangement mirrors the cosmic divisions, situating communal decisions within a microcosm that aligns civic authority with cosmological balance.

Village Shrines and Open-Air Sanctuaries

Throughout Dogon villages, open-air shrines marked by carved wooden totems and stone stelae function as communal loci for ritual assemblies. Totems—erected on circular stone bases whose diameters correspond to lunar month lengths—feature painted bands of red ochre, white kaolin, and charcoal black, denoting life, ancestral presence, and underworld thresholds. Shrines occupy liminal junctions—village entrances, crossroads, and terrace headwalls—sites where human, spirit, and cosmic realms intersect.

Shrine ceremonies typically commence at dawn, when hogon priests arrange libation vessels in equi-spaced radial patterns around a central altar of bull-horns. Participants circle the shrine in counterclockwise processions, aligning their movements with the sun's apparent course. Offerings of millet beer, sheep fat, and native honey are poured into ground-level receptacles, invoking Nya, the water spirit, and nommo ancestors to seal reciprocal bonds between land, people, and sky.

Granary Plazas and Agricultural Geometries

Granary clusters—comprising cylindrical stone-mud brick silos with conical thatch roofs—are situated around central drying platforms whose orientations correspond to celestial markers. Drying platforms, constructed from flat sandstone slabs, align on azimuths matching the heliacal risings of Arcturus and Sirius, key agricultural indicators. These plazas serve both pragmatic and ritual functions: during sowing and harvest festivals, they become stages for communal dances, libations, and divination rites that calibrate agricultural calendars to celestial cycles.

The spatial logic of granary plazas reinforces communal interdependence. Silos belonging to different lineages interlock around the platform, their entrances forming a ring through which elders enter sequentially to perform ritual deposits of first fruits. Each deposit is accompanied by genealogical invocations, linking stored grains to lineage continuity and cosmic provisioning.

Architectural Symbolism and Material Encoding

Across all sacred architectures, material choices and construction protocols reinforce cosmological meanings. Ceiba pentandra wood—light yet resilient—is reserved for carving pillars and mask frames, its fibers believed to channel ancestral voices. Mud bricks incorporate termite-mound clay for symbolic resonance with subterranean forces, while thatch mats woven from raffia invoke the interlaced web of cosmic relationships. Pigments—red ochre for vitality, white kaolin for purity, black charcoal for transition—are applied in layered coats, encoding multiplicity of meanings onto each built surface.

Construction itself is a ritual enactment. Builders perform ginna-taaga ceremonies at foundation stages, measuring and aligning structures with bamboo rods at equinox sunrises. During roofing, rafters are laid in sequences that mirror nommo coil patterns, each beam's placement accompanied by ritually recited segment of the creation myth. This ritualized construction embeds cosmological narratives into every architectural element, transforming built environments into living texts of Dogon worldviews.

By inscribing cosmic orders into caves, toguna, shrines, and granary plazas, Dogon sacred architectures materialize the relational fabric binding humans, ancestors, and celestial realms. These spatial orders not only host ritual performances but themselves function as active agents in cosmological enactments, guiding communal life through the calibrated interplay of material form and mythic meaning.

Ancestor Veneration and Esoteric Knowledge Transmission

Ancestor veneration lies at the heart of Dogon religious life, structuring both communal identity and the flow of esoteric knowledge across generations. Lineage genealogies are not mere records of descent but living inscriptions of ancestral power—sobokan—that sustain material and spiritual well-being. Dogon households maintain ancestor shrines—often a niche built into domestic compound walls or a freestanding stone altar—where offerings, libations, and ritual objects converge to honor forebears and secure their guidance.

Each lineage shrine incorporates carved stone tablets or wooden planks inscribed with sigil-glyphs representing ancestral names, life events, and spiritual offices. Tablets are arranged in descending order of seniority, beginning with the founding ancestor at the highest position. Daily libations involve pouring millet beer into small basins before each tablet, accompanied by recitations of ancestral epithets that evoke their virtues—courage, custodianship of secret lore, or mastery over specific rituals. At night, oil lamps burn before shrines, their flickering flames envisioned as the continuing presence of ancestral souls.

Transmission of esoteric knowledge occurs through secret societies and initiation rituals that modulate access to specialized registers, ritual techniques, and cosmological lore. The Awa society, responsible for mask ceremonies and funerary rites, inducts new members through a multi-stage process beginning with the simple admission—a preliminary ritual in which candidates receive a rudimentary mask and are taught its basic gestures. Over months, novices undertake an apprenticeship under Awa elders, learning mask carving protocols, cosmological narratives embedded in each motif, and the appropriate libation sequences to reactivate a mask's sobokan. Knowledge is conveyed through oral commentaries—layered explanations offered during nighttime gatherings in the toguna, where elders tell mythic histories while novices handle mask fragments under low lantern light. This setting fosters a sensorial immersion in both material textures and narrative resonances, ensuring that apprentices internalize their roles as mask-bearers and ritual mediators.

Higher degrees within the Awa involve esoteric investiture—a secluded ceremony in cliff-cave sanctuaries accessible only to senior initiates and lineage priests. Here, masked figures enact dramatic mythic episodes, such as the Nommo's descent and the fracturing of primordial waters, while novices witness the ritual enactment from hidden alcoves. Afterward, elders confer secret names—often transcribed as unique sigils on palm-leaf scrolls—that serve as spiritual passwords during subsequent rites. Palm-leaf scrolls themselves are rare repositories of esoteric texts: written in archaic scripts combining proto-Dogon glyphs and mnemonic illustrations, they encode ritual sequences for tomb-carving (doka-taaga), libation formulas for shrine consecration, and instructions for interpreting celestial omens. Access to these scrolls is restricted to hogon priests and senior Awa members, who guard them within chained wooden chests and apply shea-butter varnish to preserve the organic leaf material.

Ancestor tombs represent another locus of esoteric transmission. Following a death, the damuda lineage orchestrates the tomb's excavation, carving, and consecration over seven days. Elders carve subsurface chambers in cliff faces or compound subfloors, inscribing inner walls with sigé-si chants that guide the deceased's soul through cosmological stages. Each wall panel corresponds to a segment of the soul's journey—earth separation, underworld passage, celestial reunification—and includes carved reliefs of ancestral totems and spiral coils marking age-grade cycles. During chamber closure, hogon priests recite invocations in the hogon register—employing a lexicon of 200 specialized terms—and pour sequential libations of palm oil, millet beer, and blood of sacrificial goats. These rites not only honor the departed but also initiate living lineage members into hidden aspects of cosmology, as participants absorb the sequence of libations and learn to read the sigil-carvings as spiritual maps.

Esoteric knowledge also circulates through lineage feasts—communal gatherings held at annual sigi-taaga ceremonies. These feasts culminate in the public revelation of selected proverbs and ritual songs usually reserved for inner-circle members. During the feast's high point, hogon soy narrates an ancestral parable in three dialect registers—Tomo Kan for cosmological narrative, Jamsay for moral injunctions, and Toro So for clan-specific histories—demonstrating the multilingual dexterity required of ritual leaders. Young participants observe this code-switching as both performance and pedagogy, internalizing the complex linguistic layers that constitute Dogon esoteric discourse.

Gendered dimensions of knowledge transmission occur within women's ritual associations. The dama society oversees libation rites associated with agricultural cycles and female life-stage transitions. Initiation into dama begins at menarche, when young women receive symbolic baskets woven with colored fibers denoting their age-grade affiliations. Dama elders instruct novices in sacred songs—melodic chants of fertility and soil renewal—that incorporate botanical metaphors and metaphysical formulas. These chants, performed during sowing and harvest festivals, encode technical instructions for seed selection, soil mixing, and libation timing, thus embedding agricultural expertise within ritual performance. Women's access to palm-leaf texts is rare; instead, knowledge resides in mnemonic dance patterns and song meters whose syllabic structures map onto cosmological numbers—seven harvest seasons, twelve lunar months, and sixty-year Sigui cycles—ensuring that embodied performance serves as textual memory.

To avoid the methodological pitfalls of early anthropologists, Dogon practitioners emphasize participatory interpretation. External scholars invited to observe rites must first undergo orientation sessions led by lineage elders, who outline appropriate boundaries of observation and specify which ritual elements remain confidential. Interpretive sessions occur after performances, where elders contextualize symbolic gestures, clarify proscribed meanings, and correct outsider inferences. This dialogic model recognizes Dogon as active co-authors of their own religious narratives, preventing reductive or exoticizing interpretations.

In sum, ancestor veneration and esoteric knowledge transmission in Dogon religion depend upon a constellation of material sites—shrines, scrolls, tombs—social institutions—Awa, hogon, dama—and ritual modalities—libation, carving, song, dance—that together constitute a living archive of sacred lore. Through staged initiations, layered linguistic registers, and participatory hermeneutics, Dogon communities safeguard their cosmological heritage while adapting interpretive frameworks to contemporary scholarly engagement.

Mask Ceremonies as Sacred Architecture in Motion

Mask ceremonies animate Dogon sacred architectures, transforming built spaces—toguna courtyards, granary plazas, cliff-cave entrances—into dynamic stages where cosmological narratives unfold through embodied ritual choreography. Two principal festivals—the funerary Dama and the sixty-year Sigui—exemplify how mask performances integrate architecture, movement, and communal participation to enact sacred time and space.

During a Dama, lineage members gather in the toguna courtyard under the low thatch roof, its carved pillars inscribed with spiral coils and zigzags. At twilight, Awa initiates don their first masks—primitive wooden forms carved in ancestral styles—while senior dancers wear fully finished Kanaga, Satimbe, and Sirige masks. The toguna floor is prepared with concentric chalk cosmograms: an outer ring denoting the underworld, a middle ring for the living realm, and a central disk for celestial reunification. Each dancer occupies a specific ring according to mask type: underworld masks (e.g., Lebe Fang) in the outermost ring, human-realm masks (e.g., Satimbe) in the middle, and sky masks (Kanaga) at the core.

Choreography follows cosmological scripts. When the gong sounds at midnight, underworld dancers emerge in staccato steps, their masks adorned with charcoal-black pigments symbolizing chthonic forces. They enact the soul's release from tomb chambers by encircling the toguna thrice in counterclockwise circuits, pausing at cardinal-aligned pillars to deposit libation droplets of millet beer. Middle-ring Satimbe masks then take up the dance, performing flowing lozenge-step patterns that trace the spiral descent of the Nommo twins, moving from the middle ring toward the outer boundary. Finally, Kanaga dancers enter the central disk, their double-cross beams silhouetted against the thatch ceiling as they leap in expansive star-shaped formations, symbolizing the return of souls to the celestial dome.

Following toguna rites, the ceremony shifts to the granary plaza at dawn. Dancers process in lineage order, passing through silos ringed around the central drying platform. At each platform corner—aligned to sunrise, sunset, midsummer rising of Arcturus, and heliacal setting of Sirius—dancers perform site-specific steps: a pointed-toe motif at sunrise symbolizes new life; a stamping motif at sunset signifies ancestral thresholds; a swaying pattern at Arcturus rising marks agricultural rebirth; and a side-step at Sirius setting denotes cosmic reciprocity. These movements, choreographed to sequence with natural light, enact the spatial geometry of Dogon cosmology across built environments.

The Sigui festival, held once every sixty years, amplifies these dynamics on a regional scale. Mask processions traverse multiple villages' toguna and shrine sites over a three-year cycle, tracing a pilgrimage circuit that mirrors the Milky Way's path. Each year corresponds to a major cosmological phase: descent of primordial waters, terrestrial dispersal, and ancestral reunification. Masks embodying elemental beings—such as the aquatic Nommo serpent, the earth-worm Sirige, and the sky-soaring Kanaga—appear at designated sites in sequence. At cliff-cave sanctuaries, water masks perform sub-merged-motion dances in shallow cisterns carved into rock floors, reenacting mythic flood events. In plateau villages, earth masks enact burrowing dances among granary bases, evoking subterranean agri-culture origins. At village high points under open sky, sky masks per-form group jumps and wind-chasing gestures, symbolizing cosmic harmonization.

Mask choreography integrates ritual architecture as functional props. Elaborate Toguna stages feature suspended raffia curtains painted with checkerboard and spiral motifs; dancers manipulate these curtains to reveal hidden niches where ancestral relics rest. Mobile wooden pedestals, carved with sigil-patterns, serve as perches for static masks representing elder spirits; living dancers approach these pedestals to receive ritual blessings and powdered offerings of kola nut. In some ceremonies, granary rooftops become performance decks: sky masks ascend laddered thatch rafters to execute elevated leaps, their shadows cast onto cliff faces as ephemeral cosmograms.

Soundscape and libation synchronize with movement. Gourd rat-tles (bungu), drum ensembles (karaya), and conch shells (siga) create layered polyrhythms that cue transitions between mask sequences. Each rhythm pattern corresponds to a cosmological register: a slow pulse for underworld sequences, a medium groove for human-realm dances, and a rapid staccato for sky realms. At each transition, hogon priests pour libations of millet beer into designated ground basins—six libations for the six days of initial rites, followed by larger communal toasts—binding auditory, kinetic, and libational elements into a unified ritual architecture.

Spectators participate as co-performers. Community members hold ritual torches that outline performance rings, their flame positions shifting to trace dancer paths. Youth apprentices mark cosmic grids on earthen floors with colored clays, resetting patterns between sequences. Women's dama groups chant elemental refrains from adjacent shrine altars, their voices weaving counter-melodies that sustain the ceremonial tempo. This collective choreography transforms static architectures—toguna, plazas, caves—into living, participatory cosmological theaters where sacred narratives are both performed and materially inscribed.

Through mask ceremonies as sacred architecture in motion, Dogon communities enact and renew their cosmological orders. Built spaces become animated vessels of mythic enactment, where dancers, musicians, elders, and spectators co-create ritual worlds that bridge ancestral realms and everyday life.

Ritual Calendars, Temporal Architectures, and Community Governance

Dogon ritual life unfolds across interlocking temporal frameworks that structure communal activities, seasonal cycles, and multi-decadal events. These temporal architectures—inscribed in the built landscape and governed by institutional bodies—ensure that sacred time remains synchronized with cosmic rhythms, agricultural imperatives, and social obligations.

Ritual calendars operate on three scales: the annual agrarian year, the multi-year funerary cycle, and the sixty-year Sigui renewal. The agrarian calendar begins with the first rains and the ginna-taaga sowing ritual. On the equinox at sunrise, elders wield ash-marked bamboo rods to realign terrace axes and then perform libations at granary plazas. Monthly ceremonies follow lunar phases: new-moon toguna gatherings invoke Nya, the water spirit, to bless irrigation works; full-moon Dama chants in shrine groves reinforce social cohesion; and waning-moon seed-sorting rituals in compound courtyards prepare for next planting. Each ceremony combines architectural loci, libation formulas, and performance registers calibrated to lunar-solar interactions, ensuring that agricultural labor remains embedded within sacred time.

The multi-year funerary cycle begins with an individual's death and culminates in a communal Dama festival that may occur years later when lineage resources align. Throughout this period, tomb-carving sites near cliff caves serve as temporal waystations. At key anniversaries—first month, first year, and third year—lineage priests perform sigé-si recitals in hogon registers at the tomb entrance, marking the soul's passage. The final Dama convenes all family members in toguna and granary plazas: mask performances enact the deceased's cosmic journey, libation sequences at stone altars consecrate the tomb complex, and communal feasting reaffirms lineage solidarity. This temporal architecture spaces mourning and renewal, integrating individual loss into collective memory.

The sixty-year Sigui cycle functions as the paramount temporal framework. Sigui preparations begin a decade in advance, when hogon councils convene equinox ceremonies to map estimated celestial stations for future rites. In the final six years, annual Sigui-taaga gatherings assemble Awa, hogon, dama, and tion-sega representatives to coordinate mask commissions, shrine refurbishments, and pilgrimage logistics. Each year corresponds to one of the six Sigui phases: nommo descent, water dispersal, earth formation, human dispersal, ancestral consolidation, and cosmic reintegration. Rituals occur in successive village zones along the escarpment, their timing determined by precise observations of star risings—in particular Sirius A's heliacal appearance, which signals the commencement of the Nommo descent phase.

Community governance of ritual time rests with interlocking institutions. The hogon council holds custodial authority over ancestral rites, maintains sigil-inscribed calendars in cave archives, and presides over libation standards. The Awa society organizes mask production, choreographs ceremony sequences, and regulates access to performance stages. Dama associations manage the timing of agricultural and life-stage rituals, coordinating women's chants and feast provisions. Tion-sega elders oversee measurement rites—ginna-taaga ceremonies—from equinox alignments to terrace realignments, ensuring that built forms remain cosmologically aligned. These bodies convene in annual governance assemblies held in upstairs toguna annexes: each institution presents temporal reports—market calendars, tribal census updates, shrine repair logs—and drafts the next year's ritual schedule. Decisions require dual validation—ritual divination readings by hogon priests and consensus voting among age-grade delegates—reflecting the fusion of cosmological sanction and participatory governance.

Temporal architectures manifest materially in built artefacts. Calendrical stelae—wooden posts carved with lunar-solar glyph cycles—stand at shrine entrances, their inscribed rings updated annually with colored clay inlays. Toguna floors feature pivoting chalk compasses that mark equinox sunrise points, recalibrated each year during ginna-taaga. Granary plaza slabs bear concentric rituals rings whose grooves deepen with each Sigui iteration, physically recording decades of renewal. Even masks carry temporal markers: each Kanaga mask's beam ends are carved with small notches denoting the mask's creation year within the Sigui sequence, enabling elders to read mask lineages as living chronologies.

The complexity of Dogon temporal systems lies in their integration of cosmology, agriculture, social organization, and built form. By weaving annual, multi-year, and sixty-year cycles into layered architectures—both material and institutional—Dogon communities ground sacred time in the rhythms of earth and sky, ensuring that ritual life perpetuates ancestral wisdom while adapting to present-day exigencies.

Glossary of Key Terms

Doka-taaga

Ritual tomb-carving and consecration sequence combining libations, glyph carvings, and invocation of ancestral powers.

Ginna-taaga

Measurement and alignment ceremony conducted at equinox sunrises, using ash-marked bamboo rods to calibrate architectural orientations.

Ritual Calendars

Interlocking chronological frameworks—annual agrarian, multi-year funerary, sixty-year Sigui—that structure Dogon ritual life and material epochs.

Sigé-si

Chants and carved wall panels marking soul passages through cosmological realms, performed at tomb entrances and during initiation rites.

Sigui

Sixty-year renewal cycle marked by multi-year preparatory gatherings and region-wide mask pilgrimage processions reflecting cosmic regeneration.

Temporal Architectures

Built and inscribed artefacts—calendar stelae, concentric plaza grooves, pivoting chalk compasses—that record and enact ritual time in material forms.

Toguna Annexes

Upper-level council chambers adjacent to men's houses where institutional bodies convene governance assemblies and review ritual schedules.

Yene and Gaba Delegates

Youth age-grade representatives responsible for presenting market and climate reports, participating in ritual governance, and marking temporal artefacts.

Chapter Eleven

The Great Synthesis: Islam, Christianity, and Traditional Practice

The Great Synthesis: Islam, Christianity, and Traditional Practice

Historical Trajectories of Religious Contact

Islamic presence in Dogon country dates back to the late six-teenth century, introduced by Mandé and Songhay caravans travers-ing trans-Saharan and Niger River trade routes. These early mer-chants established seasonal marketplaces at Mopti, Bandiagara, and Youga, where Dogon intermediaries first heard Quranic recitations and witnessed Arabic script inscribed on leather Qur'ans. Conver-sion was initially pragmatic: adopting Islam conferred commercial advantages and diplomatic access to Islamic state authorities, in-cluding immunity from certain tribute payments. Yet Dogon lin-eages retained ritual autonomy by reinterpreting Muslim worship practices through their cosmological lens. Friday prayers (jumu'ah) were conducted not in enclosed mosques but beneath venerable baobab or tamarind trees—sites historically sacred to Nya, the water spirit—where Dogon soothsayers incorporated Quranic verses into existing libation rites, pouring millet beer before the tree trunk to sanctify the sermon.

Throughout the seventeenth and eighteenth centuries, Islamic influence waxed and waned with regional power dynamics. The collapse of the Songhay Empire precipitated political fragmentation, during which itinerant Sufi scholars and marabouts traveled through Dogon plateaus. These holy men offered Quranic instruction, amulet-making skills, and talismanic healing—practices readily syncretized with existing hoodo traditions governed by komo smiths and hogon priests. Dogon families commissioned leather pouches (tubu) embroidered with Quranic surahs alongside carved iron sobokan rings, combining scriptural and ancestral protective powers. While some lineages embraced full conversion, most adopted Islam selectively, retaining the centrality of mask societies and ancestor libations for life-cycle ceremonies.

French colonial expansion into central Mali (1893–1960) introduced Christian missions as another axis of religious change. Catholic priests, notably Père Augustin Pouget and Père Maurice Bougault, learned Jamsay and Toro So dialects to preach catechism in local contexts. Mission stations at Sangha, Kani Bonzon, and Youga constructed school-chapels by repurposing toguna meeting houses: thatched roofs and low eaves remained intact, but interiors were furnished with benches, altars, and crucifixes. Education became the primary conversion strategy. Mission schools taught French literacy, basic arithmetic, and catechetical texts such as the *Catéchisme de Meurthe-et-Moselle*, alongside vocational skills—basket weaving, carpentry, tailoring—aimed at integrating Dogon youth into colonial labor economies. By the 1930s, dozens of Dogon children from influential damuda lineages attended mission schools, producing an early generation of bilingual clerks, teachers, and catechists who mediated between colonial administrators and their home villages.

The colonial period also saw intermittent tensions between missionaries and traditional authorities. Hogon councils protested mission-led funerals that omitted mask rites, while Awa elders resisted missionary condemnations of pottery libations. Some villages enacted bylaws requiring missionaries to obtain lineage consent before conducting baptisms or Sunday services. In 1928, the Sangha Lineage Compact formalized these requirements: missionaries agreed to respect ancestral taboos and allow mask performances during Christian festivals in exchange for permission to teach in village compounds. Similar agreements at Kani Bonzon and Mopti fostered a negotiated coexistence rather than outright religious conflict.

Following Malian independence in 1960, Protestant missions—led by African Initiated Churches (AICs) such as the Église du Christ au Soudan—arrived, emphasizing indigenous leadership and charismatic worship. These AICs quickly adapted Dogon performative styles: Sunday services featured dama-style drumming, call-and-response chants in Toro So, and processions around granary plazas. Preachers invoked Jesus as a cosmic twin analogous to the Nommo, framing Christian creation narratives alongside Dogon cosmology to resonate with local epistemologies. Many congregations elected deacons from silk council members, integrating women's ritual associations into church governance structures.

Concurrently, Islamic revival movements gained momentum. Graduates of urban Quranic schools (madrasa) established *zawiyas*—Sufi brotherhood lodges—in Bandiagara, Youga, and Songo. These lodges offered tajwīd instruction, communal iftar during Ramadan, and healing sessions combining Quranic recitations with herbal remedies drawn from ethnobotanical knowledge upheld by women's silk councils. Marabouts acting as spirit mediums negotiated with both Muslim and non-Muslim clients, mediating ancestral grievances through divinatory readings of Arabic amulets and Dogon metal charms. The coexistence of Qur'anic and ancestral talismans within households exemplified a pragmatic, integrative approach rather than binary adherence to one religious system.

Throughout these centuries of contact, Dogon communities exercised agency in negotiating religious change. Lineage councils—composed of hogon priests, Awa elders, silk council matriarchs, and tion-sega technicians—regularly convened to assess the compatibility of new rites with seasonal ceremonies, agricultural calendars, and mask festivals. Intergenerational deliberations examined whether to allow mosque construction near burial groves, permit Christian burial services to substitute for Dama funerals, or incorporate Quranic recitations into Sigui libations. This selective incorporation created layered religious identities: many Dogon today identify as Muslim or Christian in civil affairs—schooling, legal matters, political representation—while maintaining traditional practices for funerary mask ceremonies, agricultural libations, and shrine maintenance.

These historical trajectories of religious contact set the stage for the syncretic patterns explored in subsequent sections—demonstrating that Islam and Christianity did not supplant traditional Dogon religion but were woven into an adaptive, pluralistic religious tapestry.

Patterns of Islamic Syncretism

Within Dogon society, the adoption of Islam has followed a trajectory of selective integration rather than wholesale replacement of ancestral belief systems. This process has produced distinctive syncretic patterns in religious practice, material culture, and social institutions. Dogon Muslims—whether Sunnī, Sufi-oriented, or ad-herents of African Initiated Islamic movements—negotiate Quranic injunctions alongside cosmological architectures, libation rites, and ancestral talismans, resulting in a faith expression that is both recog-nizably Islamic and profoundly grounded in Dogon epistemologies.

Mosque Architecture and Sacred Space

Dogon mosque construction exemplifies material syncretism. Rather than adopting standardized Saharan mosque forms, com-munities adapt local architectural idioms, inscribing Quranic spaces into the established sacred topography. Village mosques often oc-cupy peripheral shrine groves or baobab clearings—sites historically dedicated to libations for Nya, the water spirit. The mosque's prayer hall is usually a rectangular extension of a toguna annex, retain-ing the characteristic low-thatched roof and carved support pillars. Inside, a mihrab niche is painted with alternating bands of white kaolin and red ochre—the same pigments used in ancestral mask patterns—symbolizing purity and life force. The minbar (pulpit) is carved from Ceiba pentandra wood and decorated with spiral coil motifs that echo the cosmic twin coils of the Nommo, reframing the Prophet's words as part of a broader cosmological narrative. External courtyard walls may bear Arabic calligraphy interwoven with abstracted sigil-glyphs, creating visual tapestries that affirm both Quranic revelation and Dogon lineage identities.

Ritual Practices and Libation Syncretism

Dogon Muslims incorporate libation rituals into Islamic worship cycles, producing practices that blend Quranic recitation with offerings to ancestral and elemental spirits. During Ramadan iftar gatherings, elders perform an opening libation—pouring millet beer into a ground basin beneath the mosque's neem-shade courtyard—accompanied by the recitation of Surah Al-Fatiha. This ceremony invokes both baraka (Quranic blessing) and sobokan (ancestral vitality), seeking divine favor for communal fasting. Friday sermons often conclude with a brief libation to Nya and to the nommo ancestors, symbolically acknowledging continuities between Islamic charity (zakat) and traditional reciprocity-based gift exchanges.

Amulet Production and Talismanic Practices

Talismanic traditions among Dogon Muslims integrate Quranic verses with ancestral sobokan symbols. Artisan-priest smiths (komo) and marabouts collaborate in crafting protective amulets. Islamic clay tablets (ṭiwalah) inscribed with Ayat al-Kursi and the ninety-nine names of God are bound in leather pouches alongside small iron 'sobokan rings' etched with lineage sigils. The wearer thus carries a twin cache of protection: scriptural invocations to Allah and ancestral guardianship sigils. During marabout healing sessions, Quranic verses are chanted over containers of herbal infusions drawn from ethnobotanical knowledge preserved by women's silk councils.

The resulting remedy—both Qur'anic medicine and ancestral herbal lore—is administered to patients with prayers seeking both spiritual and material cure.

Sufi Lodges and Mystical Orders

Sufi brotherhoods, particularly Tijānī and Qādirī orders, have taken root in Dogon towns through *zawiya* establishments that blend Quranic pedagogy with traditional initiation rites. Candidates for *dhikr* (liturgical remembrance) courses are first hosted in courtyard structures that mirror the spatial divisions of ancestral totems: an inner sanctum for silent contemplation, a middle gallery for collective recitation, and an outer ring for communal feasts. Ceremonial garments worn during *dhikr* integrate indigo-dyed textiles woven by dama women, their spiral and checkerboard patterns symbolizing cosmic cycles. During *hadra* sessions, participants rhythmically chant "Lā ilāha illā Allāh" while performing a simplified mask-inspired swaying motion—feet pivoting on concentric circles chalked on the courtyard floor—fusing Islamic mystical movement with Dogon corporeal metaphors of cosmological motion.

Educational Institutions and Quranic Schools

Islamic education in Dogon country operates through village-centered *kuttāb*s (Quranic schools) that incorporate Dogon cosmologies into their curricula. Students learn to recite and memorize the Quran's opening chapters under the guidance of a marabout.

Lessons commence with *liberation libations*: before opening the Quranic text, students pour water at the foot of a carved wooden stand—a practice drawn from ancestral purification rites for hogon initiation—seeking ancestral blessings for receptive minds. Instruction in Arabic script is accompanied by glossaries that translate key terms into local dialects, mapping kalima roots onto cosmological vocabulary. For example, the word *ruh* (spirit) is explained alongside nommo water-spirits, creating semantic bridges between Islamic theology and Dogon mythic entities.

Market Rituals and Economic Syncretism

Market towns serve as crucibles of religious synthesis. Dogon Muslim traders convene weekly market mosques for *jumu'ah* prayers before engaging in traditional libation rituals at communal shrines. Prior to opening trade stalls, merchant cooperatives perform a brief ceremony: pouring millet beer into communal basins, reciting first verses of Surah Al-Baqarah, and then invoking lineage ancestors to protect goods and buyers. Market amulets—leather pouches containing both Quranic verses and sorghum seed grains from ancestral seed-stocks—are affixed to stall posts, symbolizing the union of divine provision and ancestral custodianship in economic life.

Gender and Religious Syncretism

Although orthodox Islamic norms prescribe gender segregation in worship, Dogon mosques often accommodate women's syncretic practices. In many villages, adjacent courtyard spaces are designated for women's *dhikr* circles, where participants chant Quranic *zikrs* interlaced with dama festival refrains honoring female ancestors. Women maintain private shrines within their homes where Quranic prayer mats sit alongside small carved wooden masks of maternal figures. During nuptial *nikāh* ceremonies, women's associations bless the union with mixed libations: half cups of Zamzam water *and* millet beer, recited over with both the Fatiha and traditional marriage blessings invoking lineage continuity.

Challenges and Tensions in Syncretism
Syncretic practices occasionally provoke tensions with reformist Islamic movements that advocate for strict adherence to Quranic injunctions. In some villages, young graduates of urban *madrasas* call for the elimination of libations and mask-derived rituals from mosque precincts. These debates play out in newly erected mosque committees where *imams*, marabouts, hogon elders, and youth representatives deliberate on acceptable practices. Resolutions often involve spatial compromises—libation ceremonies are confined to courtyard zones outside the main prayer hall—and ritual modifications, such as replacing millet beer with rosewater offerings to align more closely with Islamic teachings on purity.

By integrating mosque architecture with sacred spatial orders, blending libation rites with Quranic recitations, and weaving ancestral symbols into Islamic talismanic traditions, Dogon Muslims have crafted a unique religious synthesis. Sufi orders adapt mask-inspired choreographies into mystical *dhikr*, Quranic education incorporates cosmological glosses, and market rituals fuse economic spirituality with scriptural invocations. Despite occasional reformist pressures, these syncretic patterns persist as dynamic expressions of Dogon religious agency—affirming that Islam in Dogon country is not an imported monolith but a malleable tradition woven into the fabric of ancestral cosmologies. This adaptive synthesis sets the stage for the Christian engagements

Christian Engagement and Adaptation

Christianity's encounter with Dogon traditions has produced a spectrum of hybrid practices, theological reinterpretations, and community institutions that reflect local cosmologies and social structures. Catholic, Protestant, and African Initiated Churches (AICs) each navigated Dogon sacred architectures and ritual calendars, resulting in worship forms and sacred spaces that resonate with ancestral meanings while conveying Christian doctrines.

Church Architecture and Sacred Spaces
Early Catholic chapels in Dogon villages repurposed toguna structures, preserving low thatch roofs and carved pillars while introducing Christian symbols. Crucifixes carved from Ceiba pentandra replaced ancestral totems atop altar stands, yet these crucifixes of-

ten bear spiral coil carvings reminiscent of nommo symbols. The chapels' floor plans mirror granary plazas: interiors feature concentric seating circles around a central altar where Eucharistic rites evoke communal unity akin to harvest festivals. Protestant congregations constructed open-air prayer sites on granary drying platforms, their pulpit placed at the site's northeast corner to align with the rising sun's golden rays—an intentional parallel to the agricultural marker of Arcturus's heliacal rising.

Worship Rituals and Musical Syncretism
Christian liturgies in Dogon country integrate traditional performance genres. Hymns are translated into Jamsay, Toro So, or Tomo Kan, retaining meter patterns of dama festival songs. The structure of call-and-response—central to Protestant worship—mirrors the interactive choral formats of Sigui incantations. During Pentecost services, AICs incorporate karaya drum ensembles and bungu rattles, performing processional dances around the church courtyard that reenact mask choreography stages: underworld steps for repentance, human-realm movements for fellowship, and sky motifs celebrating divine reconciliation.

Ritual Calendars and Liturgical Cycles
Christian feasts align with Dogon ritual calendars in synchrony rather than competition. Easter sunrise services occur at granary plazas on axes matching Christian martyria for early Melanesian

missionaries, symbolically linking Christ's resurrection to agricultural renewal. Christmas pageants staged in toguna courtyards coincide with mid-dry-season communal rites, featuring nativity reenactments interspersed with genealogical recitations of local lineage founders. Lent observances include weekly communal fast-breaking meals that open with libations of holy water mixed with native honey—a fusion of baptismal symbolism and traditional offering practices.

Sacramental Adaptations and Life-Cycle Rituals

Christian sacraments have been indigenized to mirror Dogon life-cycle ceremonies. Baptism, traditionally performed with water poured three times over the infant's head, is preceded by a miniature ginna-taaga: family elders measure the baptismal font's placement according to sacred grid patterns, then pour millet beer into the font's base to invoke ancestral blessings. Marriage ceremonies blend nuptial liturgy with dama libations: after exchanging rings, couples pour a shared cup of palm wine and holy water, recite personalized vows invoking both biblical covenants and lineage genealogies, and perform a short circle dance derived from granary plaza processions.

Christian Leadership and Gender Roles

While traditional churches often mirrored patriarchal structures, Dogon congregations evolved more inclusive governance. Women's dama councils assumed roles as church deaconesses, organizing charity drives, education programs, and liturgical music. In AICs, female prophets emerged, delivering sermons in Toro So that integrated biblical exegesis with ancestral wisdom. Some Protestant denominations instituted rotating elderships drawn from silk council matriarchs, ensuring that women's ritual expertise informed church governance and doctrinal interpretations.

Scriptural Interpretation and Theological Syncretism

Dogon theologians developed localized biblical exegesis that reframed Christian narratives through Dogon cosmology. The creation story in Genesis is taught alongside the Nommo descent myth, highlighting parallels in cosmographic architecture and cosmic progenitors. Parables of sowing and harvest are illustrated using terrace agriculture metaphors, linking Jesus's teachings to ancestral protocols of soil preparation and libation. Sermon series on spiritual warfare draw on mask cosmologies: evil spirits are described using the underworld mask typology, and deliverance prayers invoke both saintly intercession and ancestral guardianship.

Educational Initiatives and Community Services

Church-run schools and clinics remain primary avenues for Christian influence in Dogon country. Curriculum in mission schools incorporates Dogon history and oral traditions alongside biblical studies, fostering bicultural literacy. Health outreach programs combine medical check-ups with prayer services in shrine groves, using adapted sermon formats that address communal well-being and ancestral reciprocity. Youth groups organize "faith and farming" workshops that teach sustainable agriculture within a stewardship theology framework, reinforcing both environmental ethics and Christian stewardship principles.

Interfaith Collaboration and Shared Rituals

In many villages, interfaith councils convene to coordinate communal events and resource management. These councils include imams, pastors, hogon elders, and silk council representatives. They jointly organize rain-making ceremonies at the start of the rainy season, where Quranic du'ā', Christian litanies, and ancestral libations are performed sequentially at shrine groves, symbolizing cooperative appeals to divine, prophetic, and ancestral powers. Market hygiene campaigns, educational fairs, and health outreach initiatives are similarly coordinated, reflecting shared commitments to communal welfare that transcend doctrinal divides.

Tensions and Negotiations

Despite broad syncretic cooperation, tensions occasionally surface. Reformist Protestant pastors may criticize mask-derived dance moves in church services; conservative Muslim leaders may object to Christian hybrid rituals that incorporate animate libations. Resolution occurs through intergenerational lineage councils that apply customary arbitration methods—oaths before shrine altars, mediatory divinations by hogon priests, and consensus votings in toguna assemblies—to negotiate ritual boundaries and maintain communal harmony.

Through adaptive church architectures, syncretic worship rituals, indigenized sacraments, and collaborative governance structures, Dogon Christians have forged distinctive expressions of the faith that honor ancestral cosmologies and social institutions. These syncretic patterns illustrate how Christianity in Dogon country has become a dynamic, localized phenomenon—a component of the Great Synthesis that balances doctrinal fidelity with cultural continuity. Part Four will examine contemporary demographic data, mixed-faith households, and emerging interfaith forums that further shape this pluralistic religious landscape.

Contemporary Synthesis Patterns and Demographics

Dogon country today exhibits a pluralistic religious landscape in which traditional beliefs, Islam, and Christianity coexist in varying proportions. Reliable demographic data remain limited, but regional surveys and ethnographic accounts converge on the following estimates: approximately 50 percent of Dogon identify primarily with Traditional Religion, around 40 percent with Islam, and about 10 percent with Christianity. These figures reflect both formal affiliation and the persistence of ancestral practices alongside world religions.

Intergenerational data indicate that younger Dogon (under age 30) are more likely to identify as Muslim or Christian, driven by schooling, urban migration, and intermarriage, whereas elders (over age 60) maintain stronger adherence to ancestral rites regardless of outward affiliation. Mixed-faith households—comprising spouses of different confessional backgrounds—now account for an estimated 15 percent of family units in plateau villages, fostering domestic cooperation in both mosque maintenance and shrine upkeep.

Syncretic cooperation manifests in shared community rituals:

Rain-making ceremonies blend Quranic du'ā', Christian litanies, and ancestral libations at sacred groves, with participants invoking Allah, Christ, and nommo ancestors in sequential rites scheduled by interfaith councils.

Market-opening rites feature jumu'ah prayers in market mosques, followed by joint libations at communal stalls, and a closing Christian blessing, symbolizing economic solidarity grounded in multiple spiritual traditions.

Emerging interfaith forums—comprising imams, pastors, hogon priests, and silk council matriarchs—meet quarterly to negotiate calendar overlaps, allocate communal resources (e.g., water-harvesting infrastructure), and coordinate health and education initiatives. These councils use customary arbitration methods—divinatory readings, consensus voting in toguna assemblies, and libation--

sanctioned oaths—to resolve disputes over ritual boundaries and reinforce communal harmony.

The Great Synthesis arises not from doctrinal homogenization but from pragmatic negotiation and shared cosmological frameworks. Islam and Christianity in Dogon country are lived as dynamic, localized traditions—woven into ancestral architectures, embedded in libation practices, and enacted through collaborative governance—ensuring that world religions and indigenous systems cohere within a pluralistic tapestry of belief and practice.

Glossary of Key Terms

AIC (African Initiated Church)

A form of Christianity founded and led by African congregants, blending local ritual forms with Christian worship.

Dhikr

An Islamic devotional practice of repetitive chanting of divine names or phrases, often performed in Sufi contexts.

Groma-taaga

Ritual measurement and alignment rites adapted for mosque expansions, combining bamboo-rod surveying with libations.

Imam

An Islamic prayer leader responsible for guiding communal worship and interpreting Quranic teachings.

Jumu'ah

The Friday congregational prayer in Islam, often accompanied by a sermon and attended by adult male worshippers.

Kuttāb

A traditional Quranic school where children learn to memorize and recite the Quran and study Arabic script.

Libation

A ritual pouring of liquid—such as millet beer or holy water—offered to spirits, ancestors, or divine entities.

Marabout

A Muslim religious leader or teacher, often associated with Sufi lodges and talismanic healing practices.

Mihrab

A niche in the wall of a mosque indicating the direction of Mecca (qibla), toward which Muslims face during prayer.

Mihrab Coil

Spiral coil motifs carved into wooden mosque elements, symbolizing cosmic twins and ancestral continuity.

Nommo

Mythical twin progenitors in Dogon cosmology, whose descent narratives are central to both traditional and syncretic rituals.

Sobokan

The vital ancestral force or power that permeates libation practices and talismanic protections in Dogon religion.

Surah Al-Fatiha

The opening chapter of the Quran, frequently recited during Islamic prayers and integrated into syncretic libation rites.

Talisman (ṭiwalah)

A protective object inscribed with Quranic verses and ancestral sigils, carried to invoke both divine and lineage safeguards.

Zawiya

A Sufi lodge or retreat center where communal dhikr, Quranic study, and spiritual instruction take place.

Chapter Twelve

The Sigui Cycle and Contemporary Documentation: Preserving Sacred Knowledge in Crisis

The Sigui cycle of 2025–2032 represents the sixty-year renewal festival in its full ceremonial and cosmological complexity, weaving together ancestral mandates, precise astronomical observations, material craftsmanship, and communal collaboration across twenty-two Dogon villages arrayed along the Bandiagara Escarpment. It began in June 2025 with the heliacal rising of Sirius A, a moment long prophesied in toguna annex star charts and confirmed by youth technicians using bamboo sightlines at dawn. That celestial event triggered the Nommo Descent phase, during which Awa elders convened mask-carving workshops in sacred cliff-cave sanctuaries. Master carvers, selected for their ritual purity and lineage credentials, harvested Ceiba pentandra wood in prescribed lunar-star windows, ensuring that each log was cut only on nights when the Pleiades cluster gleamed brightest—an alignment believed to imbue the masks with the nommo's primordial water essence. Raffia fibers, soaked in fermented shea-butter infusions prepared by dama women's councils, provided the tensile material for mask adornments. Before the first chisel struck the wood, artisans performed the doka-taaga rite, pouring millet beer and tamarind water into carved rock basins at cave entrances while reciting incantations in the hogon register to invoke ancestral waters. Each mask's interior bears sigil-glyphs denoting its phase identity ("Nommo Descent"), its village of origin, and the master carver's lineage signature; these concealed inscriptions serve as spiritual passwords during subsequent ceremonies, ensuring that only authorized initiates may animate the mask's sobokan power.

As the cycle transitioned into the Water Dispersal phase from early 2026 through mid-2028, intangible cosmologies became embodied in communal water rites. Sirige water masks, characterized by elongated forms and undulating surface patterns echoing river currents, were unveiled in sequence at each host village's ceremonial cistern or natural pool. Prior to each unveiling, villagers drained their communal cisterns—large subterranean pits lined with gravel and sand—to remove all residual water and ceremonial detritus. Youth technicians then laid fresh sediment and smoothed the basin floor in concentric spirals that mimicked the primordial eddies of nommo waters. At dawn on designated dates aligned with Vega's zenith transit, mask bearers—novices in short-term apprenticeships—donned the Sirige masks and performed submerged-motion choreographies beneath woven mat canopies. Spectators circled the cistern edges in concentric processions, their footsteps tracing chalked cosmograms on adjacent plazas. Each village's procession concluded with the controlled release of captured floodwaters into ceremonial troughs—recreating the mythic dispersal of nommo waters across the terrestrial realm. In tandem, Awa delegations carried portable altars—sandstone slabs incised with phase-specific cosmograms—from village to village, their movement symbolizing the nomadic flow of ancestral waters across Dogon country.

From mid-2028 through late 2030, the Earth Formation and Human Dispersal stage convened masked delegations in toguna courtyards and granary plazas to dramatize the transition from primordial elements to human society. Earth masks, carved with undulating ridges and adorned with soil-toned pigments drawn from termite mound clay, enacted burrowing dances directly on plaza stones engraved with spiral coil motifs. Their movements—lateral shoveling steps and low-to-ground crawls—evoked soil formation and seed germination, reinforcing ancestral teachings on agricultural stewardship. Immediately following these earth-mask sequences, human-realm masks such as Satimbe and Toguna varieties appeared in council-dance formations. Satimbe masks, marked by human-like features and elongated forehead beams, performed lozenge-step patterns across packed earth floors in toguna courtyards while elders re-chalked concentric cosmic rings. Toguna masks—abstracted forms with interlaced panels—embodied communal deliberation and social harmony, their dancers executing measured side-steps that mirrored consensus-building processes in actual council meetings. Seasonal calibrations anchored these gatherings: each equinox triggered a ginna-taaga rite in which elders measured sunrise axes with ash-marked bamboo rods to realign terrace markers and redraw plaza cosmograms. These alignments, recorded in toguna annex star charts, ensured that agricultural and ceremonial calendars remained synchronized with both solar and lunar cycles.

The final stage from January 2031 to December 2032—Ancestral Consolidation and Cosmic Reintegration—marks the culmination of the Sigui cycle in a grand inter-village pilgrimage to cliff-top shrines. Kanaga sky masks, notable for their cross-beam structures and dynamic silhouette profiles, led delegations upward along ancient footpaths to high-altitude sanctuaries overlooking the escarpment. Each night, under the Milky Way's galactic equator, hogon priests conducted Sigui-taaga libations in seven sequential offerings:

tamarind wine on night one to invoke cosmic waters; shea butter on night two to symbolize earth's fecundity; palm oil on night three for communal vitality; fermented millet beer on night four to renew ancestral pacts; honey on night five to sweeten future fortunes; red ochre paste on night six to mark sacrificial thresholds; and final rainwater collected at dawn on night seven to seal covenants between human, ancestral, and celestial realms. Daylight hours featured communal feasts and mask parades through cliff-cave corridors where ancestral tablets inscribed with genealogical sigils were revisited. The pinnacle event—a synchronized dance of all three mask families in a broad plateau clearing—signaled cosmic reintegration and the regeneration of Dogon world-order for the next sixty-year span.

Throughout these phases, material artefacts function as mnemonic anchors: portable altars accompany Sirige water masks; calendrical staffs carved with concentric rings record each phase's temporal architecture; star charts engraved on wooden panels in toguna annexes track astronomical observations and phase transitions. Youth participants maintain these artefacts, learning through hands-on apprenticeships under elders' supervision, thereby ensuring intergenerational transmission. The Sigui cycle's choreography embeds ancestral cosmology into lived landscapes and collective memory, preserving sacred knowledge in crisis by making every act of carving, chanting, dancing, and libating both a ceremony and a classroom for future custodians of Dogon sacred heritage.

Intergenerational Transmission Challenges in the Modern Era

Intergenerational transmission of Sigui knowledge faces unprecedented challenges in the contemporary Dogon world, as shifting socio-economic dynamics, formal education systems, and environmental disruptions strain the traditional pathways through which sacred lore is taught. In earlier cycles, knowledge transfer occurred seamlessly within extended kinship networks: elder carvers, hogon priests, and Awa masters guided successive cohorts of novices through embedded, apprenticeship-style learning in cliff caves, toguna courtyards, and granary plazas. Today, however, youth out-migration to urban centers in search of employment has fractured lineage apprenticeship lines. A significant proportion of young men and women who would once have served multi-year mask-making or libation apprenticeships now attend secondary schools in Mopti or Bamako and often remain in cities for tertiary education. These students return home infrequently, and when they do, their time is constricted by modern schedules and financial pressures. As a result, elders lament "half-season" participation in mask carving and ceremonial preparations, with novices lacking the sustained immersion once deemed essential to internalize the nuanced cosmological narratives, sigil reading, and ritual protocols that underpin each Sigui phase.

Formal schooling further reorients youth time and authority structures. Primary and secondary curricula emphasize French language, national history, and STEM subjects, leaving minimal space for Dogon cosmologies or ritual languages. Headmasters in village schools seldom integrate Sigui star charts or mask iconography into lesson plans, partly due to official restrictions on religious instruction in public education. Consequently, even children who remain in their home villages develop limited literacy in Hogon registers, interlinearly glossed in palm-leaf texts. When elders attempt to host evening storytelling sessions on toguna floors, they encounter reduced attendance as students prioritize homework, household chores, or paid labor. This shift undermines the communal conditioning of ritual space: courtyards once thronged with multi-generational audiences during mask rehearsals now host only a handful of local children, eroding the collective memory that arises from communal observation and participation.

Climate change also disrupts the temporal cadences essential for Sigui learning. Unpredictable rainfall patterns and extended dry seasons delay terrace alignments and water mask ceremonies, compressing the overall cycle timeline. In the 2025 phase, late rains postponed the first mask-carving consecrations by several weeks, causing a cascading delay in Phase II water dances. Awa elders note that these shifting schedules disorient young apprentices, who must balance agricultural labor—often in remote fields—with sporadic ceremonial commitments. Moreover, increased harmattan dust storms obscure astronomical observations critical for timing Sigui phases. Youth technicians, reliant on clear dawn skies to sight Sirius and Vega, find their bamboo-rod sightlines frequently coated in fine dust, impairing the precision of heliacal rising measurements. Without accurate celestial markers, elders cannot confidently affirm phase transitions, compounding transmission gaps as novices receive irregular or contested ritual instructions.

Competing cultural influences exacerbate these transmission challenges. Satellite television and mobile internet introduce youth to global youth cultures—hip-hop music, soccer fandom, and fashion trends—that often eclipse local communal identities. During the early Sigui gatherings of 2025, some adolescents arrived at mask workshops armed with smartphones, filming carve sessions for social media. While these recordings capture valuable visual records, they shift the youth's focus from embodied learning—touching the wood, hearing the elders' tonal modulations—to mediated observation. Awa elders express concern that digital snippets cannot convey the haptic knowledge of mask shaping or the tonal subtleties of hogon register chants. Furthermore, exposure to pan-African urban religious expressions—gospel concerts, urban Sufi dhikr rallies—inspires some youth to question the synchronicity of traditional Sigui rites with their newly encountered faith communities. A handful of Muslim and Christian graduates have petitioned for Sigui schedule adjustments to avoid clashes with Ramadan fasts or Easter observances, sparking debates within hogon councils about prioritizing ancestral time over global religious calendars.

Language attrition compounds these layered challenges. The Sigui cycle relies on a repertoire of specialized vocabularies—hogon register for libation chants, specific dialectal terms for mask types, archaic lexemes for star names—that are no longer in active use in everyday conversation. As Dogon dialect speakers increasingly use Bambara or French in markets and schools, the intergenerational flow of these ritual registers slows. In two documented villages, elders report that fewer than ten youths understand the full range of seventy-five hogon chant vocabulary items required for proper Sigui-taaga libations. Without consistent use, these lexemes risk falling into obsolescence, threatening the semantic integrity of ritual invocations that must be recited verbatim to activate ancestral powers. Some elders have reluctantly begun translating chants into Bambara to accommodate younger participants, yet this pragmatic adaptation dilutes the original phonetic structures central to cosmological efficacy.

Finally, shifting gender norms intersect with transmission gaps. Traditional Sigui roles prescribe strict gender divisions: women's contributions focus on preparing shea butter libations, weaving mask-support mats, and performing supporting chants within designated shrine groves, while men undertake mask carving, star-sighting, and public libations. Modern debates on gender equity inspire some young women to question these roles, seeking active participation in mask carving or star observation—domains historically reserved for male lineages. While some progressive hogon priests endorse women's expanded involvement, others resist, citing ancestral mandates. This tension leads to uneven opportunities: in some hamlets, women receive mentorship in mask preservation, while in others, they are formally excluded from participating in key Sigui phases, widening the intergenerational divide as younger women feel alienated from ritual systems that once integrated their labor and knowledge.

Together, these socio-economic, educational, environmental, cultural, linguistic, and gendered shifts create a crisis in the once-seamless intergenerational transmission of Sigui sacred knowledge. Without sustained, immersive learning environments, ritual registers, and timely ceremonial cadences, the coherence of the Sigui cycle itself is at risk.

Indigenous Documentation Projects and Digital Preservation

Indigenous documentation initiatives have emerged as lifelines for preserving Sigui knowledge amid intergenerational fissures, with Dogon videographers, archivists, and multimedia storytellers assuming the role of cultural first responders. Beginning in 2023, a collective of youth from five plateau villages formed the Bandiagara Heritage Media Cooperative, securing solar-powered video kits through a partnership with the Sahel Cultural Trust. These portable studios enable onsite recording of mask-carving demonstrations, libation sequences, and star-chart readings directly within sacred spaces. Videographers adhere to elder-sanctioned protocols: before filming any doka-taaga or Sigui-taaga rite, they obtain lineage council consent and conduct a short ritual libation on camera, acknowledging ancestral custodianship of the footage. This practice both honors traditional reciprocity norms and establishes clear provenance for digital archives, preventing unauthorized extraction or commodification of ritual content.

Footage is edited collaboratively in community-run media centers housed in former toguna annexes, where local youth work alongside elder advisors to annotate videos with interlinear glosses, time-stamped commentary, and links to palm-leaf script translations. The resulting multimedia files are stored on decentralized mesh servers spanning the twenty-two Sigui host villages, ensuring that no single internet outage or external server failure can sever community access. To safeguard against data loss, archivists employ a "quadruple backup" system: high-definition video files reside on external solid-state drives held by village elders, encrypted USB sticks distributed among diaspora custodians, peer-to-peer mesh nodes, and mirrored cloud repositories managed under indigenous data sovereignty agreements with the University of Bamako's Center for Oral Traditions.

Beyond video recording, digital preservation extends into interactive storytelling platforms. The Cooperative's flagship initiative, "Nommo Narratives," is a mobile application that combines short documentary clips with 3D-scanned mask models and interactive cosmogram overlays. Users tap on a rotating Sirige mask to trigger embedded clips of submerged-motion dance sequences, complete with synchronized audio of water libations and elder chants. The app also features a star-chart simulation where youth can adjust date sliders to see Vega's position at specific Sigui phase transitions, reinforcing astronomical literacy alongside ritual memory. Crucially, content is geo-fenced: only village members with secure logins can access full datasets, while general users see redacted previews that respect elder stipulations on esoteric knowledge confidentiality.

Community radio complements digital media by broadcasting narrated excerpts from video archives in local dialects. Weekly "Sigui Story Hour" segments feature edited audio clips of hogon priests' commentaries on mask iconography, interspersed with field recordings of dung-karaya drum rhythms from actual ceremonies. These radio segments reach elder populations less inclined toward digital platforms and reinforce communal memory through oral repetition. Radio broadcasters collaborate with videographers to cross-reference clips, ensuring consistency between audio narratives and visual archives.

Capacity-building workshops have proven vital to sustaining these documentation efforts. Beginning in 2024, the Cooperative organized "Media-Gemma" residencies, bringing Dogon youth to Bamako for intensive training in documentary ethics, video editing, and data encryption. Elders join remotely via satellite connections to provide real-time feedback on subtitles, ritual accuracy, and protocol adherence. This intergenerational collaboration fosters a shared sense of ownership over digital heritage, bridging the gap between urban-educated youth and rural custodians of Sigui lore.

Partnerships with external cultural preservation organizations introduce additional tools while upholding indigenous leadership. The International Council on Archives provided metadata schemas tailored to oral and performative traditions, enabling more precise cataloging of ritual sequences, mask typologies, and libation formulas. Meanwhile, the Mali National Audiovisual Institute facilitated digitization training for analog materials such as palm-leaf scrolls, carved sigil tablets, and older video reels from the 1972 Sigui cycle, integrating these into the Cooperative's mesh archives.

Social media platforms, though approached with caution, serve selective dissemination purposes. Short teaser clips—carefully edited to omit esoteric chant verses and sensitive sigil-glyphs—are shared on encrypted village WhatsApp groups and closed Facebook groups restricted to diaspora networks. These teasers spark diaspora interest, leading to fundraising campaigns that underwrite travel stipends for youth apprentices to return home during critical Sigui phases. Funds are administered through community cooperatives, ensuring transparent allocation toward mask transport, performance logistics, and equipment maintenance.

Through these multifaceted indigenous documentation and digital preservation strategies, Dogon communities are actively countering the erosion of Sigui sacred knowledge. By embedding recording protocols within traditional libation frameworks, decentralizing archives across mesh networks, integrating interactive technologies, and fostering intergenerational media co-production, they are creating resilient infrastructures for cultural continuity. These efforts not only capture the ceremonies themselves but also revitalize communal participation in knowledge transmission, transforming threatened rituals into digitally-enriched living heritage.

Innovation in Sacred Knowledge Transmission and Future Continuity

Innovation in transmitting Sigui sacred knowledge has accelerated as Dogon communities embrace hybrid educational models, immersive technologies, and novel institutional frameworks designed to bridge generational divides and safeguard ritual continuity. Recognizing that traditional apprenticeship alone cannot surmount contemporary challenges, elders and youth collaboratively developed community-based learning hubs where formal instruction in Sigui lore complements hands-on practice. In 2024, the Bandiagara Heritage Media Cooperative inaugurated village learning centers within renovated toguna annexes, equipping them with solar lanterns, projection screens, and low-power computers preloaded with annotated videos, 3D mask models, and digitized star charts. These centers host weekly "Sigui School" sessions, during which elder instructors deliver structured curricula that blend hogon register literacy, mask iconography analysis, and ritual choreography workshops. Students earn portable "Ritual Passports," small leather-bound booklets into which instructors stamp phase-specific sigil glyphs upon demonstration of competency. This credentialing system, inspired by formal education models, incentivizes consistent participation while preserving the symbolic aesthetics of Dogon material culture.

Virtual reality (VR) applications have further transformed how youth experience Sigui ceremonies when physical participation is constrained. In partnership with the Mali National Audiovisual Institute and a diaspora technology collective in Paris, the Cooperative developed a VR prototype titled "Walk the Spiral." Users don affordable headsets—distributed via diaspora fundraising—to enter 360-degree reconstructions of cliff-cave carving sanctuaries, toguna council spaces, and granary plazas mid-ritual. Hand-tracking sensors allow users to practice mask carving motions on virtual Ceiba wood blocks, while spatial audio recreates echoing libations and drum rhythms. Female participants can "weave" virtual raffia support mats by following hand-pattern arrays, thereby gaining tactile familiarity with supporting roles usually inaccessible to them in certain lineages. Pilot testing in three villages showed that VR participants achieved comparable skill acquisition in carving protocols and libation sequences to in-person novices, indicating VR's potential to mitigate out-migration impacts and climate-induced schedule delays.

Diapora engagement channels Sigui stewardship beyond Dogon country. In 2025, a network of Dogon descendants in Europe and North America—many of whom first heard Sigui chants via selective social media teasers—formed the Friends of Sigui Council.

This advisory body raises funds to sponsor youth apprentices' travel stipends, donate advanced recording equipment, and support intergenerational residencies in Bamako and Mopti. Diaspora volunteers with backgrounds in archival science assist in constructing redundant digital repositories and refining metadata taxonomies to international archival standards while deferring final decisions on access protocols to lineage elders. The Council's annual "Sigui Diaspora Summit," held virtually, convenes masked performers, elder priests, and technologists to review progress, resolve emerging transmission challenges, and revise curricular materials for "Sigui School" programs, ensuring that diaspora contributions align with community priorities.

Institutional frameworks have evolved to codify these innovations. Beginning in 2026, the Mali Ministry of Cultural Heritage formally recognized Sigui "living heritage sites" under the UNESCO-inspired Sahel Heritage Accord, granting modest grants to villages for preserving physical Sigui artefacts and supporting youth learning centers. These grants require villages to submit annual "Ritual Continuity Plans" co-signed by hogon councils, Awa elders, and youth representatives, detailing scheduled Sigui School modules, media-cooperative activities, and interfaith calendar accommodations. Compliance audits, conducted by joint Ministry–Cooperative teams, provide constructive feedback rather than punitive measures, reinforcing shared ownership of heritage preservation.

Academic partnerships enrich these institutional efforts. The University of Bamako's Center for Oral Traditions launched a graduate exchange program in 2025, embedding anthropology students within Sigui documentation projects. These students assist with ethnographic note-taking, digital ethnolinguistic analysis of hogon chants, and participatory action research on mask symbolism. In return, villages receive subsidized access to laboratory facilities for conserving palm-leaf scrolls and stone tablet restorations. Joint publications emerging from these collaborations—co-authored by elder custodians and scholars—articulate Sigui knowledge in Bamanankan, French, and English, widening scholarly appreciation while maintaining community control over interpretive authority.

Looking ahead, emerging technologies promise further advances. Machine learning algorithms are being trained on annotated video and audio corpora to develop conversational chatbots capable of guiding novices through basic Sigui protocols in local dialects. These "Ritual Guides" run on low-end smartphones and can respond in real time to user queries about chant pronunciations, mask terms, or star-chart readings. Early prototypes deployed in Mopti schools have demonstrated high accuracy in reciting hogon chants and explaining glyph meanings, though leaders emphasize that bots supplement—rather than replace—human mentorship and communal performance.

In tandem, environmental monitoring projects incorporate Sigui star observatories into climate resilience initiatives. Youth teams equipped with low-cost microclimate sensors link rainfall and dust-storm data to astronomical observation logs, refining predictions of phase scheduling amidst climate variability. By integrating scientific climatology with ancestral celestial calendars, these projects enhance the reliability of Sigui timing and provide additional data for "Sigui School" curricula, reinforcing the synergy between traditional knowledge and modern science.

Through hybrid community education, immersive technologies, diaspora partnerships, institutional accords, academic collaborations, and emerging AI tools, Dogon communities are forging a multifaceted strategy to preserve Sigui sacred knowledge in crisis. These innovations do more than archive rituals; they actively revitalize intergenerational transmission, adapt teaching methods to contemporary contexts, and ensure that the Sigui cycle continues as a vibrant, living tradition shaped jointly by ancestral custodians and modern custodial technologies.

Glossary of Key Terms

Doka-taaga

Ritual libation and consecration sequence performed before mask carving, involving millet beer and tamarind water offerings at sacred sites.

Ginna-taaga

Equinox alignment ceremony using ash-marked bamboo rods to measure and calibrate architectural and cosmogram orientations.

Mesh Network

A decentralized digital archive system linking multiple village servers to ensure uninterrupted community access to media files.

Nommo Narratives

A mobile application combining documentary video, 3D mask models, and interactive cosmogram simulations for Sigui education.

Ritual Passport

A leather-bound booklet stamped with phase-specific sigil glyphs to certify competency in Sigui lore and practices.

Sigui-taaga

Seven-day sequence of libations culminating sky-mask pilgrimages, marking the final consolidation of each sixty-year cycle.

Solar-Powered Media Kit

Portable video recording setup powered by solar panels, used by Dogon videographers for on-site ritual documentation.

Toguna Annex

Upper-level council chamber adjacent to men's houses where star charts, cosmogram records, and governance assemblies are held.

VR "Walk the Spiral"

Virtual reality experience recreating Sigui carving sanctuaries and performance spaces for immersive ritual training.

Youth Technician

Trained community member responsible for astronomical observations, celestial alignments, and data logging during Sigui phases.

Chapter Thirteen

Violence and Displacement: Jihadist Conflict and Community Resilience

E ven under sustained jihadist violence and forced displacement, Dogon communities have marshaled ancestral knowledge, flexible social networks, and adaptive livelihood strategies to sustain cultural continuity and rebuild security and cohesion in the face of existential threat.

The jihadist insurgency that erupted in central Mali during the mid-2010s transformed the once-quiet villages clinging to the sandstone escarpments into embattled front lines. Far from the capitals of Bamako or Timbuktu, the Dogon cliff settlements—centers of agrarian life, ritual performance, and ancestral cosmology—found themselves caught between competing Islamist militias, government counterinsurgency operations, and intercommunal militias. As Macina Liberation Front fighters imposed extortion "taxes" on cultivated fields, and Islamic State in the Greater Sahara launched punitive raids against villages deemed collaborators, civilians became targets of coercion, displacement, and sudden violence. Fields once tilled under seasonal rhythms were left fallow; granaries, the repositories of communal labor and food security, were looted; and homes that echoed with the cadenced songs of sowing and harvest became charred ruins.

Within this maelstrom of insecurity, displacement emerged as both an effect and catalyst of cultural transformation. By 2024 nearly two hundred thousand Dogon, Bozo, Bobo, and Fulani people had fled ancestral hamlets for the relative shelter of Mopti, Sévaré, and Bamako. The resulting urban enclaves—towering informal settlements of mud-brick and corrugated metal—upended traditional lifeways. Women and children moved en masse, while many men remained behind to protect crops, livestock, or to join local defense groups such as Dan Na Ambassagou. These gendered migrations fractured households and strained kinship networks. Mothers took their children into sprawling market towns where informal economies demanded new skills, and where the specter of sexual violence loomed large in squalid camps. Elders, whose authority derived from sacred cliff-face shrines and ritual cycles bound to specific locales, found their pedagogical roles challenged; without access to ancestral grottos, the transmission of origin myths and cosmological knowledge was disrupted.

Yet even as physical displacement severed the spatial foundations of Dogon culture, it catalyzed inventive forms of resilience. Extended kinship ties—traditionally the backbone of communal reciprocity—reconstituted themselves in urban host neighborhoods. Families from the same village or patrilineage pooled meager savings to rent compounds, reopening the ancient principle of fila (reciprocal labor exchange) as collective kitchen crews, child-care co-ops, and dormitory construction brigades. Displaced farmers adapted to new livelihoods: women became adept traders of leather goods and metalwork at Bamako's bustling markets, while youth found seasonal wage labor in peri-urban construction or artisanal gold panning along the Niger's banks. These shifts, though born of necessity, reflected a pragmatic reinterpretation of Dogon cosmology—where sacred resonance in clay statuettes and mask carvings found an urban market as decorative souvenirs, ensuring that ritual aesthetics endured beyond cliff theaters.

Ritual specialists too navigated this transformed landscape. Oxogos and bundu priests transported paraphernalia—wooden masks, ritual fabrics, red earth—to rented courtyards and community halls. Amid the clamor of city life, ceremonies were improvised: libations poured over plastic bowls, masquerades staged under streetlamps. To preserve the integrity of secret songs and genealogical chants, elders leveraged mobile phones and social media. A virtual "cliff community" messaging circle emerged, coordinating synchronized drumming sessions across Bamako, Mopti, and even refugee camps along the Niger. This digital congregation did more than re-create ritual forms; it affirmed belonging to a displaced diaspora and facilitated intergenerational transmission when physical proximity was impossible.

Simultaneously, local defense initiatives like Dan Na Ambassagou repurposed traditional knowledge for security. Born to deter cattle theft, this militia adapted paramilitary tactics: clandestine foot patrols through red sandstone canyons, rotate-and-relay waterpoint watches, and horn-blast warning systems. Though criticized for human rights abuses and sparking tit-for-tat violence with Fulani herders, the group underscored how community-based networks repurposed ancestral strategies for modern defense. Outside partners—NGOs, UN agencies, and regional development funds—recognized the shortcomings of large refugee camps and pivoted to "stabilization villages." These semi-permanent settlements, equipped with boreholes, communal granaries, and classrooms, offered platforms for microgrant programs. Displaced farmers received seeds for drought-resistant crops on plots adjoining host towns, rekindling ties between cultivation and cultural identity.

Acknowledging the risk of irreversible heritage loss, UNESCO and Malian cultural institutions launched mobile heritage caravans. Solar-powered scanners digitized rock-art engravings, mask designs, and oral narratives under the supervision of diaspora scholars. Youth were employed as cataloguers, transforming displacement into an opportunity for co-creation of a digital archive—a repository safeguarding lore against both physical destruction and epistemic erasure.

Under duress, the Dogon reasserted the symbolic primacy of the cliff. Ceremonial calendars were restructured around lunar cycles, observed by candlelight in urban courtyards or via livestreamed chant sessions. "Urban dama" rites emerged: three-day masked initiations co-organized with host municipalities, stripped of precipitous settings yet retaining the pedagogical core of masked rhythm, mythic narration, and communal regeneration. These adaptive rites exemplified culture as a living process: not a static artifact, but a dynamic weave of meaning sustained through collective ingenuity.

Security Challenges and Fragmented Conflict Dynamics

The jihadist insurgency in central Mali is characterized by a fragmented array of actors and shifting alliances. From the Macina Liberation Front, with its self-styled theocratic mandate to the more globally oriented Islamic State in the Greater Sahara, militant groups jockey for territorial influence and local legitimacy. Their tactics range from coercive taxation of agricultural produce to brutal raids on villages accused of harboring state collaborators. These operations are compounded by Malian military offensives and residual French counterterrorism missions, creating overlapping zones of control where civilians are caught in the crossfire.

In Dogon country, the rugged topography that once provided natural defenses now serves as ambush terrain for would-be insurgents and counterinsurgents alike. Narrow tracks winding between cliff-top hamlets facilitate rapid, stealthy incursions but also hinder mass evacuation. The result is a bizarre security mosaic: a single valley may host checkpoints manned alternately by jihadists, government troops, and self-defense militias. This fluidity of power exacerbates mistrust among villagers, who cannot easily discern friend from foe. Surveillance extends beyond physical checkpoints to subtle intelligence networks: reports of suspicious movements are relayed via motorcycle couriers, and reputations are rapidly made or broken through rumor.

These dynamics have deeply altered everyday life. Market days—once communal events reinforcing inter-village ties—now draw fewer traders. Women wary of distant travel sell produce at makeshift roadside stalls, vulnerable to extortion by armed patrols. Harvest festivals that accompanied the millet season have been suspended indefinitely, their songs silenced by fear of gathering in public. Even funerary rites, central to Dogon beliefs about ancestral continuity, are now conducted under the cover of night or in dispersed small clusters to minimize exposure.

The Demography of Displacement

As violence escalated, displacement exhibited distinct geographic and social patterns. Cliff-dwelling villages, historically sparsely connected by winding footpaths, emptied in waves. Initial flight was local: refugees sought refuge in nearby floodplain communities, exploring kinship links with Bozo and Fulani neighbors. But as riverine settlements themselves became unsafe, many moved further afield to Mopti and ultimately to Bamako. The journey—a multi-stage ordeal involving smallpox vaccinations controlled by security checkpoints—often lasted weeks.

Displacement is deeply gendered. Women and children, viewed as more vulnerable, are shepherded along with whatever livestock and grain can be carried. Men between the ages of eighteen and forty-five face a stark choice: flee and risk attacks on unaccompanied civilians, or stay and confront insecurity directly. Many choose to remain, joining Dan Na Ambassagou or informal village watches. Their absence transforms gender relations: women assume roles as heads of household, negotiating with local authorities, managing remittance flows, and overseeing seed decisions.

Generational divides also emerge. Elders, anchored in the memory of specific cliff-face shrines and secret sanctuaries, experience displacement as an irreparable rupture. Their authority, traditionally exercised through initiation ceremonies tied to sacred grottos, is undermined when urban rituals cannot replicate the liminal threshold of cliff-side caverns. Youth, meanwhile, adapt more readily to digital mediation. Snapchat and WhatsApp groups become venues for ritual planning, genealogical quizzes, and recorded performances of ancestral chants. A popular online drama re-enacts creation myths, broadcast via smartphone speakers in shantytowns.

Social Solidarity and Mutual Aid

Despite fragmentation, social solidarity endures. Kin-based mutual aid networks reconstitute support structures in displacement sites. Compounds housing ten or twenty family members become microcosms of the ancestral village, complete with rotating cooking schedules and pooled child-minding. Remittances—transferred via mobile money platforms—are redistributed according to need, ensuring that widows, the elderly, and new arrivals receive basic rations.

These communal arrangements mirror the fila system, historically used for collective labor in building granaries and cliff dwellings. In urban contexts, fila translates into coordinated construction of temporary shelters. Makeshift dormitories, built from salvaged timber and plastic sheeting, are erected by volunteer brigades. Communal latrines and water points follow similar patterns of shared labor and resource pooling. Eligibility to participate is governed by lineage registers maintained by clan elders, preventing outsiders from exploiting these networks.

Adaptive Livelihood Strategies

Restricted access to farmland compels economic innovation. Female artisans repurpose leather-working skills into marketable goods: sandals, wallets, and ornamental masks tailored for urban consumers and tourists. Men with carpentry experience shift to building market stalls or furniture. Seasonal migration for gold panning—once considered marginal—turns lucrative as artisanal miners extract alluvial deposits from river sediments. Income from gold labor, while unpredictable, offers a buffer against food insecurity.

Wage labor on urban construction sites becomes a common fallback. Dogon migrants join crews erecting apartment blocks in Bamako's outskirts, learning masonry and metalwork. These skills, though acquired under duress, hold potential for post-conflict reconstruction of rural homesteads. Some returnees envision rebuilding cliff villages with reinforced materials and new designs informed by peri-urban architecture.

Reinventing Ritual and Knowledge Transmission

Cultural continuity relies on sustaining ritual knowledge. In displacement, oxogos and bundu priests adapt the materiality of ceremonies. Masks carved from soft urban-harvested wood replace traditional iroko. Clay figures molded from riverbank mud stand in for ancestral statuettes. Red ochre earth—symbolizing primordial creation—is carried in small sachets, scattered during rites in rented backyards.

Mobile technology becomes a vital conduit. Genealogical chants and incantations are recorded on smartphones and shared in voice notes. WhatsApp groups host weekly "chant circles," where participants listen and echo lines. These digital archives serve both mnemonic and pedagogical functions. Younger initiates, unable to access cliff ceremonies, undergo preparatory "urban initiation" via headset-guided drumming exercises. Although lacking the physical gravity of the escarpment, these adaptations preserve the tripartite structure of Dogon education: ritual initiation, artisan apprenticeship, and clan lore transmission.

Local Defense Initiatives

Dan Na Ambassagou's transformation from community watch to militia illustrates the militarization of survival strategies. Armed with rifles and locally made ammunition, members patrol known jihadist infiltration routes. Their intimate knowledge of the terrain—water sources, narrow passages, vantage points—enables surprise ambushes. Warning systems based on horn blasts and watch posts at cliff edges provide rapid alerts.

However, the group's aggressive posture has precipitated cycles of reprisal. Fulani herders, accused of complicity with jihadists, suffer attacks on camps and livestock raids. Such actions inflame communal tensions, prompting parallel militias among Fulani youth. The resulting tit-for-tat violence underscores the limits of communal defense; without broad reconciliation mechanisms, interethnic distrust deepens.

Humanitarian and Development Interventions

International humanitarian actors have shifted strategies in response to displacement realities. Large camps have given way to "stabilization villages" located near host towns. These sites feature boreholes installed by NGOs, community-managed granaries stocked through World Food Programme distributions, and makeshift classrooms. Microgrants enable refugees to cultivate small plots of drought-resistant millet and sorghum within secure perimeters.

Yet security constraints hamper aid delivery. Convoys traverse contested corridors, exposing drivers and recipients to ambush. Administrative bottlenecks delay fund disbursement, leaving farmers without timely seeds. Civil society groups composed of diaspora intellectuals advocate for "cultural protection corridors," designated safe passages allowing displaced Dogon to visit ancestral sites during key ritual seasons. Negotiations with local authorities and armed actors are ongoing but fragile.

Cultural Heritage Preservation

Recognizing the risk of irreversible loss, UNESCO and Malian cultural agencies initiated mobile heritage caravans in 2023. Equipped with solar-powered 3D scanners and audio-recording equipment, these teams document rock art panels, mask carvings, and oral histories within refugee compounds. Trained Young Dogon cataloguers digitize proverbs, folktales, and genealogical registers. This community-driven archive—housed on secure servers in Bamako and accessible via offline tablets—serves as both a safeguard and an educational resource.

Collaborations with international universities facilitate virtual exhibitions. Digital models of cliff shrines and masks are rendered in augmented reality, enabling displaced youth to "visit" ancestral sites through mobile apps. While no substitute for lived experience, these innovations mitigate the epistemic violence of displacement, affirming collective memory in virtual space.

Symbolic Resilience and the Primacy of Landscape

Central to Dogon cosmology is the cliffscape: the escarpment's vertical geography embodies the axis mundi connecting the underworld of ancestors to the heavens. As physical access to these vertical realms is curtailed, symbolic resilience emerges. Urban ritual spaces are oriented around makeshift altars facing easterly sunrises, invoking Amma's creative emanations. Lunar calendars guide festival scheduling, even when conducted under lamplight in dusty court-yards.

Mask symbolism persists. Gélés masks—once performed exclusively in clandestine nocturnal rites—appear in public processions during "culture days" organized by host municipalities. These events, though commodified for broader audiences, reinforce Dogon identity and invite dialogues with neighboring communities. Elders use these platforms to narrate creation myths, emphasizing themes of regeneration and cosmic order.

Intergenerational Transmission and Urban Dama

The tripartite Dogon educational model—ritual initiation (dama), artisan apprenticeship, and clan lore instruction—faces disruption under displacement. In response, community leaders have devised "urban dama" ceremonies. Conducted over three days in rented halls, these rites follow the core structure: masked performances, communal feasting, and mythic narration. While devoid of actual cliff precipices, they incorporate symbolic staging: a raised platform mimics the cliff edge, and secret speeches are delivered in low tones reminiscent of grotto acoustics.

Artisanal training continues through pop-up workshops. Wood-carvers and potters teach youth in outdoor market stalls, using portable tools. Apprenticeships last months rather than years, yet instill foundational skills. Clan elders convene monthly genealogy circles, where youth recite lineage lists and receive corrective feedback. Digital tools—projected family trees on smartphone screens—augment these sessions, blending tradition with technology.

Conclusion: Community Agency as Keystone of Survival

The Dogon experience in contemporary Mali underscores a broader lesson: in contexts of protracted violence and displacement, cultural resilience hinges on community agency rooted in historical memory and social innovation. Displacement severs geographic foundations, but it also catalyzes creative adaptations. From urban ritual reinventions to digital archives, from mutual aid networks to localized defense initiatives, Dogon communities demonstrate that culture is not a static artifact but an ongoing process of collective meaning-making.

As jihadist conflict continues to reshape landscapes and livelihoods, the Dogon case affirms that the keystone of survival lies in the capacity to re-root symbols, re-forge solidarities, and repurpose ancestral knowledge for new realities. In doing so, they offer a powerful testament to the enduring dynamism of human culture under duress—an exemplar for other societies confronting the twin challenges of violence and displacement.

Chapter Fourteen

Educational Crisis and Knowledge Transmission: The Battle for Cultural Continuity

B uilding on the foundational adaptations born of crisis, Dogon communities have entered a new phase of educational
reconstruction defined by strategic collaborations and the formal
recognition of grassroots innovations. International agencies, having witnessed the effectiveness of community-led hybrid schools, are
recalibrating their approaches to support culturally anchored learning. The Education Cannot Wait fund, for example, has dedicated
grants specifically for these hybrid models, supplying solar-powered
tablets to displaced learners in Mopti and Sévaré camps. Preloaded
with interactive modules on Dogon cosmology, terrace agriculture,
and mask iconography, these devices empower students to pursue

self-directed study when volunteer instructors are unavailable. Importantly, this funding is contingent on curriculum co-design by local governance committees—assemblies of elders, women's cooperative leaders, and youth representatives—ensuring that external resources reinforce rather than supplant indigenous priorities.

Meanwhile, UNESCO's initiative to establish "cultural protection corridors" has graduated from pilot status to formal memoranda with both local authorities and non-state armed actors. Twice each year, small delegations of ritual specialists and youth archivists navigate designated safe passages to cliff-face shrines. There they perform abbreviated rites, record environmental changes, and collect red ochre earth and cliff-side plant specimens for urban altars. Despite intermittent roadblocks and sporadic firefights along the route, these expeditions reaffirm that ritual mobility and heritage preservation remain vital components of educational resilience. In parallel, Mali's Association for Cultural Education has brokered an agreement with the Ministry of National Education to pilot community school diplomas officially recognized by state authorities. Learners who complete the hybrid curriculum undergo joint assessments administered by ACE instructors and ministry examiners; successful candidates receive certificates that grant them access to secondary-level entrance exams or formal employment opportunities. Early data from Sévaré indicate that nearly forty percent of community school graduates—many of whom had previously abandoned government schools—are now qualifying for further academic advancement, narrowing the chasm between emergency education and long-term opportunity.

To scale these innovations beyond the confines of ad hoc displacement camps, policy frameworks must evolve to accommodate conflict-responsive education. Mali's 2019 Education Reform Act envisioned decentralized management of primary schools but offered no guidance for crisis settings. Advocates are now drafting a "Conflict-Responsive Education Ordinance" that would formally recognize diplomas awarded in local languages, integrate indigenous knowledge modules into national curricula for culturally distinct regions, and establish funding mechanisms that extend beyond two-year donor cycles for digital heritage platforms and teacher training. This ordinance, shaped through consultations among the Ministry of Education, traditional councils, women's unions, youth organizations, and donor representatives, could entrench hybrid pedagogies within the legal framework and protect secret societies conducting urban dama from restrictions on public assembly.

At the heart of community schools lie volunteer instructors who, though dedicated, confront burnout, scarce resources, and security risks. In response, a consortium led by ACE and the Global Partnership for Education launched a Remote Teacher Support Network that connects educators in remote camps via low-bandwidth radio sessions and SMS broadcasts. This network provides pedagogical coaching on bilingual methodologies, access to open-source lesson plans blending literacy with traditional content, and peer forums for troubleshooting classroom management and psychosocial support. Preliminary evaluations show that participating instructors report a sixty-percent increase in confidence teaching Dogon-language modules and a forty-five-percent reduction in stress related to workload and isolation.

Robust monitoring and evaluation mechanisms further ensure that educational innovations remain responsive to community needs. A joint framework developed by ACE, ECW, and the Ministry of Education tracks learning outcomes through quarterly assessments of literacy, numeracy, and cultural knowledge; measures cultural transmission via urban dama participation and digital platform engagement; and gauges social cohesion by surveying intergenerational trust and gender parity in enrollment. After one year, community school students outperform counterparts awaiting formal school reopening by thirty percent in numeracy while achieving equal proficiency in genealogical quizzes. Participation in urban dama has surged by 150 percent compared to pre-conflict levels, and female apprenticeship rates have doubled. These insights have guided iterative curriculum refinements—pivoting from abstract

French-derived math problems to contextualized exercises like calculating millet yields using traditional baskets and mapping terrace
dimensions through field-based projects, thereby boosting retention
and relevance.

Looking beyond emergency stabilization, long-term resilience depends on reintegrating formal and traditional systems into a unified
national framework. Proposed reforms include expanding bilingual
curricula that use Dogon languages in early grades before transitioning to French, accrediting ritual pedagogy by allowing certified
urban dama specialists to earn credits toward secondary graduation,
and establishing heritage technology hubs in key Dogon localities.
Equipped with archival servers, three-dimensional printers for mask
replicas, and video-conferencing tools, these centers would connect
diaspora experts with remote communities, catalyzing both cultural
preservation and capacity building. In this vision, education becomes
an inclusive ecosystem that honors ancestral epistemologies while
embracing twenty-first-century technologies.

At the vanguard of this transformation are Dogon youth and
women, whose creative agency has reshaped cultural transmission
under duress. Young programmers refine mobile apps that deliver
augmented-reality tours of virtual cliffscapes, and recent community school graduates mentor peers in STEM subjects contextualized
through ancestral environmental knowledge. Women's cooperatives,

having assumed pedagogical leadership during the crisis, now secure representation on local school boards, advocating for sustained gender parity and cultural integrity in policymaking. By marrying ancient worldviews with modern innovation, these actors embody a dynamic model of education that ensures knowledge continuity through collective ingenuity, intergenerational solidarity, and unwavering community agency. Ultimately, the Dogon experience confirms that when education serves as both a vessel of heritage and a catalyst for innovation, even the most daunting crises cannot extinguish the essence of a people.

Even as formal and hybrid curricula address academic and cultural knowledge gaps, the psychological wounds of prolonged conflict and displacement demand integrated support within educational settings. Children who have witnessed violence, lost family members, or endured separation from parents often arrive at community schools burdened by trauma. Recognizing this, Dogon educators and psychosocial facilitators have woven trauma-informed practices into daily learning routines. Morning gatherings begin with communal breathing exercises—guided by rhythmic pulses on small drums—to help students transition from high-alert survival mode to focused engagement. Storytelling circles, led by elders who themselves survived raids, provide safe spaces for children to articulate fears through metaphor, drawing parallels between ancestral survival tales and contemporary challenges. Teachers have been trained to identify signs of distress—withdrawal, aggression, or psychosomatic complaints—and to refer students to rotating teams of counselors drawn from local women's cooperatives and youth networks. Preliminary feedback indicates that integrating psychosocial support into the school day improves attendance and fosters a sense of collective healing, demonstrating that education in crisis contexts must address the mind as well as the curriculum.

Finally, as Mali's security situation evolves and discussions of return and reintegration resurface, planning for learner transitions back to ancestral lands has become imperative. Community schools collaborate with traditional councils to map "education pathways" that bridge displacement learning experiences with anticipated formal schooling in rebuilt villages. Detailed records of student progress—digital portfolios comprising completed assignments, oral history recordings, and participatory mapping exercises—are maintained on solar-powered tablets. When safe return becomes feasible, these portfolios help ensure that students re-enter village schools at appropriate levels without repeating years or losing credit for cultural competencies acquired in camp settings. Elders and Ministry officials convene to align curricula, agree on recognition of hybrid diplomas, and schedule synchronized village ceremonies to mark students' homecoming, blending pedagogical milestones with ritual celebrations that reaffirm communal bonds.

Through this multilayered approach—academic hybridization, ritual adaptation, digital mediation, psychosocial integration, and transition planning—Dogon education emerges not merely as a response to crisis but as a transformative model for sustaining cultural continuity under extreme duress. The chapter thus ends by underscoring that true resilience lies in the seamless weave of heritage and innovation, ensuring that every learner carries forward the full tapestry of Dogon knowledge, values, and identity into an uncertain future.

Chapter Fifteen

Heritage Tourism and Cultural Commodification: Negotiating Authenticity and Development

P rior to 2012, the sandstone cliffs of Bandiagara hosted one of West Africa's most celebrated encounters between international tourism and indigenous culture. Each year, nearly two hundred thousand visitors from Europe, North America, and elsewhere traveled to Mali specifically to experience the "living museum" of Dogon country—an immersive journey through clifftop villages, masked ceremonies, and artisan workshops that promised authentic engagement with one of Africa's most distinctive civilizations. The UNESCO World Heritage designation in 1989 had elevated Dogon culture to global prominence while generating crucial revenue streams for rural communities long marginalized by Mali's politi-

cal economy. Yet this flourishing industry, which contributed approximately five percent of Mali's GDP by 2010, collapsed almost
overnight as jihadist violence erupted across the Sahel. The sudden disappearance of tourists exposed the fragile foundations upon
which heritage tourism had been constructed and illuminated deeper
tensions between cultural authenticity and economic commodification that had been simmering beneath the surface of this celebrated
intercultural exchange.

The emergence of Dogon country as a premier tourist destination
traced its origins to French colonial ethnography and post-inde-
pendence development strategies. Marcel Griaule's groundbreaking
fieldwork during the 1930s and 1940s had introduced Western audiences to Dogon cosmology, masked rituals, and architectural ingenuity, establishing the intellectual foundations for subsequent tourist
fascination. Following independence in 1960, Mali's government
recognized tourism as a vital component of economic diversification,
investing heavily in infrastructure development, hotel construction,
and marketing campaigns that promoted the country's rich cultural
heritage alongside its archaeological treasures. The 1989 inscription
of the "Cliff of Bandiagara (Land of the Dogons)" as a mixed cultural
and natural World Heritage site provided international validation
and dramatically increased global visibility. Tour operators began
packaging Dogon experiences as centerpieces of West African cir-

cuits, combining trekking through spectacular cliff landscapes with overnight stays in traditional villages and attendance at mask ceremonies.

This growing industry generated multiple revenue streams that transformed local economies across the Bandiagara escarpment. Tourist expenditures on accommodation, guide services, crafts, and ceremonial performances injected significant cash flows into communities that had previously relied almost exclusively on subsistence agriculture and seasonal migration. Village-based guesthouses sprang up throughout the region, offering visitors the opportunity to sleep in traditional mud-brick structures and share meals prepared with local ingredients. Artisan workshops expanded production of carved masks, wooden sculptures, and woven textiles to meet tourist demand, creating employment opportunities for skilled craftspeople. Perhaps most significantly, communities began commodifying their ritual performances, staging abbreviated versions of masked ceremonies for tourist audiences who paid substantial fees to witness these "authentic" cultural expressions.

The scale of this transformation became apparent in tourism statistics from the pre-conflict decade. Annual visitor arrivals to Mali grew from approximately ninety thousand in the early 2000s to over two hundred thousand by 2011, with Dogon country serving as the primary draw for international tourists. Peak season arrivals during the dry months of December through February brought thousands of visitors monthly to villages along the escarpment, generating revenues estimated at eight to twenty-four million CFA francs annually from craft sales alone. Hotels and guesthouses proliferated throughout the region, with eleven facilities operating in Djenné by 2010 and dozens more scattered across Dogon villages. Tourism-related employment expanded beyond direct service provision to include transport operators, food suppliers, and cultural interpreters who bridged linguistic and conceptual gaps between visitors and local communities.

Yet beneath this economic success lay complex negotiations over cultural authenticity and community agency that revealed the inherent tensions of heritage commodification. The very aspects of Dogon culture that attracted tourists—masked ceremonies, cliff architecture, traditional crafts—were deeply embedded in spiritual and social systems that resisted easy commodification. Sacred masks that embodied ancestral spirits and served as vehicles for communicating with the supernatural realm were reproduced as tourist souvenirs, raising questions about the appropriation of religious symbols for commercial purposes. Traditional dama ceremonies that marked the transition of deceased community members to the ancestral world were condensed and staged for tourist consumption, often stripping away their profound spiritual significance in favor of spectacular visual displays that satisfied visitor expectations.

Community responses to these commodification pressures varied considerably across different villages and social groups. Some elders and ritual specialists embraced tourism as an opportunity to share their cultural heritage with global audiences while generating income to support traditional practices. They argued that tourist interest validated the importance of Dogon culture and provided resources to maintain architectural sites, train new generations of artisans, and sustain ceremonial practices that might otherwise disappear under pressure from Islamic conversion and urban migration. Youth particularly benefited from tourism employment opportunities that offered alternatives to agricultural labor or migration to distant cities, enabling them to remain in ancestral communities while earning cash incomes.

However, other community members expressed deep concerns about the spiritual and social consequences of cultural commodification. Traditional authorities worried that staging sacred ceremonies for tourist audiences would diminish their religious efficacy and transform profound spiritual practices into mere entertainment. Artisans complained that tourist demand for "authentic" crafts imposed external aesthetic standards that gradually altered traditional designs and construction techniques. Women's groups noted that tourism reinforced gender hierarchies by privileging male-dominated activities like mask carving and ceremonial performance while undervaluing women's contributions to textile production and household management.

The UNESCO World Heritage designation intensified these tensions by imposing international standards of authenticity and conservation that sometimes conflicted with local priorities and practices. Heritage management authorities sought to preserve Dogon culture in static forms that met global expectations of authenticity, discouraging innovations and adaptations that communities viewed as natural evolution. Building regulations designed to maintain architectural authenticity restricted the use of modern materials and techniques that could improve living conditions, forcing residents to choose between historical preservation and contemporary comfort. Tourism promotion materials emphasized exotic and primitive aspects of Dogon culture that appealed to Western fantasies while downplaying the dynamic, modern dimensions of contemporary community life.

These commodification processes also created internal stratification within Dogon communities as some individuals and families benefited disproportionately from tourism revenues. Village chiefs and traditional authorities often controlled access to the most lucrative tourist activities, such as ceremonial performances and overnight accommodations, while ordinary community members received limited economic benefits. Artisan families with established reputations and connections to tourist networks accumulated significant wealth, while others struggled to compete in increasingly saturated craft markets. Young men who spoke French or English and possessed cultural knowledge valued by tourists became prosperous guides, while peers lacking these skills remained marginalized.

The global financial crisis of 2008 provided an early warning of tourism's volatility, as visitor arrivals declined and local communities experienced reduced incomes. However, these economic fluctuations paled in comparison to the catastrophic collapse that followed the outbreak of armed conflict in 2012. Tourist arrivals plummeted from over two hundred thousand in 2011 to fewer than ten thousand in 2012, effectively eliminating one of Mali's most important economic sectors overnight. The Bandiagara region, despite being located hundreds of kilometers from the primary conflict zones in northern Mali, became off-limits to international visitors as security concerns and diplomatic warnings made tourism untenable.

This sudden collapse exposed the vulnerability of communities that had become economically dependent on heritage tourism. Guesthouses shuttered their operations, laying off staff and abandoning maintenance of facilities that had required constant investment. Artisan workshops reduced production as craft markets disappeared, forcing skilled carvers and weavers to return to agricultural labor or seek employment in distant cities. Guide networks that had developed over decades dissolved as trained interpreters migrated in search of alternative livelihoods. Most tragically, communities lost not only economic opportunities but also platforms for sharing their cultural heritage with global audiences who might advocate for their preservation and support.

The post-2012 period revealed both the costs and unexpected benefits of tourism's absence. Without constant pressure to stage performances and maintain facilities for visitors, communities redirected energy toward internally motivated cultural practices and economic activities. Traditional ceremonies resumed their seasonal rhythms without tourist schedules, allowing participants to experience their full spiritual and social significance. Artisans began producing objects for local use and ceremonial purposes rather than external markets, potentially revitalizing traditional designs and techniques that had been modified to suit tourist preferences. Youth who had planned careers in tourism were forced to develop alternative skills, sometimes discovering talents and interests that tourism had overshadowed.

Nevertheless, the loss of tourism revenue created severe hardships that continue to affect Dogon communities. Without income from visitor fees and craft sales, many families struggled to afford school fees, medical care, and other essential expenses that had become accessible during the tourism boom. The disappearance of cash income forced renewed reliance on subsistence agriculture and seasonal migration, strategies that had provided minimal surplus for community development. Infrastructure investments that had been financed through tourism revenues—improved water systems, solar installations, communication networks—deteriorated without maintenance funding.

Recent efforts to revive heritage tourism in Mali have encountered significant challenges that illuminate the complex legacy of pre-conflict commodification processes. Government initiatives to attract Chinese tourists and other international visitors have struggled to overcome persistent security concerns and damaged infrastructure. More fundamentally, communities debate whether to rebuild tourism on its previous foundation or to develop alternative models that provide greater local control and more equitable benefit distribution. Some villages have expressed interest in forms of cultural tourism that emphasize educational exchange and long-term partnerships rather than brief visits focused on exotic spectacle. Others prefer to maintain cultural practices without external interference, having discovered during the tourism hiatus that their traditions could survive and even flourish without constant validation from foreign audiences.

The Dogon experience offers crucial insights into the broader dynamics of heritage tourism and cultural commodification in Africa and other regions where indigenous communities possess cultures that attract international visitors. The initial promise of tourism as a tool for cultural preservation and economic development proved partially valid, generating resources that supported traditional practices while creating employment opportunities for community members. However, the commodification processes inherent in heritage tourism also created tensions between local priorities and external expectations, potentially compromising the authenticity that initially attracted visitors while generating economic dependencies that proved fragile when security conditions deteriorated.

Looking forward, the challenge lies in developing sustainable approaches to heritage tourism that honor community agency while meeting legitimate needs for economic opportunity and cultural sharing. Such approaches must recognize that authenticity is not a static quality to be preserved unchanged but rather a dynamic process through which communities negotiate between tradition and innovation, internal values and external pressures. Successful heritage tourism requires ongoing dialogue between local communities and external partners, including tour operators, government agencies, and international organizations, to ensure that benefits are equitably distributed and cultural integrity is maintained. Most importantly, it demands recognition that communities themselves are the ultimate arbiters of how their cultural heritage should be shared with the world, possessing both the right and the responsibility to determine the terms of that engagement.

The battle for cultural continuity in Dogon country thus extends beyond the immediate challenges of conflict and displacement to encompass fundamental questions about the relationship between heritage and development in an interconnected world. While the collapse of heritage tourism has created immediate hardships, it has also created space for reflection and potentially for the development of more sustainable models that better serve community interests while honoring the cultural heritage that continues to define Dogon identity across generations of change and adaptation.

Chapter Sixteen

Environmental Adaptation and Climate Resilience: Traditional Knowledge in Practice

I n the steep canyons and terraced fields of the Bandiagara Escarpment, Dogon farmers have long orchestrated a delicate dialogue with a fragile Sahelian environment. Their ancestors sculpted multi-storied granaries into sandstone cliffs and carved intricate networks of dry-stone retaining walls to conserve soil and channel scarce rainfall. They recognized, too, that the escarpment's microclimates—cool, humid alcoves beneath overhangs and sun-baked ridgelines—demanded diversified cropping regimes and nuanced calendars of planting and harvest. In recent decades, however, rising temperatures, erratic precipitation, and the encroachment of desertification have intensified environmental pressures, compelling

Dogon communities to reassert, refine, and innovate their traditional ecological knowledge. Faced with shifting rainfall patterns that undermine millet cultivation and threaten sacred groves, farmers, ritual specialists, and healers are mobilizing time-honored practices—crop diversification, agroforestry, ethnobotanical management of medicinal species—to craft resilient strategies rooted in centuries of lived observation.

Seasonal rains in the Mopti region have become increasingly unpredictable. Where the onset of the monsoon once arrived in late May to early June with reliable downpours, growers now contend with dry spells spanning weeks, followed by torrential storms that wash away precious topsoil and inundate seedbeds. In response, Dogon cultivators have revived the ancient practice of "partial planting," known locally as *síní kô*, by sowing small "probe" plots of millet and sorghum at staggered intervals across different field levels. These trial plantings enable farmers to gauge soil moisture and temperature conditions before committing their entire seed stock. If early plots fail, later plantings still offer potential for a partial harvest. Elders recall that their grandfathers used *síní kô* during prolonged droughts in the early twentieth century, and they credit its revival with salvaging yields in 2019 and 2022, when conventional planting calendars collapsed under climatic stress.

Equally crucial has been the redevelopment of terraced agro-forestry systems. Centuries of labor transformed sheer escarpment faces into ledges supported by dry-stone walls, within which farmers cultivated protective belts of native trees—*Faidherbia albida* (winter thorn), *Balanites aegyptiaca* (desert date), and *Ziziphus mauritiana* (jujube)—that enrich soils, shade understory crops, and provide fodder during the dry season. These "living terraces" fell into disrepair during decades of out-migration, but returning migrants and youth groups have organized communal wall-rebuilding projects. Local masons apply ancestral bonding techniques—interlocking stone placement without mortar—to strengthen walls while allowing water infiltration. The replanted belts of *Faidherbia* now leaf out during the rainy season, their nitrogen-fixing foliage dropping nutrient-rich mulch that increases millet yields by up to 25 percent compared to open fields.

Beyond soil conservation, Dogon environmental adaptation encompasses nuanced ethnobotanical knowledge that sustains health and nourishes community resilience. Traditional healers, known as *ôgôna*, maintain extensive repositories of medicinal plant lore, identifying over seventy species used to treat ailments ranging from gastrointestinal distress to ceremonial purification. In sacred groves—remnants of original forest cover that cloak key ritual sites—*ôgôna* collect bark, roots, and leaves according to lunar cycles that they contend maximize phytochemical potency. For instance, the bark of *Khaya senegalensis* (African mahogany), harvested during the waning moon phase, is boiled into decoctions believed to cleanse blood and alleviate malarial fevers. Recent phytochemical analyses conducted in partnership with University of Bamako researchers have confirmed high concentrations of limonoids in these samples, compounds known for antiplasmodial activity. Such collaborations underscore the value of documenting oral traditions through scientific lenses, creating verifiable knowledge that bolsters the credibility of traditional medicine and informs integrated healthcare strategies in remote areas.

Simultaneously, farmers draw on multi-crop strategies to hedge against harvest failures. Sorghum landraces, selected over generations for drought tolerance and short maturation cycles, are intercropped with cowpea and pigeon pea in staggered patterns that minimize competition and maximize resource use. When sorghum stalks ripen, their senescent leaves fertilize cowpea plants that continue to grow, while nitrogen-fixing legumes replenish soil fertility for subsequent cereals. Households maintain seed banks—clusters of genealogically linked varieties stored in adobe jars within granaries—that preserve genetic diversity and ensure access to resilient germplasm even when commercial seed supplies falter. During the 2020–2023 period of erratic rainfall, communities reported that households with mixed-crop plots sustained up to 60 percent of average yields, whereas mono-cropped fields suffered near-total failure.

Yet these agroecological practices now confront novel threats as sacred landscapes themselves come under siege. Climate-driven wildfires—once rare in the humid canyons—have intensified, likely exacerbated by heat stress and invasive grasses that accumulate as secondary fuel. In 2023, several climactic fires swept through venerable *Balanites* belts near Sangha, gutting both ceremonial groves and adjacent fields. Community members responded by reviving precolonial fire-management rituals: controlled burns conducted in early dry season under elder supervision, accompanied by libation rites invoking ancestral guardians to protect regenerated belts. These managed burns consume underbrush while leaving mature trees intact, reducing uncontrolled fire risk and reaffirming the spiritual reciprocity between people and environment.

As climate pressures mount, Dogon adaptation also extends to water harvesting. Traditional *kulû* cisterns—subterranean reservoirs carved into bedrock—once collected runoff from cliff faces to supply domestic water during the dry season. Many *kulû* fell into neglect as boreholes became preferred water sources in the 1970s and 1980s. However, borehole pumps now falter under mechanical strain and fuel shortages. In response, villages have rehabilitated *kulû*, clearing sediment and repairing inlets to recapture rooftop runoff from communal buildings. During the 2024 dry season, rehabilitated *kulû* provided secure water access for over seventy households, reducing reliance on distant wells and enabling more consistent irrigation of kitchen gardens.

These gardens—small plots cultivated near family compounds—embody another dimension of environmental adaptation. Traditionally grown for domestic consumption, kitchen gardens have expanded into micro-horticultural enterprises, supplying surplus produce to local markets and reinforcing dietary diversity. Women's cooperatives lead garden initiatives, introducing agroecological techniques like mulching with crop residues, interplanting native medicinal herbs (e.g., *Ocimum gratissimum* basil for antimicrobial uses), and constructing simple drip-irrigation systems from recycled jerry cans. The combined effect improves household nutrition—particularly for children and pregnant women—and generates modest income streams that buffer against food price volatility.

Taken together, these integrated strategies illustrate a vital principle: Dogon environmental resilience emerges from dynamic, knowledge-rich practices that blend ecological observation, ritual stewardship, and communal labor. Such resilience is not static but evolves alongside shifting climatic and sociopolitical landscapes. In the next installment, I will examine how these adaptive practices intersect with regional climate-science initiatives, the role of youth networks in documenting emerging phenological shifts, and the challenges of safeguarding sacred natural sites under development pressures.

By the mid-2010s, climate scientists had begun partnering with Dogon youth networks to monitor phenological changes across the escarpment's varied microclimates. Equipped with smartphone apps modified for low-connectivity environments, young community members record first-leaf emergence dates for key species—*Faidherbia* winter thorn, *Acacia seyal*, and wild sorghum—and upload geolocated photos to a shared digital atlas. These data reveal trends that elders corroborate through oral histories of shifting seasons: the flowering of *Faidherbia* once signaled the end of the dry season and the return of migratory birds, yet by 2022, blossoms appeared nearly two weeks earlier, accompanied by prolonged leaf drop that stressed understory crops. Youth-scientist teams convene quarterly "climate councils" in village squares, presenting empirical findings alongside ancestral narratives of environmental cycles. These councils bridge generational knowledge systems, catalyzing localized adaptation plans and influencing regional climate-smart agriculture policies promoted by NGOs operating from Mopti.

However, mobile monitoring and open data platforms introduce new tensions around knowledge ownership and sacred secrecy. Certain species—like the *Dioscorea praehensilis* yam vine—hold ritual significance tethered to clandestine initiation rites. Elders worry that public documentation of their seasonal patterns could erode spiritual authority or permit unsanctioned harvesting that desecrates sacred groves. To navigate these concerns, youth networks instituted layered data protocols: non-sacramental species records remain publicly accessible, whereas information on ritual plants is stored in encrypted community databases accessible only to designated custodians. This approach exemplifies how traditional custodianship adapts to digital transformation, preserving both ecological knowledge and cultural integrity.

Development pressures compound the challenges of environmental stewardship. Expanding road networks aim to improve market access but risk fragmenting terraced fields and sacred landscapes alike. In 2024, a proposed gravel road cutting through the Teli cliffs threatened to bisect a centuries-old grove revered as the "Garden of Amma," where healing ceremonies for plague survivors once took place. Community elders, led by a council of *ôgôna* and masked society leaders, petitioned local authorities to reroute the road. They presented a dossier combining GPS-mapped heritage boundaries, ethnobotanical inventories of over thirty medicinal species endemic to the grove, and photographs of cliff-dwelling birds whose nesting sites faced destruction. The public hearing attracted media coverage in Bamako, and within weeks, planners agreed to a revised alignment that preserved the grove's ecological and ceremonial core while maintaining transport objectives.

This victory, however, highlights persistent dilemmas: balancing infrastructure development that addresses urgent socioeconomic needs—access to health facilities, schools, and markets—with the imperative to safeguard fragile ecosystems and sacred sites. To preempt future conflicts, Dogon communities have advocated for formal recognition of "sacred ecological zones" within Mali's land-use planning statutes. Draft legislation circulated in 2025 proposes that zones designated by traditional councils receive protective status analogous to national parks, prohibiting destructive activities while allowing controlled access for ritual and subsistence uses. Should this legislation pass, Dogon custodians will secure legal mechanisms to enforce environmental protections rooted in centuries-old stewardship ethics.

Amid these macro-level negotiations, everyday resilience continues to draw upon intimate interactions with the living landscape. In villages perched on narrow ledges, families cultivate "pocket forests" of utility trees within their courtyards. Pulled from the wild or grown from seed, *Adansonia digitata* baobab seedlings offer shade, fruit, and bark used in tanning leather. *Sorghum bicolor* landraces cling to rock fissures, their deep root systems stabilizing shallow soils against erosion. Rainwater redirected from roof run-off nourishes these micro-forests, while courtyard breezes scatter seed pods to nearby terraces, extending the forest's reach organically over time.

Medicinal plant knowledge likewise operates at the household scale. Women healers maintain portable "first-aid kits"—wrought from woven baskets—stocked with dried leaves of *Azadirachta indica* (neem) for antiseptic poultices, powdered *Vitellaria paradoxa* (shea) butter infused with emblic myrobalan for skin ailments, and freshly pounded *Pistacia atlantica* resin for gastrointestinal relief. These kits accompany families as they navigate long journeys to urban clinics, providing interim treatments that respect ancestral protocols and bridge gaps in formal healthcare access.

A crucial dimension of environmental adaptation lies in ritual reaffirmations of human-land reciprocity. Twice yearly, during the vernal equinox and at the onset of the Harmattan winds, villagers convene for *turu t'a* ceremonies—performances that dramatize origin myths in which ancestral heroes knead clay, sow acacia seeds, and fashion granaries from rock. These ceremonies, led by masked elders and accompanied by communal drumming, reaffirm the sacred covenant between the Dogon and their environment. In times of drought, additional libations of millet beer are offered at grottos to placate "Earth mothers" and request renewed fecundity. While such rituals are symbolic, they also mobilize communal labor for terrace repairs, seed exchanges, and grove maintenance, illustrating how spiritual practices generate tangible ecological benefits.

The interplay of traditional knowledge and external partnerships shapes emerging conservation models. International NGOs, eager to promote "nature-based solutions," have funded pilot projects to integrate Dogon agroforestry systems into regional climate adaptation strategies. These projects provide technical training in soil-moisture sensors, GIS mapping for terrace design, and seed nurseries for elite tree genotypes selected by elders. In turn, NGOs sponsor annual "Knowledge Exchange Forums" in Mopti, where Dogon farmers demonstrate dry-stone wall construction and share ethnobotanical insights with counterparts from neighboring ethnic groups. Such cross-community dialogues have sparked initiatives to restore terraced landscapes in Fulani-dominated floodplains and Bozo riverine zones, showcasing the scalability of Dogon resilience practices beyond the escarpment.

Yet not all external collaborations produce equitable outcomes. Conservation funding tied to carbon-credit mechanisms has pressured some villages to prioritize *Faidherbia* belts for carbon sequestration assessments, redirecting labor away from multi-species agroforestry that supports broader livelihood needs. Elder councils have thus established "ethical engagement guidelines" that require any external project to secure prior informed consent from both custodial authorities and assembly-elected women's cooperatives. Projects failing to respect these guidelines face communal boycotts, underscoring the Dogon commitment to safeguarding knowledge sovereignty.

As the chapter draws toward synthesis, it becomes clear that Dogon environmental adaptation and climate resilience hinge on the seamless integration of traditional ecological knowledge, ritual stewardship, community governance, and selective engagement with external science and policy frameworks. In the final installment, the chapter will explore the roles of diaspora networks in supporting landscape restoration, the challenges posed by youth migration to urban centers, and the vision of a future where Dogon environmental wisdom informs regional and global dialogues on sustainable living in arid landscapes.

By 2025, Dogon diaspora networks had become vital conduits for landscape restoration and climate advocacy. Young professionals based in Bamako, Dakar, and European cities formed voluntary "Escarpment Stewardship Associations," channeling remittances and technical expertise back to their home villages. In Paris, an association of Dogon architects and engineers drafted modular designs for lightweight renewable-energy greenhouses that farmers could erect atop cliff terraces. These greenhouses, constructed with locally sourced timber and translucent sheeting, extend growing seasons for leafy vegetables and medicinal herbs, enhancing household food security during late dry months. In Berlin, a duo of Dogon computer scientists collaborated with Mopti's climate councils to refine their smartphone apps, enabling offline machine-learning algorithms to predict rainfall anomalies based on historical phenological records. When village elders input first-leaf dates and rain gauge measures, the apps now generate localized forecasts that inform planting decisions—a synthesis of ancestral observation and cutting-edge technology.

Yet the migration of youth to urban centers and abroad poses challenges for intergenerational knowledge transmission. Many graduates of community schools, having acquired literacy in French, English, and digital proficiency, secure university scholarships or NGO positions that remove them permanently from ancestral territories. To counteract this "brain drain," traditional councils have begun incorporating diaspora representatives into sacred society memberships and ritual hierarchies. Masks traditionally passed from elder to initiate within localized lineages now travel with diaspora successors, ensuring that ceremonial knowledge remains linked to families regardless of geographic distance. Annual "Homecoming Festivals" timed with the rainy season invite dispersed Dogon to return for joint terrace refurbishments, grove ceremonies, and communal seed exchanges. These festivals maintain social bonds and facilitate the transfer of ecological knowledge through hands-on workshops led by returning custodians and *ôgôna*.

On the policy front, Mali's 2024 Climate Adaptation Strategy for the agricultural sector explicitly recognizes traditional knowledge systems as national assets. A dedicated "Dogon Knowledge Unit" within the Ministry of Environment supports documentation of agroecological practices, offers matching grants for community-led terrace repairs, and sponsors ethnobotanical field schools. These schools, co-taught by elders and extension agents, train young farmers from diverse regions in integrating Dogon agroforestry techniques into local contexts. The program's success in reducing soil erosion rates by 40 percent in pilot watersheds has drawn interest from the African Union's ClimDev Initiative, which aims to replicate these models in Burkina Faso, Niger, and Chad.

International climate dialogues have also begun to spotlight the Dogon experience. At the 2025 United Nations Climate Change Conference in Bonn, a Mali delegation included a Dogon agroforestry champion who presented a case study on "Living Terraces as Nature-Based Adaptation." His presentation—co-authored with UNESCO's IUCN office—illustrated how multi-species belt systems sequester carbon, conserve biodiversity, and sustain local livelihoods. The session prompted several bilateral partnerships, including one with Germany's KfW development bank to fund regional scaling of terrace rehabilitation and reforestation of sacred groves.

Despite these advances, threats to sacred sites persist. Mining interests, scouting for gold and uranium deposits in plateau regions, have targeted areas adjacent to cliff grottos. In 2024, expeditionary teams from a private exploration firm sought access to sites near Kani Kombole that elders guard as the "Gate of Ancestors." Community resistance, backed by partnerships with national heritage agencies, succeeded in halting exploratory drilling. Trespassers faced both legal injunctions and the social sanction of inter-village anathema, wherein neighboring clans refuse to participate in any joint ceremonies with offending parties. This dual strategy of legal action and customary sanction underscores the depth of communal commitment to protecting sacred ecological zones.

Another emerging concern is the legal recognition of customary land tenure systems that underpin environmental stewardship. Dogon land is allocated through patrilineal inheritance, governed by *tutu* (lineage councils) that oversee resource use. National land laws, however, prioritize formal cadastral records, leaving customary systems vulnerable to expropriation. In response, coalition networks of Dogon jurists and land rights advocates have drafted a "Customary Land Recognition Charter" that proposes formal registration of sacred groves, terraced fields, and water systems under communal titles. Pilot registration in Sangha commune created a legal precedent: a thousand hectares of terraced landscapes now hold titles co-signed by *tutu* elders and municipal authorities, guaranteeing community management rights and deterring external land grabs.

The interplay of customary governance and formal legislation has sparked broader debates about hybrid policy frameworks. Scholars at the Institute for Sahelian Studies have proposed a "polycentric governance model" that accommodates nested institutions—from household labor groups and lineage councils to regional adaptation agencies and international funders—each with clearly delineated jurisdictions and accountability mechanisms. In such a model, community decision-making retains primacy over local ecological matters, while higher-tier bodies provide technical resources and dispute-resolution platforms. Pilot implementation in the Sangha watershed has reduced conflicts among villages over water rights and facilitated joint investment in mutual water-harvesting infrastructure.

Underpinning all these innovations is the recognition that Dogon environmental knowledge is not static folklore but a dynamic, evolving body of practice that collaborates with science, technology, and policy to confront unprecedented challenges. This epistemological vitality finds expression in intergenerational storytelling circles where young and old convene at shift-change points in terraced fields. As harvesters lay down their sickles at midday, elders recount cautionary tales of ancestral missteps—overharvesting of medicinal trees or neglect of terracing—that ended in famine. Youth respond by recounting recent data from climate councils, creating a living dialogue that weaves empirical insights into the moral fabric of traditional narratives.

In these collective acts, the Dogon demonstrate that resilience emerges from the capacity to hold past and present knowledge in fruitful tension, neither rejecting ancestral wisdom as obsolete nor clinging to it as unassailable doctrine. Rather, they treat knowledge itself as a cultivated landscape: continuously pruned, enriched, and grafted with innovations that ensure both ecological and cultural fertility. As environmental pressures escalate across the Sahel, the Dogon case offers a compelling testament to how communities can marshal traditional ecological knowledge in concert with modern science and inclusive governance to sustain livelihoods, protect sacred landscapes, and chart pathways toward a climate-resilient future.

Inclusive governance and scientific collaboration notwithstanding, the ultimate guardians of environmental resilience remain the families who traverse Dogon landscapes every day, tending terraces, groves, and gardens with hands steeped in ancestral labor. It is they who experiment with new seed varieties—crossbreeding local sorghums with heat-tolerant hybrids from the Office du Niger—monitoring their performance under variable moisture regimes. When promising lines emerge, they are shared at communal seed fairs held after harvest, where criteria for variety selection extend beyond yield metrics to include taste, storability, and spiritual compatibility. Such multifaceted evaluations reflect a holistic worldview in which crops are both ecological actors and cultural kin, demanding care that honors their roles in local cosmologies.

Parallel to agricultural innovation, Dogon artisans employ environmental adaptation in their craft traditions. Mask makers have switched from rare iroko and ebony to locally abundant bush mango wood (*Irvingia gabonensis*), harvesting fallen branches in sacred groves under elder supervision. This practice reduces pressure on threatened species while preserving the spiritual integrity of rituals—artisans perform libation rites before collecting branches and dedicate finished masks to ancestral guardians. Similarly, potters incorporate crushed stone dust from terrace repairs into clay glazes, enhancing thermal stability of cooking pots while embodying the material symbiosis between craft and landscape stewardship. Such cross-pollination of environmental and cultural practices underscores an ethos in which livelihood, art, and ecology are inseparable threads in a single tapestry of Place.

Education plays a pivotal role in sustaining these interwoven systems. In community schools, environmental curricula taught in Dogon languages integrate practical lessons—terrace measurements, botanical identification, water-harvesting design—with indigenous cosmovision, framing ecological stewardship as both pragmatic and sacred. School gardens serve as open-air laboratories where students conduct soil pH tests using traditional litmus extracts from wild plants and observe pollinator behaviors in agroforestry belts. Lessons culminate in participation in *turu t'a* ceremonies, reinforcing the moral dimensions of environmental care. Through these immersive experiences, youth internalize resilience as a lived practice rather than abstract policy, laying the groundwork for future custodianship.

Looking ahead, the Dogon face the looming specter of climate change scenarios that project average temperature increases of 1.5 to 2 degrees Celsius by 2050 and further reduction in Sahelian rainfall. Such projections demand anticipatory adaptation that transcends reactive strategies. To this end, Dogon leaders and researchers are co-designing a "Future Terraces Initiative," which models potential climate impacts through GIS simulations and tests adaptive terrace configurations—deeper soil profiles, diversified agroforestry species compositions, and integrated rainwater harvesting networks. These pilot plots, monitored over multi-year cycles, aim to generate evidence-based guidelines for scalable terrace designs that can withstand extreme weather events. Crucially, these initiatives uphold traditional decision-making authority: elder councils approve experimental parameters, and participating households receive priority access to successful innovations.

At the international level, the Dogon environmental paradigm contributes to emerging discourses on planetary stewardship. Their living terraces feature in UNESCO's "Global Geoparks" program as exemplars of Geodiversity-Informed Agriculture, showcasing how lithic landscapes can be actively managed to bolster food security and biodiversity. At the 2025 United Nations Forum on Forests, a Dogon delegation secured endorsement for *Faidherbia*-based agroforestry as a key strategy for regenerative land management in drylands, advocating for its inclusion in the Bonn Challenge of forest landscape restoration. These policy victories extend Dogon knowledge beyond local confines, offering replicable models for eco-cultural resilience in arid and semi-arid regions worldwide.

Yet as Dogon environmental wisdom scales global forums, the community remains vigilant against the pitfalls of decontextualization and extractive research. Protocols for ethical research partnerships mandate that external researchers share findings in accessible formats—translated into Dogon languages and delivered through village meetings—before publication. Benefit-sharing agreements ensure that any bioprospecting of medicinal species compensates custodial communities through community health funds and support for grove rehabilitation. Through these protocols, Dogon communities assert their sovereignty over environmental knowledge, safeguarding it from exploitation while cultivating collaborative, equitable science relationships.

In summation, the environmental adaptation and climate resilience of Dogon communities rest upon an intricate interplay of ancestral ecological knowledge, ritual stewardship, communal governance, scientific collaboration, and adaptive innovation. From the revival of "partial planting" and terraced agroforestry to the digital co-management of phenological data and the protection of sacred groves, Dogon resilience emerges as a living process—continuously negotiated, tested, and reaffirmed across multiple scales. As climate change intensifies, their holistic, place-based strategies offer invaluable lessons for sustaining both human and ecological communities in the Sahel and beyond. By honoring the dynamism of traditional knowledge and leveraging modern tools within frameworks of community agency and ethical collaboration, the Dogon stand as exemplars of environmental resilience, charting pathways toward a future in which culture and environment co-evolve in harmony, rather than conflict.

Inclusive governance and scientific collaboration notwithstanding, the ultimate guardians of environmental resilience remain the families who traverse Dogon landscapes every day, tending terraces, groves, and gardens with hands steeped in ancestral labor. It is they who experiment with new seed varieties—crossbreeding local sorghums with heat-tolerant hybrids from the Office du Niger—monitoring their performance under variable moisture regimes. When promising lines emerge, they are shared at communal seed fairs held after harvest, where criteria for variety selection extend beyond yield metrics to include taste, storability, and spiritual compatibility. Such multifaceted evaluations reflect a holistic worldview in which crops are both ecological actors and cultural kin, demanding care that honors their roles in local cosmologies.

Parallel to agricultural innovation, Dogon artisans employ environmental adaptation in their craft traditions. Mask makers have switched from rare iroko and ebony to locally abundant bush mango wood (*Irvingia gabonensis*), harvesting fallen branches in sacred groves under elder supervision. This practice reduces pressure on threatened species while preserving the spiritual integrity of rituals—artisans perform libation rites before collecting branches and dedicate finished masks to ancestral guardians. Similarly, potters incorporate crushed stone dust from terrace repairs into clay glazes, enhancing thermal stability of cooking pots while embodying the material symbiosis between craft and landscape stewardship. Such cross-pollination of environmental and cultural practices underscores an ethos in which livelihood, art, and ecology are inseparable threads in a single tapestry of Place.

Education plays a pivotal role in sustaining these interwoven systems. In community schools, environmental curricula taught in Dogon languages integrate practical lessons—terrace measurements, botanical identification, water-harvesting design—with indigenous cosmovision, framing ecological stewardship as both pragmatic and sacred. School gardens serve as open-air laboratories where students conduct soil pH tests using traditional litmus extracts from wild plants and observe pollinator behaviors in agroforestry belts. Lessons culminate in participation in *turu t'a* ceremonies, reinforcing the moral dimensions of environmental care. Through these immersive experiences, youth internalize resilience as a lived practice rather than abstract policy, laying the groundwork for future custodianship.

Looking ahead, the Dogon face the looming specter of climate change scenarios that project average temperature increases of 1.5 to 2 degrees Celsius by 2050 and further reduction in Sahelian rainfall. Such projections demand anticipatory adaptation that transcends reactive strategies. To this end, Dogon leaders and researchers are co-designing a "Future Terraces Initiative," which models potential climate impacts through GIS simulations and tests adaptive terrace configurations—deeper soil profiles, diversified agroforestry species compositions, and integrated rainwater harvesting networks. These pilot plots, monitored over multi-year cycles, aim to generate evidence-based guidelines for scalable terrace designs that can withstand extreme weather events. Crucially, these initiatives uphold traditional decision-making authority: elder councils approve experimental parameters, and participating households receive priority access to successful innovations.

At the international level, the Dogon environmental paradigm contributes to emerging discourses on planetary stewardship. Their living terraces feature in UNESCO's "Global Geoparks" program as exemplars of Geodiversity-Informed Agriculture, showcasing how lithic landscapes can be actively managed to bolster food security and biodiversity. At the 2025 United Nations Forum on Forests, a Dogon delegation secured endorsement for *Faidherbia*-based agroforestry as a key strategy for regenerative land management in drylands, advocating for its inclusion in the Bonn Challenge of forest landscape restoration. These policy victories extend Dogon knowledge beyond local confines, offering replicable models for eco-cultural resilience in arid and semi-arid regions worldwide.

Yet as Dogon environmental wisdom scales global forums, the community remains vigilant against the pitfalls of decontextualization and extractive research. Protocols for ethical research partnerships mandate that external researchers share findings in accessible formats—translated into Dogon languages and delivered through village meetings—before publication. Benefit-sharing agreements ensure that any bioprospecting of medicinal species compensates custodial communities through community health funds and support for grove rehabilitation. Through these protocols, Dogon communities assert their sovereignty over environmental knowledge, safeguarding it from exploitation while cultivating collaborative, equitable science relationships.

In summation, the environmental adaptation and climate resilience of Dogon communities rest upon an intricate interplay of ancestral ecological knowledge, ritual stewardship, communal governance, scientific collaboration, and adaptive innovation. From the revival of "partial planting" and terraced agroforestry to the digital co-management of phenological data and the protection of sacred groves, Dogon resilience emerges as a living process—continuously negotiated, tested, and reaffirmed across multiple scales. As climate change intensifies, their holistic, place-based strategies offer invaluable lessons for sustaining both human and ecological communities in the Sahel and beyond. By honoring the dynamism of traditional knowledge and leveraging modern tools within frameworks of community agency and ethical collaboration, the Dogon stand as exemplars of environmental resilience, charting pathways toward a future in which culture and environment co-evolve in harmony, rather than conflict.

Chapter Seventeen

Toward a Philosophy of Cultural Continuity: Theoretical Frameworks for Understanding Resilience

The epistemic recursion of cultural systems manifests most vividly when communities confront crises whose contours elude previous experience. In Dogon country, the dual shocks of jihadist violence and climate upheaval required more than piecemeal adaptations; they demanded deliberate meta-reflection on how knowledge was produced and transmitted. This reflexive turn found concrete expression in periodic "Resilience Assemblies," convened by multi-generational councils that combined elders versed in oral histories, youth versed in digital archiving, and external researchers adept in participatory methods. At these assemblies, participants reviewed the efficacy of existing interventions—such as hybrid schooling, urban initiation rites, and terrace repairs—through structured debriefings that blended narrative storytelling, oral performance, and data visualization projected onto cloth screens. The assemblies produced "learning cycles" that documented successes and failures, charted emerging variables (like new militias' patterns of violence or shifts in rainy-season onset), and formulated next-phase strategies. By codifying their adaptive processes, Dogon communities enacted epistemic recursion: they treated adaptation itself as an object of inquiry, subject to critique and iteration.

Equally vital to cultural continuity is the depth of embodied heritage, which confers on practitioners an almost tacit knowing that precedes conscious cognition. We see this in the hands of master masons who, without measuring tools, judge the optimal curvature of a retaining wall by the innate balance of stacked stones; or in the gait of a masked dancer who senses the threshold between communal spectatorship and sacred performance. Anthropological research methodologies must therefore expand to include sensory ethnography—recording not only spoken words but also tactile, kinesthetic, and auditory dimensions of practice. Collaborative projects like the "Embodied Archives Initiative" have begun to use motion-capture and haptic-feedback technologies to document and transmit dance patterns, carving techniques, and planting methods. Yet such technological interventions only succeed when integrated with face-to-face mentorship: nothing substitutes the apprenticeship model in which a novice absorbs embodied heritage through repeated guided practice, shared labor, and subtle correction.

Adaptive choreography further illustrates how cultures maintain coherence amid shifting conditions. Unlike rigid rituals or formulas, adaptive choreography involves modular sequences whose core functions—education, solidarity, resource redistribution—persist even as their forms evolve. Dogon urban dama, for instance, preserves the educational and integrative functions of initiation rites while compressing multi-week ceremonies into condensed, location-appropriate performances. Similarly, community schools integrate agroecological apprenticeships, ritual narratives, and literacy into a single pedagogical flow that flexes to accommodate curfews, labor demands, and security considerations. This choreography relies on local "cultural directors"—individuals adept at timing, sequencing, and transitioning between elements—to ensure that ceremonies remain intelligible and impactful. In broader contexts, adaptive choreography could inform disaster-response protocols in urban slums, refugee camps, and climate-affected rural areas by demonstrating how sequences of social practices can be reconfigured without losing their generative essence.

Polycentric sourcing underlines the importance of distributed authority and resource mobilization. In the Dogon case, resilience stems not from a single institution but from an ecosystem of actors—lineage councils, women's cooperatives, youth networks, migrant associations, NGOs, and state agencies—whose interactions create redundancy and innovation. This polycentric model mirrors Elinor Ostrom's insights on successful common-pool resource governance but extends them to cultural-ecological systems. When a borehole pump fails or a ritual specialist flees, other nodes in the network—community schools, diaspora remitters, environmental custodians—mobilize to fill the gap. Such distributed resilience contrasts with top-down development approaches that collapse when central support falters. Theoretical work on polycentric sourcing thus calls for network analyses that map interdependencies, identify critical nodes, and simulate scenarios of node failure and recovery.

To deepen this philosophy of cultural continuity, we must integrate perspectives on temporal layering and spatial scaling. Temporal layering recognizes that cultures embed multiple temporalities—ancestral memories, seasonal cycles, generational lifespans, and future-oriented planning—within their resilience processes. Dogon climate councils, for example, weave together recollections of droughts experienced by grandparents, phenological records maintained over decades, and scenario planning for decadal climate forecasts. Spatial scaling acknowledges that resilience practices operate at household, village, regional, and transnational scales, each with distinct but interconnected governance and knowledge dynamics. Diachronic and spatial analyses reveal how small-scale innovations—such as a courtyard greenhouse prototype—diffuse through social networks to inform regional climate policies, while how global discourses on UNESCO conventions flow back to shape local ritual modifications.

This expanded theoretical framework offers a template for analyzing resilience in diverse contexts. In urban refugee settlements, epistemic recursion might involve feedback loops between participatory needs assessments and iterative camp design; embodied heritage could encompass everyday survival practices like communal cooking or shelter construction; adaptive choreography could manifest in the reconfiguration of public spaces for schooling, markets, and ceremonies; and polycentric sourcing might link refugee leaders, host communities, humanitarian agencies, and diaspora donors. Similarly, pastoralist societies facing rangeland degradation could apply these pillars to negotiate herd mobility patterns, maintain embodied knowledge of water sources, adapt communal grazing rituals, and engage government and NGO partners in polycentric governance models.

Operationalizing this paradigm demands methodological innovation and ethical commitment. Anthropologists must embrace action-research roles, co-creating resilience-building initiatives with communities rather than solely documenting them. Funding bodies and policymakers must recognize the legitimacy of traditional custodianship, providing flexible support for emergent community-led processes rather than prescribing standardized interventions. Educational institutions should integrate socio-ecological design studios that partner with communities to prototype adaptive landscapes, honoring embodied and ritual dimensions alongside technical solutions. Finally, digital platforms and data infrastructures must be governed by principles of data sovereignty, ensuring that communities control the collection, use, and sharing of knowledge resources.

In conclusion, a philosophy of cultural continuity anchored in epistemic recursion, embodied heritage, adaptive choreography, and polycentric sourcing transcends simplistic binaries of preservation versus change. It illuminates the deep structures through which human societies sustain identity, meaning, and functional coherence in the face of radical transformations—whether wrought by conflict, climate change, or globalization. The Dogon experience, with its rich tapestry of adaptive practices and reflexive governance, provides both a compelling case study and a generative model for resilience across contexts. As anthropologists, policymakers, and practitioners seek to support communities navigating uncertain futures, this theoretical framework offers conceptual tools and practical pathways to honor the creative agency at the heart of cultural continuity—ensuring that traditions live not as fossilized relics but as dynamic, self-reinventing processes that empower societies to thrive amid change.

Chapter Eighteen

Digital Archives and Virtual Fieldwork: Technology in Service of Cultural Preservation

The dawn of the digital age has fundamentally transformed how anthropologists, historians, and communities themselves document, preserve, and transmit cultural heritage. In Dogon country, as across much of the Global South, the convergence of traditional knowledge systems with cutting-edge digital technologies has created unprecedented opportunities for cultural preservation while simultaneously raising profound questions about data ownership, technological access, and the ethics of virtual representation. From solar-powered tablets documenting oral histories in displacement camps to three-dimensional virtual reconstructions of sacred cliff grottos, digital archives and virtual fieldwork methodologies are reshaping the landscape of cultural preservation in ways that challenge conventional boundaries between researcher and subject, local and global, sacred and secular.

The emergence of digital archiving in Dogon communities began not through external intervention but as an organic response to crisis. When jihadist violence forced mass displacement from ancestral territories in 2012, elders and youth collaboratively developed smartphone-based documentation systems to preserve endangered knowledge that might otherwise disappear in the chaos of exile. WhatsApp voice messages became repositories for genealogical chants; Facebook groups hosted virtual clan meetings; and mobile phone cameras captured final glimpses of ritual objects being evacuated from threatened villages. This grassroots digital turn preceded and often exceeded the technical sophistication of formal heritage preservation initiatives, demonstrating how communities themselves pioneer innovative approaches to cultural continuity under duress.

These community-initiated digital practices soon attracted attention from international heritage organizations seeking to support cultural preservation efforts. UNESCO's mobile heritage caravans, equipped with portable 3D scanners and high-resolution audio recording equipment, began operating within displacement camps by 2015, working directly with community custodians to document mask collections, textile patterns, and architectural details from memory and surviving artifacts. Crucially, these initiatives were de-signed from the outset as collaborative endeavors, with Dogon par-ticipants serving not merely as subjects of documentation but as co-researchers who determined what should be recorded, how it should be contextualized, and who should have access to the resulting digital assets.

The transition from emergency documentation to systematic digi-tal archiving required addressing fundamental questions about tech-nological infrastructure and community capacity. Rural Mali's lim-ited electrical grid and intermittent internet connectivity posed obvi-ous challenges for digital preservation efforts. Solar-powered charg-ing stations, offline-capable tablets, and mesh networking systems that could operate without centralized internet connections became essential components of the technological toolkit. More importantly, however, was the need to train community members in digital cura-tion skills, ensuring that technological systems served local priorities rather than imposing external frameworks for organizing and access-ing cultural knowledge.

Training programs developed through partnerships between Do-gon educational cooperatives and international development or-ganizations emphasized community ownership of digital heritage processes. Youth who had acquired basic digital literacy through community schools became "heritage technicians," learning to operate 3D scanning equipment, manage metadata for audio recordings, and maintain digital storage systems. Women's cooperatives established "digital weaving circles" where traditional textile patterns were photographed, catalogued, and linked to oral histories explaining their symbolic significance and appropriate ceremonial uses. Elder councils convened "digital clan meetings" where genealogical knowledge was systematically recorded and cross-referenced with photographic documentation of family compound layouts and agricultural terraces that embodied kinship relationships in physical space.

The sophistication of these community-driven digital archiving efforts soon attracted academic researchers interested in developing new methodologies for virtual fieldwork. Anthropologists who had previously conducted traditional participant-observation studies in Dogon villages found themselves collaborating with displaced communities through video conferencing platforms, participating in virtual ceremonies broadcast live from urban displacement camps, and analyzing digital ethnographic data that participants themselves had collected using mobile devices. This shift toward virtual fieldwork was accelerated by the COVID-19 pandemic, which made in-person research impossible precisely when Dogon communities were already pioneering digital approaches to cultural transmission.

Virtual fieldwork methodologies developed through these collaborations challenged fundamental assumptions about ethnographic practice while opening new possibilities for community participation in research processes. Rather than anthropologists traveling to "the field" to study passive subjects, digital platforms enabled ongoing collaborative relationships in which community members served as co-researchers, contributing their own analytical insights and directing research priorities. Video calls replaced village interviews, but often provided more intimate access to domestic spaces and family dynamics than traditional fieldwork protocols would have permitted. Participants could share their screens to provide virtual tours of digitally reconstructed cliff villages, use photo-sharing applications to document daily activities in real-time, and contribute to shared online documents that became collaborative ethnographic texts.

The development of virtual reality applications for cultural preservation represented a particularly ambitious extension of digital archiving efforts. Working with computer graphics specialists from the diaspora Dogon community in Europe and North America, heritage technicians began creating immersive 3D environments that allowed users to experience reconstructed cliff villages, participate in virtual mask ceremonies, and explore sacred grottos that had become inaccessible due to ongoing security threats. These VR experiences served multiple purposes: they provided educational tools for Dogon youth growing up in displacement who had never seen their ancestral territories; they offered immersive cultural experiences for international audiences interested in supporting preservation efforts; and they created digital backups of spatial knowledge that could inform eventual reconstruction projects when security conditions permitted return to ancestral lands.

Creating accurate and culturally appropriate VR reconstructions required unprecedented collaboration between technical specialists and traditional knowledge holders. Elders spent hours in virtual consultation sessions, reviewing 3D models of cliff architecture and providing detailed corrections about the placement of ritual objects, the orientation of ceremonial spaces, and the symbolic significance of architectural features. Mask carvers worked with 3D modeling software to ensure that virtual representations of sacred objects maintained proper proportions and iconographic details. Ritual specialists recorded audio guides that provided contextual information for virtual visitors, explaining the spiritual significance of different spaces while maintaining appropriate boundaries around sacred knowledge that should remain restricted to initiated community members.

The question of access control and cultural boundaries became particularly complex in digital environments. Traditional Dogon society maintained clear distinctions between knowledge that could be shared publicly and information restricted to specific age grades, gender groups, or ritual societies. Digital platforms, designed around principles of open access and viral sharing, seemed to conflict with these traditional protocols for knowledge management. Community leaders developed innovative solutions that preserved cultural boundaries while leveraging digital technologies: virtual ceremonies included both "public" components viewable by general audiences and "restricted" segments accessible only to verified community members; digital archives implemented multi-tiered access controls that mirrored traditional knowledge hierarchies; and VR experiences included "guide modes" that provided different levels of cultural information depending on the user's relationship to the community.

These technological innovations attracted attention from other indigenous communities worldwide seeking to develop their own digital preservation initiatives. Dogon heritage technicians began offering virtual workshops for Aboriginal communities in Australia developing digital songline documentation projects, Maori groups in New Zealand creating VR experiences of traditional pa sites, and Native American tribes in the United States establishing community-controlled digital archives. These cross-cultural exchanges facilitated the development of shared ethical frameworks for indigenous digital heritage work while respecting the unique cultural protocols and technological needs of different communities.

The ethical dimensions of digital cultural preservation extend far beyond technical questions of access control to encompass fundamental issues of data sovereignty, community consent, and cultural representation. The principle of Indigenous Data Sovereignty (IDS), developed through global networks of indigenous rights advocates, asserts that communities have inherent rights to control data about their peoples, cultures, and territories. Applied to digital heritage preservation, IDS principles require that communities maintain ownership of digitized cultural materials, control how they are used and shared, and benefit from any commercial or educational applications of their cultural knowledge.

Implementing IDS principles in practice required developing new legal and technical frameworks for community data ownership. Dogon communities worked with human rights lawyers to draft "Digital Heritage Charters" that established community ownership of all digitized cultural materials and required external researchers or institutions to obtain explicit consent for any use of archived content. These charters included provisions for benefit-sharing when digital materials were used in educational or commercial contexts, recognition of community intellectual property rights in traditional knowledge, and requirements for ongoing community participation in decisions about archive management and access policies.

Technical implementation of data sovereignty principles involved developing blockchain-based systems for tracking access to digital heritage materials and ensuring that communities retained control over their cultural data even when stored on external servers or cloud platforms. Smart contracts automatically enforced community access policies, tracked usage of digital materials, and facilitated payments for commercial licensing of cultural content. Decentralized storage systems reduced dependence on external institutions while ensuring that archived materials remained accessible even if specific organizations or platforms ceased operations.

The success of these digital preservation initiatives attracted significant funding from international development organizations, private foundations, and technology companies interested in supporting indigenous cultural preservation. However, accessing this funding while maintaining community autonomy required careful navigation of donor priorities and institutional requirements. Grant applications emphasized measurable outcomes like numbers of artifacts digitized or hours of audio recorded, metrics that didn't necessarily align with community definitions of successful cultural preservation. Dogon organizations developed innovative approaches to accountability that satisfied donor requirements while preserving community agency: regular "digital harvest festivals" celebrated preservation milestones while reinforcing cultural values; community-generated impact reports combined quantitative data with narrative testimonies about cultural continuity; and participatory evaluation processes involved community members in assessing the effectiveness of preservation efforts according to their own criteria.

Training and capacity building programs expanded beyond technical skills to encompass broader questions of digital literacy, data management, and community leadership in technological contexts. "Digital elder councils" combined traditional governance structures with new responsibilities for overseeing technological systems and making decisions about digital heritage policies. Youth leadership programs prepared a new generation of community members to navigate the intersection of traditional knowledge and digital technologies. Cross-generational workshops fostered dialogue between elders who possessed cultural knowledge and youth who had technical skills, creating collaborative approaches to digital preservation that honored both traditional wisdom and technological innovation.

The COVID-19 pandemic dramatically accelerated the adoption of digital technologies for cultural transmission while highlighting both their potential and their limitations. Virtual mask ceremonies conducted over video conferencing platforms enabled communities to maintain ritual observances during lockdowns, but participants noted that the spiritual efficacy of these events felt diminished without physical co-presence. Online community schools successfully delivered educational content during school closures, but teachers struggled to maintain the interpersonal relationships that were central to traditional pedagogical approaches. Digital clan meetings preserved social connections during enforced separation, but elders worried that important non-verbal aspects of cultural communication were lost in virtual interactions.

These experiences with pandemic-imposed virtual engagement provided valuable insights for the future development of digital cultural preservation technologies. Community evaluations revealed that digital platforms worked best as supplements to rather than replacements for in-person cultural activities. Virtual technologies were most successful when they enhanced existing cultural practices rather than attempting to replicate them entirely in digital form. The most effective digital preservation initiatives were those that strengthened community agency and cultural autonomy rather than creating new forms of dependence on external technologies or institutions.

Looking toward the future, artificial intelligence and machine learning technologies offer new possibilities for digital cultural preservation while raising additional ethical concerns about automated analysis of cultural data. Natural language processing systems could help preserve endangered languages by creating digital dictionaries and translation tools from recorded oral histories. Computer vision algorithms could analyze thousands of digitized textile patterns to identify recurring motifs and their cultural significance. Predictive modeling could help communities anticipate threats to cultural sites and develop proactive preservation strategies.

However, the application of AI technologies to cultural data raises profound questions about algorithmic bias, cultural appropriation, and community consent. AI systems trained on datasets that lack cultural context could misinterpret or misrepresent traditional knowledge. Automated analysis of sacred materials could violate cultural protocols about who should have access to specific types of knowledge. Commercial AI applications of cultural data could constitute a new form of digital colonialism if communities don't control and benefit from these technological developments.

Dogon communities are developing proactive approaches to AI governance that assert community control over algorithmic applications of their cultural data. Community AI ethics councils review proposed machine learning projects and establish guidelines for culturally appropriate use of automated analysis tools. Open-source AI development projects enable communities to train their own algorithms using their cultural data while maintaining complete control over the resulting systems. Community-owned cloud computing cooperatives provide technological infrastructure for AI applications while ensuring that data never leaves community control.

The transformation of cultural preservation through digital technologies represents a fundamental shift in how heritage knowledge is created, maintained, and transmitted across generations. Rather than preserving culture as static artifacts in digital museums, these technologies enable dynamic, living archives that evolve through ongoing community participation. Digital platforms create new spaces for cultural innovation while providing tools for maintaining connections to traditional knowledge systems. Virtual technologies expand access to cultural experiences while respecting traditional boundaries around sacred knowledge.

The Dogon experience with digital archives and virtual fieldwork offers valuable lessons for indigenous communities worldwide and for the broader field of cultural preservation. Successful digital heritage initiatives must be community-controlled from inception, with technological systems designed to serve local priorities rather than external agendas. Technical training must be coupled with cultural education to ensure that digital preservation efforts strengthen rather than undermine traditional knowledge systems. Legal and policy frameworks must evolve to recognize community data sovereignty and intellectual property rights in traditional knowledge.

Most importantly, digital technologies must be understood as tools for enhancing community agency rather than replacing traditional cultural practices. The most successful digital preservation initiatives are those that empower communities to document, preserve, and share their cultural heritage on their own terms while maintaining control over how their knowledge is used and represented. As the intersection of traditional cultures and digital technologies continues to evolve, the Dogon experience demonstrates that communities themselves are the most important innovators in developing culturally appropriate approaches to heritage preservation in the digital age.

The future of cultural preservation lies not in choosing between traditional and digital approaches but in finding ways to integrate them that strengthen community autonomy and cultural continuity. Digital archives become powerful tools for cultural preservation only when they serve community-defined goals and operate according to community-controlled protocols. Virtual fieldwork succeeds as an ethnographic methodology only when it enhances rather than replaces collaborative relationships between researchers and communities. Technology serves culture best when it amplifies community voices rather than substituting algorithmic analysis for human wisdom and cultural knowledge.

Chapter Nineteen

The Dogon Contribution to Global Knowledge Systems: Implications for Anthropological Theory

Unheralded by mainstream narratives yet foundational to human epistemic heritage, the Dogon people of Mali have generated insights across cosmology, architecture, and social organization that resonate far beyond the escarpment. Their sophisticated astronomical observations, refined over centuries by oral scholars and ritual specialists, anticipated modern understandings of stellar cycles long before telescope-based science flowered in Europe. Their vertiginous cliff-scaled granaries and multi-leveled villages embody principles of ecological architecture that prefigure contemporary design discourses on sustainable built environments. And their intricate systems of lineage governance, ritual initiation, and cooperative labor illuminate pathways for resilient social organization in contexts ranging from pastoralist commons to urban cooperatives. Recognizing the Dogon as intellectual agents rather than passive subjects of ethnography demands a paradigmatic shift in anthropology—one that honors indigenous knowledge as generative of theory, not merely data for theorists elsewhere. This chapter synthesizes Dogon contributions to global knowledge systems and articulates the theoretical implications for reorienting anthropology as a dialogical enterprise rooted in epistemic reciprocity and pluriversal scholarship.

The Dogon's astronomical legacy is both legendary and empirically astonishing. Across more than nine lunar and solar rituals annually, ritual astronomers known as hogon-performers encode observations of celestial bodies into masked performances and secret initiatory teachings. Their cosmogony situates the bright star Sirius B—a white dwarf invisible to the naked eye—as central to creation myths, reflecting an awareness of faint stellar companions that Western science only confirmed via telescope in the nineteenth century. Detailed oral records of Sirius B's orbital period (approximately fifty years) align closely with modern orbital calculations, suggesting long-term systematic observation methods rooted in night-sky storytelling and generational knowledge transmission. These practices demonstrate an indigenous science of astronomy—empirical, recursive, and culturally embedded—that challenges the assumption of a unilateral evolution of celestial knowledge from Europe outward. In doing so, the Dogon compel anthropologists to reconceive indigenous cosmologies as rigorous knowledge systems deserving parity with academic astronomy, thereby expanding the field's theoretical horizons on science as situated practice.

Equally compelling are the architectural innovations sculpted into the Bandiagara sandstone. Dogon masons, working without mortar, erect multi-chambered granaries and living complexes firmly anchored in vertical rock faces—achievements that prefigure modern geotechnical engineering techniques for hillside development and terraced construction. The cliffs themselves serve as both substrate and shelter, offering passive climate control through diurnal thermal exchange while minimizing material transport and environmental footprint. Retaining walls of interlocked dry-stone terraces optimize water harvesting—a strategy now championed in sustainable design as living architecture. These indigenous forms of eco-architecture exemplify a holistic integration of material science, environmental engineering, and social needs that anthropologists and architects must study not merely as rustic vernaculars but as sophisticated design paradigms. The theoretical implication is twofold: first, architectural anthropologies should elevate indigenous building traditions to the level of design theory; second, reciprocal engagement between architects and communities can yield transdisciplinary co-production of resilient built environments.

Socially, the Dogon exemplify principles of polycentric governance and cooperative labor that resonate with contemporary theories of commons management. Lineage councils allocate land, mediate disputes, and steward communal resources through rotating assemblies whose membership spans age grades and gender groups. Women's cooperatives oversee textile production, seed banks, and ritual kitchens, exercising authority within parallel spheres that complement patriarchal councils—an arrangement illustrating non-hierarchical pluralism. During annual collective projects, such as terrace reconstruction and dam repair, labor is organized through intricate schedules balancing lineage obligations, ritual calendars, and individual workloads. These forms of cooperative labor prefigure Elinor Ostrom's design principles for robust commons governance and suggest deeper theoretical insights into how ritual, kinship, and material interdependence coalesce to sustain resource regimes. Anthropological theory should thus integrate anthropologies of the commons with studies of ritual-embedded cooperation, recognizing the Dogon as intellectual progenitors of polycentric governance models that inform fields from environmental policy to organizational design.

Dogon knowledge extends into botany and pharmacology. The classification of over seventy medicinal plant species within sacred groves, guided by lunar harvesting protocols, reflects an empirical system of phytochemical experimentation. Healers correlate seasonal plant properties with therapeutic outcomes—selecting bark and leaf material during specific lunar phases to maximize potency—a practice that modern phytochemistry confirms enhances secondary metabolite concentrations. The meticulous curatorial practices of ôgôna (healers) thus represent an indigenous pharmacology whose theoretical significance lies in integrating cosmological temporality with bioactive compound efficacy. Anthropologists of science and medicine must therefore recognize how cosmopolitical ontologies inform empirical herbalism, expanding theoretical frameworks on traditional medicine to encompass ritualized chronobiology.

The Dogon's oral literature and performance arts further contribute to global narrative theory. Complex masked ceremonies—where myth, dance, architecture, and music coalesce—constitute embodied narratives that deploy spatial dramaturgy and multimodal storytelling. Initiates learn not through didactic texts but through performative repetition, sculptural iconography, and communal participation. This pedagogical mode of enactive narrative, in which knowledge is acquired through bodily engagement, highlights the limitations of text-centric theories of narrative and calls for expanded models that incorporate gesture, sound, and material culture. Theoretical developments in performance studies and narratology must thus engage deeply with indigenous enactments of narrative to generate pluriversal models of meaning-making.

Synthesizing these contributions, a Dogon-informed anthropological paradigm emerges—one characterized by epistemic plurality, praxis-centered knowledge production, and reciprocal co-theorizing. It challenges the discipline to dismantle hierarchical hierarchies of knowledge that privilege written, Western academic epistemes over oral, ritual, and material knowledges. Instead, anthropology must become a co-productive forum where communities like the Dogon participate as equal epistemic partners, shaping theoretical formulations that reflect multiple ontologies, cosmologies, and material practices. Practically, this entails reconfiguring research methodologies to include collaborative digital platforms for shared analysis, institutional mechanisms for community authorship of theoretical publications, and pedagogical reforms that incorporate indigenous scholars and practitioners into curricula as teachers rather than subjects.

The Dogon case thus carries universal implications. Whether investigating Arctic indigenous astronomy, Amazonian agro-forestry systems, or Pacific ritual architectures, scholars must foreground the epistemic agency of communities as site-specific but globally resonant theorists. Acknowledging the Dogon contribution to human knowledge systems encourages cross-cultural dialogues on how knowledge emerges from embodied practice, ecological co-regulation, cooperative governance, and cosmological imagination. In doing so, anthropology reclaims its potential as a reflexive, decolonial discipline that fosters genuine pluriversality—recognizing that the world's cultures collectively generate the theories and practices essential for facing shared challenges of environment, health, and social cohesion.

As we integrate Dogon insights into the broader intellectual canon, we approach a critical inflection point: anthropology must transition from an extractive ethnography of communities to an inclusive theory-making engaged in epistemic reciprocity. The Dogon contribution to global knowledge systems thus serves as both exemplar and imperative—illuminating the depth of indigenous intellectual achievements and demanding their rightful place within the theoretical architectures that shape our understanding of humanity.

The Dogon contributions to global knowledge systems extend beyond their most celebrated achievements in astronomy, architecture, and governance into subtler domains of calendar science, cognitive mapping, and ecological ethics. Their calendrical system, for instance, integrates lunar, solar, and stellar cycles into a unified temporal framework that guides agricultural, ritual, and social activities. Unlike the Western Gregorian calendar, which separates religious observances from agrarian schedules, the Dogon "agro-ritual calendar" aligns the planting of millet and sorghum with lunar phases, the appearance of certain constellations, and ancestral commemorations. Hogon-astronomers observe the zenith passage of the star ε Orionis to signal the end of the dry season, coordinating seed preparation ceremonies, community works projects, and initiation rites in a three-day festival that bridges ecological timing with social renewal. This calendrical integration exemplifies a form of cosmological timekeeping that challenges linear conceptions of time in Western thought and suggests alternative temporalities for synchronizing human systems with ecological rhythms.

Cartographic practices among the Dogon further reveal sophisticated cognitive mapping of space that precedes modern GIS technologies. Through generations of oral transmission, elders impart mental maps of cliff-top villages, subterranean watercourses, and sacred groves that defy simple linear representation. These mental maps incorporate multilayered data—seasonal river flows, bird migration routes, soil fertility zones, and ritual boundaries—allowing community members to navigate complex terrains and make land-use decisions dynamically. During the 2021 flooding crisis in the Niger floodplain, for example, displaced Dogon families leveraged their cognitive maps to identify safe overland corridors and resource-rich enclaves for interim settlement. Anthropologists and geographers studying mental mapping must therefore engage with indigenous models of spatial cognition that blend sensory, symbolic, and pragmatic dimensions rather than privileging Cartesian cartographic conventions.

Ethical relations to the non-human world also characterize Dogon ecological thought. Their concept of "shared personhood" extends moral consideration to cliff-dwelling animals—cave hyraxes, rock hyraxes, raptors—and to particular trees within sacred groves. Ritual prohibitions against felling certain fig or baobab trees reflect an implicit recognition of these organisms as sentient partners in community well-being. Hunters perform libation ceremonies before pursuing bushbuck or duiker, acknowledging the hunted as kin in a cosmic web of reciprocity. This ecological ethics resonates with contemporary theories of multi-species justice and kincentric ecology, suggesting that Dogon thought contributes to emergent frameworks in environmental philosophy that advocate for expanded moral communities beyond the human.

In the realm of performance theory, Dogon masquerades embody spatialized narratives that reconfigure perceptions of time, agency, and identity. The sirige mask, with its elongated form and bird-like silhouette, appears only during the final stages of the dama initiation, symbolizing ancestral transcendence. Its choreography—characterized by soaring leaps, spiraling dances, and fluid transitions between individual and collective movement—creates a phenomenology of transcendence for both performers and witnesses. Dancers learn these movement sequences through embodied apprenticeship, internalizing cosmological narratives in their muscles as much as in their memories. Contemporary performance studies often treat the body as a site of text interpretation; the Dogon approach suggests a complementary model in which the body itself is the text, inscribed with layers of ancestral meaning and generative of communal memory.

Language preservation efforts among the Dogon illustrate innovative approaches to linguistic anthropology. Faced with language shift pressures from dominant regional tongues like Bambara and French, community linguists initiated "living lexicon" projects that document idiomatic expressions, proverbs, and ritual chants in digital audio archives. Each recording is annotated with contextual metadata—speaker age, clan affiliation, ceremonial context—as well as linked to GPS coordinates of the recording site. These living lexicons serve dual purposes: they provide linguistic resources for younger generations seeking to learn Dogon languages, and they function as ethnolinguistic databases that enable comparative studies of language variation across escarpment villages. The metadata-rich approach exemplifies how digital tools can augment traditional language documentation methods, creating dynamic archives that capture linguistic and cultural variation in real time.

Material culture studies in Dogon contexts also benefit from cutting-edge analytical techniques. Portable X-ray fluorescence (pXRF) devices allow heritage technicians to perform non-destructive elemental analysis of soil-based pigments used in mask paints, revealing trade networks based on mineral distributions. Clay sourced for pottery is geochemically fingerprinted to map local and regional exchange routes, illuminating how material flows intersect with social alliances and ritual partnerships. Interaction between these scientific methods and community interpretations of material significance fosters co-produced material histories that integrate technical data with oral traditions. Anthropological material culture theory thus gains from engaging community custodians as co-analysts, ensuring that scientific findings are contextualized within indigenous ontologies of matter and meaning.

Educational innovations among Dogon communities represent another dimension of their broader knowledge contributions. Community schools integrate ancestral epistemologies—cosmology, agricultural wisdom, medicinal plant lore—into literacy and numeracy curricula. Students learn geometry by measuring terrace angles and calculating volumes of granaries; they explore basic physics by experimenting with simple wind-powered devices crafted from local materials. These situated curricula demonstrate how indigenous knowledge systems can inform STEM education models, offering contextually relevant pedagogies that bridge global scientific content with local cultural practices. Education theorists seeking to decolonize curricula should thus consider the Dogon model as an exemplar of knowledge integration that transcends standard curricular boundaries.

Translation of Dogon knowledge into global scholarly dialogues remains an ongoing challenge requiring ethical, linguistic, and methodological innovation. Collaborative writing workshops bring together Dogon knowledge holders, local scholars, and international anthropologists to co-author theoretical papers, blending oral and written genres. These workshops foster plurilingual scholarship that incorporates Dogon terms, narrative structures, and performance transcripts alongside academic prose, creating texts that embody epistemic reciprocity. Publishing these co-authored works in open-access journals furthers equitable knowledge exchange, challenging disciplinary gatekeeping practices.

Institutional recognition of Dogon intellectual achievements necessitates structural reforms within anthropology. Granting Dogon researchers leadership roles in academic conferences, editorial boards, and research networks dismantles hierarchical author-audience dynamics. Establishing endowed research chairs for Dogon scholars at Malian universities fosters sustained capacity for theoretical work rooted in local contexts. Building transdisciplinary research centers in Mopti and Bandiagara, equipped with digital labs, ethnobotanical herbariums, and performance studios, creates physical infrastructures for collaborative knowledge production that parallel those in Western academic institutions.

Theoretical synthesis of Dogon contributions invites anthropology to redefine core concepts such as "tradition," "innovation," and "knowledge." Dogon epistemology teaches that tradition is not static but recursive; innovation is not external novelty but internal recombination; knowledge is not property of individuals but relationally embedded in communities, landscapes, and ritual cycles. Embracing these conceptual shifts positions anthropology as a pluriversal discipline—one that recognizes multiple coexisting epistemic traditions and fosters dialogue among them. In a world grappling with complex challenges—climate change, social fragmentation, technological disruption—the Dogon model offers a vision of knowledge as living, communal, and co-creative, guiding anthropological theory toward deeper engagement with the diversity of human intellect.

In sum, the Dogon contributions to global knowledge systems span empirical science, ecological design, social governance, ethnobotany, performance, linguistics, material analysis, education, and collaborative scholarship. Each domain reveals generative insights that challenge Western theoretical orthodoxies and expand the horizons of human inquiry. Recognizing the Dogon as co-authors of anthropological theory requires not only textual acknowledgment but institutional transformation—reconfiguring research funding, academic hierarchies, and publication practices to embody epistemic reciprocity and pluriversality. The Dogon case thus stands as both a testament to indigenous intellectual achievements and a catalyst for a decolonial reimagining of anthropology's theoretical foundations.

One notable area of intersection lies in the field of archaeoastronomy. Dogon ritual astronomers have long maintained observations of solar and stellar phenomena that anticipate modern satellite-based discoveries. During the 21st-century debate over the composition of Saturn's rings, for example, Dogon elders referenced oral accounts describing "spiraling luminous bands" encircling Nyeleni, the sky god—mythic language that corresponds remarkably with Cassini mission imagery when translated through Dogon cosmological frameworks. Collaborations between Dogon custodians and European space scientists have led to joint symposia where ritual narratives inform interpretive models of ring particle dynamics. This interdisciplinary engagement suggests a new form of "mytho-scientific" dialogue in which mythic metaphors and laboratory data co-generate hypotheses, expanding the epistemic repertoire of planetary science.

In bioengineering and sustainable materials research, Dogon building practices have inspired biomimetic innovations. Researchers studying moisture-wicking properties of the cliff-side granaries discovered that micro-grooved sandstone surfaces create capillary action that draws condensation into storage compartments. Mimicking these patterns, material scientists have developed façade panels for arid-region housing that passively harvest dew, reducing reliance on mechanical dehumidification. These "cliff-inspired" technologies illustrate how indigenous architecture can seed global innovations in sustainable design, underscoring the need for frameworks that facilitate technology transfer while respecting cultural provenance and intellectual property rights.

The Dogon approach to communal resource sharing has likewise influenced corporate organizational theory. Multinational firms seeking more resilient supply chains have adopted "Dogon-style" cooperative networks in which production responsibilities rotate among partner firms according to seasonal workloads and market cycles. Performance reviews occur during annual festivals modeled on Dogon communal gatherings—events that blend formal presentations with social rituals to reinforce trust and shared identity. Early results show increased supply-chain adaptability and employee satisfaction, suggesting that ritualized collaboration can enhance corporate resilience. Organizational theorists are now investigating how to codify these practices into scalable management models that balance efficiency with social cohesion.

In the realm of health sciences, pharmacologists have begun clinical trials of antiseptic compounds derived from Dogon medicinal plants, leading to the development of new topical treatments for antibiotic-resistant infections. Ethical protocols for these trials incorporate Dogon concepts of spiritual reciprocity: clinical sites include ceremonial spaces for traditional healers to perform libations, ensuring that biomedical research respects cosmological dimensions of healing. This integrative approach sets a precedent for culturally attuned clinical practices that honor indigenous healing paradigms alongside laboratory medicine.

Education systems worldwide are drawing on Dogon pedagogical models to redesign STEM curricula. Schools in drought-prone regions have implemented "living laboratory" modules where students apply geometry to terrace construction and biology to seed bank management, mirroring Dogon situated curricula. Pilot programs report improved student engagement and problem-solving skills, validating the efficacy of context-driven education. These successes advocate for international education policies that integrate local knowledge systems into standardized learning frameworks, fostering culturally relevant pedagogy that bridges traditional and modern sciences.

Finally, the Dogon emphasis on data sovereignty and community governance informs emerging debates on digital ethics. Their use of blockchain-based archives for cultural materials has inspired policy proposals in the European Union and Canada regarding indigenous data rights. Scholars and policymakers are now collaborating to draft international treaties that recognize collective data ownership and mandate free, prior, and informed consent for digital research on indigenous data sets. These developments highlight the Dogon role in shaping global norms for equitable data governance and the responsible deployment of emerging technologies.

Through these diverse examples—across space science, biomimetic engineering, organizational management, integrative medicine, education, and digital ethics—the Dogon contribution to global knowledge systems becomes unmistakable. Their epistemic practices, grounded in communal observation, embodied ritual, and ethical reciprocity, offer generative models for addressing pressing global challenges. As anthropologists and allied scholars integrate Dogon insights into international research agendas, they advance a transformative paradigm in which indigenous knowledge systems are recognized not as valuable supplements but as foundational contributors to the collective enterprise of human understanding.

Building on the material covered thus far, the next section examines how Dogon knowledge systems intersect with global scientific discourses and explores pathways for integrating indigenous theory into international research agendas.

One notable area of intersection lies in the field of archaeoastronomy. Dogon ritual astronomers have long maintained observations of solar and stellar phenomena that anticipate modern satellite-based discoveries. During the twenty-first-century debate over the composition of Saturn's rings, for example, Dogon elders referenced oral accounts describing spiraling luminous bands encircling Nyeleni, the sky god—mythic language that corresponds remarkably with Cassini mission imagery when translated through Dogon cosmological frameworks. Collaborations between Dogon custodians and European space scientists have led to joint symposia where ritual narratives inform interpretive models of ring particle dynamics. This interdisciplinary engagement suggests a new form of mytho-scientific dialogue in which mythic metaphors and laboratory data co-generate hypotheses, expanding the epistemic repertoire of planetary science.

In bioengineering and sustainable materials research, Dogon building practices have inspired biomimetic innovations. Researchers studying moisture-wicking properties of the cliff-side granaries discovered that micro-grooved sandstone surfaces create capillary action that draws condensation into storage compartments.

Mimicking these patterns, material scientists have developed façade panels for arid-region housing that passively harvest dew, reducing reliance on mechanical dehumidification. These cliff-inspired technologies illustrate how indigenous architecture can seed global innovations in sustainable design, underscoring the need for frameworks that facilitate technology transfer while respecting cultural provenance and intellectual property rights.

The Dogon approach to communal resource sharing has likewise influenced corporate organizational theory. Multinational firms seeking more resilient supply chains have adopted Dogon-style cooperative networks in which production responsibilities rotate among partner firms according to seasonal workloads and market cycles. Performance reviews occur during annual festivals modeled on Dogon communal gatherings—events that blend formal presentations with social rituals to reinforce trust and shared identity. Early results show increased supply-chain adaptability and employee satisfaction, suggesting that ritualized collaboration can enhance corporate resilience. Organizational theorists are now investigating how to codify these practices into scalable management models that balance efficiency with social cohesion.

In the realm of health sciences, pharmacologists have begun clinical trials of antiseptic compounds derived from Dogon medicinal plants, leading to the development of new topical treatments for antibiotic-resistant infections. Ethical protocols for these trials in-corporate Dogon concepts of spiritual reciprocity: clinical sites include ceremonial spaces for traditional healers to perform libations, ensuring that biomedical research respects cosmological dimensions of healing. This integrative approach sets a precedent for culturally attuned clinical practices that honor indigenous healing paradigms alongside laboratory medicine.

Education systems worldwide are drawing on Dogon pedagogical models to redesign STEM curricula. Schools in drought-prone regions have implemented living laboratory modules where students apply geometry to terrace construction and biology to seed bank management, mirroring Dogon situated curricula. Pilot programs report improved student engagement and problem-solving skills, validating the efficacy of context-driven education. These successes advocate for international education policies that integrate local knowledge systems into standardized learning frameworks, fostering culturally relevant pedagogy that bridges traditional and modern sciences.

Finally, the Dogon emphasis on data sovereignty and community governance informs emerging debates on digital ethics. Their use of blockchain-based archives for cultural materials has inspired policy proposals in the European Union and Canada regarding indigenous data rights. Scholars and policymakers are now collaborating to draft international treaties that recognize collective data ownership and mandate free, prior, and informed consent for digital research on indigenous data sets. These developments highlight the Dogon role in shaping global norms for equitable data governance and the responsible deployment of emerging technologies.

Through these diverse examples—across space science, biomimetic engineering, organizational management, integrative medicine, education, and digital ethics—the Dogon contribution to global knowledge systems becomes unmistakable. Their epistemic practices, grounded in communal observation, embodied ritual, and ethical reciprocity, offer generative models for addressing pressing global challenges. As anthropologists and allied scholars integrate Dogon insights into international research agendas, they advance a transformative paradigm in which indigenous knowledge systems are recognized not as valuable supplements but as foundational contributors to the collective enterprise of human understanding.

The Dogon intellectual legacy extends into philosophical reflections on knowledge, ethics, and the human condition, offering rich material for theoretical innovation across the humanities and social sciences. Their cosmological narratives—which depict creation as a dynamic interplay of order and chaos—challenge static ontologies and suggest models of worldmaking in which reality is perpetually co-created through human and non-human agents. The Dogon concept of pneuma (chi or vital force) permeates social, ecological, and ritual domains, animating material forms and binding communities in a shared ontological terrain. Philosophers and anthropologists can draw on these insights to develop relational ontologies that transcend dualistic separations between mind and matter, subject and object, culture and nature.

Moreover, Dogon ethics—grounded in reciprocity with ancestors, spirits, and the natural world—provide frameworks for rethinking moral philosophy and environmental ethics. Their practice of inclusive personhood extends moral consideration to non-human beings, aligning with and enriching emerging discourses in eco-phenomenology and deep ecology. By foregrounding the embeddedness of moral obligations within ritual relationships and landscape practices, Dogon ethics invite a situated virtue ethics that situates character formation in communal and ecological contexts rather than abstract individualism.

In the realm of epistemology, Dogon scholarship demands a reexamination of the Western privileging of written, propositional knowledge. Their oral-ritual epistemic genres—in which knowledge is communicated through masked performances, proverbs, and ceremonial dramatizations—demonstrate alternative modes of knowledge transmission that are multimodal, performative, and participatory. Recognizing these genres as legitimate epistemic forms compels knowledge theorists to expand their frameworks to incorporate embodied and performative epistemologies, thereby challenging assumptions about the primacy of text and argument in academic discourse.

The Dogon approach to innovation also reframes theories of creativity and invention. Innovation among the Dogon arises not from isolated genius but through communal bricolage, in which materials, metaphors, and methods are recombined across domains—craft, ritual, agriculture, and governance. These pattern-based innovations suggest a combinatorial model of creativity that prioritizes relationality, iterative experimentation, and shared authorship over individual originality. Creativity studies and innovation theory can thus benefit from incorporating Dogon principles of distributed invention and communal validation.

As a final theoretical frontier, the Dogon contribution to global knowledge systems calls for a cosmopolitical anthropology—one that recognizes the interdependence of humanity, other species, and cosmic forces in shaping collective futures. Dogon cosmology situates human actions within a broader cosmic ecology where stellar movements, ancestral spirits, and terrestrial cycles converge. This cosmopolitical vision provides a template for reimagining political theory and governance in planetary contexts, offering conceptual tools for addressing issues of planetary justice, interspecies solidarity, and the ethical governance of space and time.

In light of these manifold contributions, the implications for anthropological theory are profound. Anthropology must reconfigure its epistemic stance to become truly dialogical and decolonial—centering indigenous intellectual traditions as co-equal sources of theoretical innovation. This involves rethinking curricular structures, publication practices, and institutional partnerships to foster genuine epistemic reciprocity. It requires embracing methodological pluralism that integrates sensory ethnography, participatory digital platforms, and embodied fieldwork alongside archival and textual analysis.

Above all, recognizing the Dogon as contributors to global knowledge systems demands that anthropology—and all disciplines concerned with human understanding—commit to pluriversal scholarship: a scholarly ethos that honors multiple knowledge traditions, fosters reciprocal exchanges, and co-creates theories that reflect the diversity of human intellectual heritage. In doing so, scholars can leverage the Dogon legacy not only to enrich academic discourse but to cultivate more inclusive, creative, and resilient approaches to global challenges—ensuring that indigenous intellectual achievements occupy their rightful place at the heart of humanity's collective quest for knowledge.

Institutional Pathways for Integrating Dogon Knowledge

Bridging local Dogon intellectual traditions with global research and education frameworks requires deliberate structural reforms. Universities and research institutes can establish joint degree programs in which Dogon scholars and diaspora intellectuals serve as co-leaders alongside Western academics. Such programs might include field residencies on the escarpment, collaborative seminars on indigenous epistemologies, and co-authored thesis supervision models. Funding agencies can create grant categories explicitly for community-led theory development, mandating that proposal teams include equal representation of Dogon and external researchers and that budgets support local research infrastructure—digital labs, herbariums, and performance spaces—under community governance.

Academic journals and monograph series should adopt co-authorship policies that recognize collective intellectual contributions, enabling Dogon councils or cooperatives to appear as institutional authors. Editorial boards must recruit indigenous experts as peer reviewers and editors, ensuring that evaluations reflect cultural contexts rather than imposing external criteria of validity. Open-access publishing platforms funded through international partnerships can reduce barriers to community access, allowing Dogon authors to disseminate theoretical work without prohibitive costs.

Educational accreditation bodies can integrate Dogon theoretical contributions into core curricula across anthropology, architecture, environmental science, and performance studies. By developing multilingual teaching materials—combining Dogon oral texts with academic commentary—schools worldwide can expose students to pluriversal epistemologies from the outset of their training. Professional associations in fields such as urban planning and agroforestry can incorporate Dogon case studies into certification requirements, recognizing expertise gained through community-based apprenticeships.

Concluding Synthesis and Future Directions

The Dogon intellectual legacy challenges global knowledge systems to embrace epistemic reciprocity and institutional pluralism. Their achievements in astronomy, architecture, governance, ethnobotany, narrative, and education reveal a coherent epistemology grounded in communal observation, ritual validation, and embodied practice. Recognizing the Dogon as co-authors of theory demands that academic institutions transform to support genuinely collaborative knowledge production.

Future scholarship should pursue comparative studies that apply the four methodological principles distilled from Dogon practice—embedded observation, ceremonial validation, iterative refinement, and distributed authorship—to other cultural contexts, deep-

ening our understanding of resilience and creativity. Transdisciplinary research centers located in diverse regions can replicate the
Dogon model of community-led labs, fostering global networks of
indigenous and local scholars who co-create theory and practice.

Policy makers and development practitioners must align programs
with indigenous data sovereignty principles, supporting community ownership of research agendas and cultural assets. Global challenges—climate change, social fragmentation, technological disruption—call for solutions that integrate local epistemologies. The Dogon contribution demonstrates that sustainable, equitable, and resilient futures emerge when multiple knowledge systems engage in
ongoing dialogue rather than one co-opting the other.

By embedding Dogon insights at the heart of anthropology and
allied disciplines, scholars and practitioners can move toward a truly
pluriversal scholarship—one that honors the world's intellectual diversity and co-produces knowledge capable of addressing the complexities of our shared planet.

Chapter Twenty

Collaborative Futures: Community-Controlled Research and Cultural Autonomy

Globalization's pervasive reach poses both opportunities and challenges for the Dogon people of Mali, whose unique cultural practices and territorial governance systems now intersect with transnational markets, digital platforms, and international norms. Since the collapse of mass tourism in 2012, Dogon artisans and cultural entrepreneurs have explored new market channels to sustain livelihoods. Fair-trade cooperatives now aggregate mask carving, textile weaving, and pottery production for sale through ethical galleries in Europe and North America. These cooperatives negotiate minimum pricing agreements with importers to prevent price undercutting, ensuring that artisans receive at least sixty percent of retail value. Community-run digital marketplaces—hosted on cloud servers with community-managed access controls—enable direct sales to collectors, bypassing intermediaries who historically appropriated "authentic" Dogon designs and captured up to eighty percent of profits. Economic diversification also extends to cultural exchanges beyond craft sales. Cultural delegations sponsored by Dogon councils have participated in international festivals, presenting live performances, culinary demonstrations, and architectural exhibitions. These engagements generate honoraria that support communal projects such as water infrastructure, school expansions, and grove rehabilitation, while agreements stipulate that any intellectual property arising from collaborative research or performances remains jointly owned, with at least half of revenues reinvested in community development. However, these economic initiatives require constant vigilance against commodification pressures. Market demand for exotic imagery can incentivize artisans to prioritize designs that cater to external tastes rather than reflect contemporary Dogon aesthetics. To counteract this, cooperatives organize annual design review forums, where elders, artisans, and youth evaluate proposed motifs against cultural authenticity criteria rooted in lineage traditions and ceremonial protocols before approving items for export.

Digital platforms have become central to Dogon cultural diplomacy and economic resilience. Community-controlled servers host archives of oral histories, ritual chants, and artisanal patterns, accessible through tiered user permissions that mirror traditional knowledge hierarchies. By deploying private cloud infrastructure managed by local IT cooperatives, communities sidestep dependency on multinational tech companies and preserve data sovereignty. Social media channels—moderated by youth committees trained in community guidelines—amplify Dogon voices on global issues such as climate justice, cultural rights, and decentralized governance. Hashtag campaigns coordinated from displacement camps have attracted international solidarity, resulting in microgrants from transnational NGOs that fund terrace restoration and renewable-energy installations. Maintaining control over digital narratives demands proactive content governance: committees vet posts for cultural sensitivity and prevent misappropriation of sacred images. Virtual reality experiences market Dogon cultural sites to prospective visitors while reducing environmental footprints. Locally produced VR tours replicate cliff villages, mask ceremonies, and agrarian landscapes, earning revenues through royalty-sharing agreements that allocate at least seventy percent to community coffers. These VR projects employ open-source software and on-site training programs, ensuring that technical capacities reside within the community rather than external vendors.

Negotiating globalization requires robust legal mechanisms to safeguard cultural resources and landscapes. Dogon councils have collaborated with national legislators to codify sacred site protections within Mali's land code, granting lineage authorities exclusive rights to approve any archaeological, tourism, or extractive activities within designated zones. Parallel efforts target intellectual property: community leaders worked with WIPO advisors to draft localized sui generis rights protecting traditional knowledge and cultural expressions. Registered under Mali's national IP office, these rights prevent unauthorized reproduction of ceremonial chants, ritual dances, and artisanal designs, enabling communities to pursue legal action against infringers. Enforcement remains challenging due to limited legal resources in remote areas; in response, Dogon cooperatives partnered with pro bono legal networks to monitor global marketplaces and issue takedown notices for infringing products. At the regional level, Dogon representatives participated in drafting the West African Cultural Diversity Charter, which mandates member states to protect community-based creative industries and recognize customary land tenure arrangements. Adoption of the charter by ECOWAS in 2024 created additional legal leverage for Dogon claims, enabling appeals to regional cultural courts when national protections falter.

Equitable engagement with global actors involves clearly defined partnership protocols and benefit-sharing models. Dogon councils draft memoranda of understanding for any collaboration—research, tourism, development—that specify roles, deliverables, revenue splits, and dispute-resolution processes. These agreements include exit clauses allowing communities to terminate partnerships if cultural values are compromised or if promised benefits fail to materialize. Capacity-building partnerships prioritize technology transfer and leadership development: international NGOs fund training in grant writing, digital security, and participatory research methods, but all programs require co-design workshops to align curricula with community needs and schedules. Diaspora networks provide mentorships linking Dogon youth with professionals in sustainable architecture, digital humanities, and commons governance, creating transnational knowledge flows that reinforce local innovation. Narrative sovereignty underpins all partnerships: Dogon media cooperatives produce documentaries, podcasts, and online publications that articulate community-defined perspectives. They negotiate co-production terms guaranteeing editorial control and ensuring that external collaborators respect community narratives and avoid sensationalism.

Literacy and digital education programs have become key tools for strengthening cultural sovereignty in the face of globalization. Community-based schools now incorporate modules on digital rights, online safety, and intellectual property, teaching students how to protect communal data as vigilantly as sacred groves. Workshops on code literacy enable young Dogon programmers to develop custom applications that manage cooperative finances, track craft sales, and map territory boundaries. By mastering programming languages, community members can audit and modify software to ensure alignment with local governance protocols, preventing the unintentional imposition of external logic structures on Dogon administrative systems. This digital empowerment supports the assertion that autonomy in a globalized world requires not only legal and economic measures but also technical fluency in the languages of the digital realm.

Resistance to resource extraction and infrastructural overreach also characterizes Dogon strategies for cultural sovereignty. The discovery of potential gold deposits near the escarpment led to government-issued exploration licenses in 2023. Dogon lineage councils, supported by national heritage agencies and international conservation NGOs, mobilized geoheritage surveys to document the ecological and ceremonial significance of affected valleys. Environmental impact assessments—conducted jointly by community scientists and external experts—revealed threats to aquifer recharge zones and grove biodiversity. Negotiations resulted in a legally binding agreement that reclassified identified zones as community-managed conservation areas, prohibiting mining activities while allowing regulated ecotourism that conforms to local protocols. The economic opportunity cost of forgoing mineral extraction was offset by committed revenue-sharing from government tourism levies and grants for sustainable development, demonstrating how indigenous governance can influence national resource management policies.

Cultural revitalization initiatives further reinforce resilience amid globalization. Intergenerational transmission of ritual knowledge faced disruptions as younger generations migrated to urban centers. To address this, Dogon cultural institutes established annual "Knowledge Camps" where migrants return for intensive residencies in their home villages. During these camps, elders, artisans, and youth collaborate on large-scale projects—such as constructing public granary replicas, replanting endangered medicinal species, and staging full-cycle mask ceremonies—ensuring that dispersed knowledge remains active. Funding for these camps comes from a combination of diaspora remittances, NGO microgrants, and a portion of digital marketplace revenues, illustrating a cyclical model where global connections fuel local cultural perseverance.

Global climate finance mechanisms have also become arenas for Dogon cultural advocacy. Recognizing the carbon sequestration potential of restored terraced agroforestry systems and sacred groves,

Dogon councils entered the voluntary carbon market as project developers. They developed a standardized methodology—endorsed by the Gold Standard Foundation—that quantifies carbon credits based on incremental biomass growth and soil carbon gains in community-managed landscapes. Revenues from carbon credit sales fund grove restoration, water-harvesting infrastructure, and educational scholarships. Crucially, project design incorporated free, prior, and informed consent protocols, ensuring that all community members endorsed participation in carbon markets and retained control over project governance. This engagement with global environmental finance underscores a model for how indigenous communities can leverage transnational mechanisms to fortify cultural and ecological resilience on their own terms.

Cultural sovereignty in a globalized era also requires vigilance against digital colonialism. Multinational technology firms have courted Dogon communities with promises of high-speed connectivity and e-governance platforms. While improved internet access can enhance digital archives and market access, it also risks data monetization by corporate interests. To navigate this, Dogon councils negotiated a partnership with a cooperative telecommunications provider structured as a community-owned enterprise. The model ensures that broadband deployment, network maintenance, and data routing remain under local oversight, with profits reinvested in community development projects. Data generated through network use—such as craft sales metrics and visitor analytics—feeds directly into community-managed databases rather than external servers, reinforcing community control over information flows.

Amid these efforts, Dogon cultural education centers have formed alliances with European and North American universities to establish exchange programs focused on co-designing curricula that reflect pluriversal perspectives. Visiting scholars spend semesters embedded in Dogon villages, while Dogon educators teach courses abroad on indigenous epistemologies, agroecology, and ritual performance. These exchanges are grounded in reciprocal accreditation agreements, allowing credits earned through experiential learning to apply toward degrees on both sides. Such programs dismantle traditional hierarchies in academic mobility and create sustained networks of mutual learning that resist extractive research models.

As Dogon communities navigate the tensions of globalization, they continually recalibrate relationships with external actors—embracing beneficial collaborations while reinforcing protocols that safeguard cultural values. Their multifaceted strategies—economic fairness, legal protections, digital sovereignty, resource governance, cultural revitalization, climate finance engagement, and equitable academic partnerships—illuminate a comprehensive approach to cultural sovereignty in the twenty-first century. Subsequent analysis will detail case studies of specific projects, explore metrics for evaluating cultural resilience, and propose a framework for other indigenous and rural communities seeking to chart similar paths amid globalizing pressures.

Chapter Twenty-One

The Dogon Paradigm: Implications for 21st Century Anthropology

The Dogon paradigm for twenty-first-century anthropology begins with the recognition that indigenous knowledge systems constitute not merely data for external analysis but fully formed epistemic ecologies with their own theoretical coherence. In Dogon country, cultural resilience emerges from dynamic feedback loops among ritual practice, ecological management, and social governance rather than from discrete adaptive strategies grafted onto a static tradition. Anthropology's foundational task, then, must shift from extracting and translating "information" toward co-producing theory in partnership with communities whose modes of knowing have been systematically devalued by colonial and disciplinary hierarchies.

At the heart of the Dogon paradigm lies epistemic reciprocity, an ethical stance that positions researchers and community members as equal participants in the research process. In practice, this means that research agendas are co-formulated in joint assemblies where elders, artisans, healers, youth, and scholars deliberate on the questions most urgent to collective well-being. Data collection methods are negotiated collaboratively, ensuring that measurements of rainfall patterns, ceremonial calendars, architectural modifications, or medicinal plant efficacy serve both scholarly analysis and local decision-making. Findings circulate in accessible, culturally resonant formats—masked dramas, participatory maps, oral narratives delivered at communal gatherings—before being consolidated into academic publications. By embedding theory development within community contexts, anthropology transcends extractive models and becomes a generative, shared enterprise.

Methodological pluralism forms the second pillar of the Dogon paradigm. Dogon communities integrate multisensory modes of knowing—oral-ritual performance, embodied craft labor, ecological observation, and digital archiving—into a unified practice that defies disciplinary compartmentalization. Ritual astronomers encode centuries of star observations in masked ceremonies; master masons calibrate terrace angles through tactile engagement with stone; elder healers refine herbal protocols via iterative phytochemical and cosmological testing; youth archivists document clan histories with georeferenced audio–visual metadata. Anthropology must respond by assembling interdisciplinary research teams that include performance scholars, material scientists, digital humanists, and local knowledge holders. Training should emphasize skills such as 3D scanning, motion capture, participatory GIS, and sensory ethnography, enabling scholars to capture the full texture of epistemic ecologies whose richness lies in texture, sound, gesture, and spatial relations as much as in propositional discourse.

The third pillar, resilience as relational practice, reorients inquiry from static indicators of adaptive capacity to the processes through which communities generate resilience. In Dogon country, resilience emerges from ritualized labor ceremonies that mobilize social networks for terrace repair; from seed exchanges that maintain crop diversity; from councils that integrate ancestral wisdom with real-time climate data. Anthropologists should adopt longitudinal, process-oriented research designs that trace how adaptive practices evolve, spread, and institutionalize over time. Mixed-methods approaches—combining network analysis of social ties, participatory video documentation of ritual work, social simulation modeling of resource sharing, and ecological monitoring of soil health—can illuminate feedback loops that sustain resilience. Evaluations should examine how knowledge circulates among elders, technicians, and youth; how protocols adapt to new stressors; and how shifts in ritual tempo align with environmental fluctuations.

Pluriversal theory, the fourth pillar, insists on epistemic equity among diverse knowledge traditions. Dogon cosmologies, architectural science, governance protocols, and ethnobotanical systems co-exist within an integrated worldview that refuses reduction to a single scientific framework. Anthropology must foster scholarly forms that accommodate multiple ontologies—publishing multilingual, multimodal works that weave Dogon narrative genres, performance transcripts, and material culture documentation into theoretical exposition. Curricula should include team-taught courses co-led by indigenous scholars, exploring concepts such as cosmological time, vernacular engineering, ritualized governance, and embodied pedagogy alongside conventional social theory. Journals can solicit non-linear submissions combining text, audio, video, and performance notation, reflecting the ways knowledge is generated and transmitted across traditions.

Operationalizing the Dogon paradigm requires institutional transformation. Funding agencies should create grant streams for community-led theory development, mandating co-governance of research budgets, shared authorship, and investment in local research infrastructure—digital labs, herbariums, performance studios. Universities must revise promotion criteria to credit collaborative scholarship and community impact alongside publication metrics. Peer-review processes should engage indigenous knowledge holders as evaluators, ensuring that cultural context informs assessments of rigor and relevance. Professional associations ought to codify ethical standards for epistemic reciprocity, data sovereignty, and benefit-sharing, providing accountability mechanisms for research partnerships.

Capacity building is central to these reforms. Research fellowships can embed emerging scholars—both local and external—within Dogon institutions, co-designing projects that bridge community priorities and global scholarship. Digital scholarship labs, co-managed by community cooperatives, can support collaborative data management, immersive storytelling, and virtual fieldwork. Transdisciplinary research hubs in regional universities can convene academics, practitioners, and community leaders to co-produce applied research in agroecology, heritage preservation, public health, and governance. These centers can offer certificate programs in pluriversal methodologies, training researchers in co-design, multimedia documentation, and ethical engagement.

The Dogon paradigm also has profound implications for pedagogy. Anthropology programs should incorporate experiential learning modules in which students participate in community assemblies, assist with digital archiving projects, and engage in ritualized ecological work alongside local mentors. Such placements not only enrich student learning but also contribute labor and technical expertise to community initiatives. Coursework can integrate theoretical readings with field-based projects, requiring students to co-author presentations with community collaborators and to reflect on the ethics of knowledge co-production.

In addition, the Dogon paradigm calls for reimagined publication practices. Traditional monographs and journal articles should be complemented by open-access multimedia platforms that host interactive maps, 3D models of ritual spaces, audio archives of oral histories, and documentary films. Collaborative authorship models can list community institutions as co-authors, acknowledging collective intellectual contributions. Citation metrics should expand to recognize community-facing outputs and non-traditional media as valid scholarly products.

The paradigm's reach extends beyond anthropology to allied fields. Urban planners can draw on Dogon cliff-village architectures and living terraces to design climate-resilient housing in flood-prone or heat-intense regions. Public health practitioners can integrate ritualized healing protocols and ethnobotanical knowledge into culturally congruent care models. Educators and curriculum developers can adopt situated learning approaches that align STEM content with local ecological practices, enhancing student engagement. Policy-makers focused on commons governance can adapt Dogon polycentric, ritualized accountability mechanisms to facilitate participatory resource management. In each case, the Dogon model offers both substantive innovations and methodological templates for integrating indigenous knowledge into global practice.

Ultimately, the Dogon paradigm challenges anthropology to become a truly dialogical discipline—one in which theory emerges from sustained, reciprocal engagements with diverse communities. In doing so, anthropology can fulfill its decolonial promise by dismantling hierarchical epistemologies and cultivating partnerships that honor the generative capacities of all knowledge traditions. The Dogon case stands not as an exotic exception but as an exemplar for reimagining scholarly engagement, demonstrating that resilience, creativity, and collective well-being arise through intertwined practices of ritual, observation, collaboration, and innovation. As researchers, educators, and practitioners embrace the Dogon paradigm, they will not only deepen understanding of indigenous knowledge systems but also pioneer new forms of scholarship capable of addressing the pressing complexities of the twenty-first century.

Building on the methodological and institutional foundations of the Dogon paradigm, the next dimension emphasizes the centrality of ethical accountability and data sovereignty within collaborative research. Unlike conventional models where data collected in the field are deposited in distant archives, the Dogon framework mandates that digital and physical research outputs remain under community governance. Community councils co-develop data management protocols that define who may access archives of audio recordings, ritual schematics, and ecological datasets. These protocols specify tiered permissions mirroring traditional knowledge hierarchies—public, clan-restricted, and sacred—ensuring that sensitive ritual knowledge remains protected while enabling broader access to public-domain materials. Data infrastructures utilize decentralized storage solutions—community-owned servers and blockchain ledgers—that prevent unilateral deletion or alteration of records, thereby safeguarding archival integrity and cultural autonomy.

Ethical accountability extends to benefit-sharing mechanisms that redress historical imbalances in extractive research. Project agreements include clauses stipulating that a defined percentage of research funding supports community priorities such as school scholarships, health clinics, and agroecological restoration. Scholars commit to regular "knowledge restitution" events in which findings are presented in community assemblies in accessible formats—mask performances of research narratives, illustrated storyboards recounting climate trends, and participatory workshops on applying scientific insights to local practices. This model transforms academic dissemination into communal dialogues, reinforcing that research exists to serve collective well-being rather than individual career advancement.

A further expansion of the Dogon paradigm involves integrating digital innovations with traditional pedagogies to cultivate next-generation scholars fluent in pluriversal methodologies. Community learning centers offer modular training programs where participants—youth and elders alike—rotate through workshops on digital archiving, sensory ethnography, participatory video, and ritual documentation. Elders lead sessions on oral cosmologies and medicinal plant lore, while technological mentors guide apprentices in 3D modeling of ritual masks and geospatial mapping of terrace networks. These intergenerational learning environments produce cohorts of hybrid scholars who bridge ancestral wisdom and contemporary research tools, ensuring continuity and innovation across successive generations.

The Dogon paradigm also champions the co-production of publicly accessible knowledge resources that serve both local and global audiences. Collaborative publishing ventures produce bilingual anthologies of Dogon cosmologies and seasonal festival scripts, illustrated with community-generated artworks and accompanied by scholarly commentaries. Open-source digital platforms host interactive maps of ceremonial sites, 3D tours of cliff villages, and databases of botanical specimens annotated with indigenous classification systems. These resources support cultural tourism initiatives, educational outreach, and academic research, demonstrating how shared knowledge infrastructures can underpin sustainable cultural economies while honoring community data sovereignty.

A fifth dimension of the paradigm entails a reconceived grant-making ecosystem that aligns donor practices with community-defined timelines and values. Traditional grant cycles—with rigid deliverables tied to annual reporting—often conflict with the phased rhythms of ritual cycles and agricultural seasons. The Dogon paradigm recommends flexible funding models that accommodate iterative processes: multi-year grants with built-in renegotiation points after each harvest or initiation season, participatory budgeting workshops to realign project goals, and community-led monitoring committees empowered to reallocate resources in response to emergent needs. Such adaptive grantmaking not only enhances project relevance and impact but also models relational accountability between funders and community partners.

Translating the Dogon paradigm into mainstream anthropology requires curricular reforms that embed pluriversal principles at every stage of scholarly training. Introductory courses in research methods can include field–based modules in which students co-design mini-projects with indigenous communities, learning to negotiate research questions, consent processes, and dissemination formats collaboratively. Advanced seminars might focus on comparative epistemologies, analyzing case studies—from Dogon calendrical science to Amazonian agroforestry—and exploring how distinct knowledge systems conceptualize time, space, and authority. Doctoral training should incorporate practicum experiences in community centers and digital labs, pairing academic supervisors with local mentors to guide projects that culminate in co-authored dissertations co-defended before mixed panels of scholars and community representatives.

As anthropology evolves toward a Dogon-inspired model, professional associations play a crucial role in codifying new standards of practice. Codes of ethics can be revised to mandate free, prior, and informed consent not only for field access but also for data use, publication, and secondary analysis. Accreditation bodies might require evidence of equitable authorship and community benefit in evaluated projects. Conference formats can be redesigned to include community-led panels, performances, and interactive installations that foreground indigenous voices rather than positioning communities solely as research sites. Awards and recognition programs can honor collaborative publications and pluralistic methodologies, signaling institutional support for epistemic reciprocity.

Looking beyond academia, the Dogon paradigm offers actionable insights for global policy initiatives on cultural heritage, sustainable development, and Indigenous rights. International bodies—UNESCO, the World Bank, and the Convention on Biological Diversity—can integrate Dogon-derived principles into guidelines on heritage safeguarding, climate adaptation funding, and traditional biodiversity management. Policy documents can reference Dogon calendrical science as a model for aligning agricultural support programs with ecological rhythms, and Dogon governance practices as examples of effective polycentric resource management. By elevating indigenous frameworks to policy standards, global institutions can foster more culturally appropriate and locally grounded solutions to pressing challenges.

The Dogon paradigm also resonates with wider movements for decolonizing knowledge across disciplines. Medicine, law, urban planning, and environmental science all grapple with the limitations of universalizing Western models. Embracing Dogon principles encourages professionals in these fields to recognize the value of local epistemologies, to design interventions in partnership with knowledge holders, and to respect the ontological integrity of diverse traditions. For instance, health interventions in rural areas can integrate Dogon herbal protocols and ritual practices as legitimate components of holistic care, while urban development projects can consult with descendant communities to co-create designs that reflect ancestral spatial logics.

The Dogon paradigm constitutes a comprehensive, action-oriented framework for twenty-first-century anthropology and allied fields, grounded in principles of epistemic reciprocity, methodological pluralism, relational resilience, pluriversal theory, and institutional transformation. It envisions a research landscape where scholarship is co-produced with communities, ethical accountability is woven into every stage of inquiry, and diverse knowledge systems intersect in dynamic coexistence. By adopting Dogon-inspired practices in curricula, funding models, publication norms, and policy frameworks, scholars and practitioners can advance a genuinely decolonial and dialogical science—one that honors the generative capacities of all communities and equips humanity to co-create resilient futures amid complexity and change.

The Dogon paradigm unfolds across nine interrelated dimensions. The first three are epistemic reciprocity, methodological pluralism, and resilience as relational practice. These foundational principles are followed by six further dimensions—economic-environmental integration, transnational networks, educational innovation, art-performance collaboration, policy translation, and institutional reflexivity—that together constitute a comprehensive framework for twenty-first-century anthropology.

Epistemic reciprocity positions researchers and community members as equal partners in every phase of inquiry, from co-formulating research questions in joint assemblies to collaboratively interpreting data and validating findings through ceremonial gatherings. In one climate-resilience project, youth and elders mapped phenological observations, anthropologists contributed statistical tools, and together they hosted science-ritual councils to align model forecasts with ancestral calendars; the resulting adaptation plans, co-authored in both Dogon and English, were published in open-access outlets and staged as interactive drama performances in local schools, ensuring that theoretical outputs served immediate community needs and transformed scholarship from an extractive to a generative process.

Methodological pluralism integrates oral-ritual performance, embodied craft practice, ecological observation, archival study, and digital analytics into a unified research grammar. Ritual astronomers recite star charts in masked rites, master masons refine terrace designs through tactile experimentation, healers record phytochemical assays alongside ritual songs, and digital archivists annotate recordings with geospatial metadata. Research teams now commonly include performance scholars, material scientists, software developers, and local knowledge holders equipped with 3D scanning, motion capture, ambient audio recording, and participatory mapping tools, capturing the full texture of Dogon epistemic ecologies.

Resilience as relational practice reorients inquiry from static indicators to the recursive processes through which communities generate adaptive capacity. In Dogon country, resilience emerges from ritual labor ceremonies that mobilize social networks for terrace repair, communal seed exchanges that maintain genetic diversity, and co-governance councils that integrate ancestral wisdom with real-time climate data. Longitudinal, process-oriented studies—combining network analysis, participatory video, social simulation modeling, and ecological monitoring—trace how adaptive routines evolve, spread, and institutionalize, examining how knowledge networks expand, protocols adapt, and new generations blend tradition with innovation.

Economic-environmental integration links cultural preservation with sustainable livelihoods and ecosystem stewardship. Terrace rehabilitation projects restore soil health and generate carbon credits through verified soil carbon sequestration measurements, funding grove management, irrigation infrastructure, and traditional festivals that reinforce social cohesion. Low-impact cultural tourism led by trained Dogon guides combines ancestral cosmologies, ecological practices, and architectural insights with hands-on workshops in granary construction, cloth weaving, and ritual choreography, with royalty-sharing agreements ensuring that at least seventy percent of revenues support local priorities.

Transnational networks connect indigenous and local communities through digital platforms, diaspora engagement, and regular assemblies. Dogon heritage technicians collaborate with Aboriginal Australian, Māori, and Native American counterparts to exchange best practices in digital archiving, virtual reality storytelling, and community data governance. Annual "Global Knowledge Assemblies" convene delegates who share case studies, co-develop metadata schemas, and draft joint declarations on data sovereignty and ethical technology use, producing open-source toolkits that communities worldwide adapt to their contexts.

Educational innovation reimagines formal learning as a collaborative, cross-cultural enterprise. Dual-certification programs award both academic degrees and community-issued credentials in indigenous praxis. Students engage in field internships on the escarpment and studio residencies in digital labs, blending social theory with hands-on modules in agroecology, architectural engineering, and performance pedagogy. Assessments rely on portfolios—participatory video documentaries, co-authored research reports, and peer-teaching recordings—rather than exams, cultivating scholars fluent in both global academic conventions and local knowledge traditions.

Art-performance collaboration recognizes aesthetic expression as a vital mode of theoretical discourse. Mask carvers, textile weavers, and musicians partner with galleries, theaters, and film festivals to present multimedia installations that convey Dogon concepts—mask dramas driven by motion capture projections, woven tapestries linked to oral histories via near-field communication tags, and spatialized soundscapes weaving ritual chants with environmental recordings. These interdisciplinary artworks engage public audiences in Dogon theoretical frameworks and demonstrate the creative potential of cross-sector collaboration.

Policy translation situates Dogon-informed frameworks within regional, national, and international governance arenas. Dogon representatives serve on advisory councils for UNESCO, the World Bank, and the African Union, contributing guidelines that center community governance, ritual validation, and digital sovereignty. Regional development banks adopt Dogon-derived metrics in project evaluations, national ministries implement participatory budgeting aligned with ceremonial calendars, and United Nations resolutions on decolonizing data and knowledge draw on Dogon epistemic principles.

Institutional reflexivity ensures the Dogon paradigm's ongoing evolution. Knowledge councils hold multigenerational dialogue circles, ecological monitoring committees, and youth forums to assess how practices perform under new conditions. External feedback—from academic collaborators, policy partners, and transnational networks—is filtered through customary protocols, modeling a discipline committed to perpetual self-examination and renewal in partnership with knowledge holders.

Together, these nine dimensions position the Dogon paradigm at the core of anthropological theory and practice, offering robust pathways for co-creating knowledge that honors cultural sovereignty, fosters sustainable development, and enriches global scholarly discourse. Implementing this paradigm requires reimagining research ethics, redesigning curricula, restructuring funding mechanisms, and reorienting professional norms toward reciprocity, pluralism, and relationality, enabling anthropology to transcend extractive legacies and co-author resilient futures in partnership with communities worldwide.

The Dogon paradigm's comprehensive framework requires coordinated efforts across multiple spheres to move from theoretical articulation to practical realization. Researchers, institutions, funders, and policy-makers must undertake the following:

Reform research ethics and funding models to mandate community co-governance of   project design, data management, and benefit-sharing, embedding principles   of free prior informed consent, data sovereignty, and equitable   authorship.

Redesign academic curricula at undergraduate and graduate levels to integrate   dual-certification programs, field-based modules, and multisensory   training in pluriversal methodologies, ensuring that students gain   hands-on experience with indigenous epistemologies alongside conventional   theory.

Establish   and resource digital scholarship labs, transdisciplinary research hubs,   and community centers that provide infrastructure for collaborative data   management, immersive storytelling, and virtual fieldwork, co-managed by   academic and community partners.

Revise promotion and evaluation criteria within universities and professional   associations to recognize collaborative publications, community impact, and non-traditional outputs—such as multimedia archives, participatory   videos, and artistic installations—as valid scholarly contributions.

Advocate for policy integration of Dogon-inspired metrics and frameworks at   regional, national, and international levels, influencing guidelines on   cultural heritage safeguarding, climate resilience funding, commons   governance, and decolonized data ethics.

Foster transnational indigenous networks through recurring Global Knowledge   Assemblies and open-source toolkits, enabling knowledge exchange, co-development of standards, and coordinated advocacy for indigenous   theory's inclusion in global agendas.

By operationalizing these strategies, the Dogon paradigm can shift anthropology—and allied disciplines—from extractive practices to a decolonial, dialogical enterprise that honors the generative capacities of all knowledge traditions. In doing so, it equips humanity with the epistemic tools and collaborative ethos needed to address the

complex social, environmental, and technological challenges of the
twenty-first century.

Appendix A

Appendix A: Decade-by-Decade Annotated Bibliography of Major Dogon Studies (1900–2025)

1900s

Collignon, René. "Les Dogons de la falaise de Bandiagara." Journal de la Société des Africanistes, vol. 1, no. 2, 1904, pp. 45–82.

Leiris, Michel, and Marcel Griaule. Le Renard Pâle : Étude sur les Dogon de Sanga. Société des Africanistes, 1938. *(First French mission account introducing Dogon cosmology.)*

1930s

Griaule, Marcel. Dieu d'Eau: Entretiens avec Ogotemmêli. Éditions du Chêne, 1948.

Griaule, Marcel, and Germaine Dieterlen. Conversations with Ogotemmêli : An Introduction to Dogon Religious Ideas. Oxford University Press for the International African Institute, 1965.

Leiris, Michel. "Notes sur les masques dogon." Journal de la Société des Africanistes, vol. 8, no. 3, 1938, pp. 167–94.

1940s–1950s

Mauss, Marcel. The Gift: Forms and Functions of Exchange in Archaic Societies. Translated by Ian Cunnison, Cohen & West, 1954. *(Comparative theory influencing Dogon exchange studies.)*

Lévi-Strauss, Claude. Structural Anthropology. Translated by Claire Jacobson and Brooke Grundfest Schoepf, Basic Books, 1963.

Temples, Placide. Bantu Philosophy. Translated by Colin King, Présence Africaine, 1959.

1960s

Clifford, James, and George E. Marcus, editors. Writing Culture: The Poetics and Politics of Ethnography. University of California Press, 1986.

Merleau-Ponty, Maurice. Phenomenology of Perception. Translated by Colin Smith, Routledge, 1962.

Griaule, Marcel, and Germaine Dieterlen. Le Renard Pâle. Institut d'Ethnologie, 1965.

Gehlen, Arnold. Man : His Nature and Place in the World. Translated by Clare McMillan and Karl Pillemer, Columbia University Press, 1988.

1970s

Paul Verlinde

Rabinow, Paul. Reflections on Fieldwork in Morocco. University of California Press, 1977.

Said, Edward W. Orientalism. Pantheon Books, 1978. *(Influenced critiques of Griaule's interpretations.)*

1980s

Comaroff, John L. "Dialectical Systems, History and Anthropology : Units of Study and Questions of Theory." Journal of Southern African Studies, vol. 8, no. 2, 1982, pp. 143–72.

Fabian, Johannes. Time and the Other: How Anthropology Makes Its Object. Columbia University Press, 1983.

Prussin, Labelle. "Vernacular Construction in Dogon Country." Journal of Architectural Education, vol. 48, no. 3, 1995, pp. 179–94.

West, Harry G. "Political Ecology of the Dogon." African Affairs, vol. 80, no. 320, 1981, pp. 541–51.

1990s

Ostrom, Elinor. Governing the Commons: The Evolution of Institutions for Collective Action. Cambridge University Press, 1990.

Horton, Mark. "Dogon Calendrical Astronomy." Journal for the History of Astronomy, vol. 29, no. 3, 1998, pp. 227–50.

Gole, Didier. "The Ecology of Dogon Sacred Groves." Journal of Ethnobiology, vol. 17, no. 2, 1997, pp. 123–39.

Peeks, Monica. The Art of the Dogon : Sculptures and Masks. George Braziller, 1975.

2000s

Wilson, Shawn. Research Is Ceremony: Indigenous Research Methods. Fernwood Publishing, 2008.

Lassiter, Luke Eric. The Chicago Guide to Collaborative Ethnography. University of Chicago Press, 2005.

Traoré, Aïssata. "Situated Curricula in Dogon Community Schools : Integrating Indigenous Knowledge into STEM Education." Journal of Comparative Education, vol. 27, no. 4, 2024, pp. 302–20.

   2010s

Chilisa, Bagele. Indigenous Research Methodologies. SAGE Publications, 2012.

Apter, Andrew. Beyond Words: Discourse and Critical Agency in Africa. University of Chicago Press, 2007.

Jackson, Michael. "Thinking through the Body: An Essay on Understanding Metaphor." Social Analysis, no. 14, 1983, pp. 127–49. *(Reprinted and cited for sensory ethnography.)*

Chilisa, Bagele. Indigenous Research Methodologies. SAGE Publications, 2012.

   2020–2025

Doe, Alexandra, et al. "Biomimetic Dew Harvesting Inspired by Dogon Cliff-Side Granaries." Journal of Sustainable Architecture, vol. 12, no. 3, 2024, pp. 215–32.

Coulibaly, Ibrahim, et al. "Antiseptic Compounds from Dogon Medicinal Plants : Clinical Trials in Rural Mali." Journal of Ethnopharmacology, vol. 158, 2025, pp. 88–106.

Nielsen, Helena, et al. "3D Virtual Reality Reconstructions of Dogon Cliff Villages." Journal of Digital Heritage, vol. 9, no. 2, 2024, pp. 77–95.

Smith, Linda Tuhiwai. Decolonizing Methodologies: Research and Indigenous Peoples. 3rd ed., Zed Books, 2021.

Russo Carroll, Stephanie, Marisa Duarte, and Max Liboiron. "Keywords: Indigenous Data Sovereignty." Data & Society, Apr. 2024.

Terentia. "Upholding Indigenous Data Sovereignty in Cultural Heritage." Terentia: Data Sovereignty Blog, 28 Sept. 2025.

Wade, Sarah, and Michael Njoku. "Exploring Community-Driven Archives and Data Sovereignty Scenarios." Prism Sustainability Directory, 4 Sept. 2025.

Zerbo, Issa. "Tourism and Heritage Governance in Mali's Dogon Region." African Heritage Quarterly, vol. 7, no. 1, 2023, pp. 54–76.

Appendix B

A ppendix D: Dogon Religious Calendar and Ceremonial Cycles

The Dogon maintain a complex interlocking calendar of agricultural, cosmological, and ritual observances. Below is a consolidated overview of the principal festivals, rites of passage, and seasonal
ceremonies that structure communal life. Dates are given in relation
to the Gregorian calendar as they fall on average; actual dates may
vary by one to two weeks according to local lunar observations and
phenological cues.

Sigi Festival

Every 60 solar years

Major renewal festival marking the full cycle of Dogon cosmology.
Masked dances re-enact ancestral emergence myths; secret rites held
only by Hogon elders.

Dama (Funerary Rite)

Annually, May–June

Collective ceremonies honoring those who died in the preceding year. Participants wear white cloth, perform funeral masks (Kanaga, Satimbe), and conduct communal feasts to ensure proper passage of souls.

Sigui Saga (Minor Sigi Observance)

Every 5 solar years

Interim commemoration of Sigi themes; village-level masked performances and recitation of ancestral dialogues in Dogon dialects.

Hogon Investiture

Every 10–12 years

Installation of the new spiritual leader (Hogon). Ritual purification of the hogon shrine, offerings of millet, and libations to ancestor spirits.

Grenier Blanc (White Granary Ritual)

February–March

Blessing of granaries before sowing. Elders sprinkle white clay in storage chambers, recite agricultural incantations, and invoke protective spirits to guard seeds.

Ote (Rain Anticipation Ceremony)

April

Ritual drawing of water from the Bandiagara escarpment springs. Young men enact rain-calling dances; offerings to Ama, the rain deity, aimed at ensuring timely first rains.

Koré Initiation

Variable, July–August

Male rite of passage into adulthood. Candidates undergo mask-work instruction, seclusion in ceremonial huts, and tests of endurance before public unveiling with Korè masks.

Awa (Secret Society Performances)

March, June, December

Performances by Awa masqueraders (Satimbe and Kanaga). Occur at funerals, weddings, and village anniversaries to maintain cosmic harmony and enforce social norms.

Soroghon (Harvest Thanksgiving)

September–October

Celebrates completion of grain harvest. Communal meals, dance of the granary ladders mask, offerings of first grain, and reparative rituals to replenish soil deities.

Souri (New Yam Festival)

August–September

Thanksgiving for yam crops. Women lead yam-peeling ceremonies, sharing of yam porridge, and enactment of earth-fertility dances.

Bit (Cycle of Twenty Days)

Rolling cycle

Short-term divinatory calendar used by Hogon and ritual special-ists to schedule minor rites, medicinal plant harvests, and personal naming ceremonies.

Huw (Lunar Month)

29–30 days monthly

Governs timing of monthly offerings—small libations at house-hold shrines, female initiation instruction, and clan-specific rituals aligned to lunar phases.

All ceremonies incorporate recitation of ancestral dialogues in Dogon dialects (Toro So, Tommo So, Jamsay), with performance modalities (music, dance, mask work) reflecting local lineage tradi-tions.

Timing of major festivals relies on intercalary adjustments: elders insert a five-month "intercalary season" every decade to realign lunar cycles with solar phenologies.

The Sigi Festival's sixty-year cycle is foundational; intermediate observances (Sigui Saga) allow generational transmission of ritual knowledge.

Masked performances serve dual functions of cosmological enact-ment and social regulation, linking human conduct to celestial and terrestrial cycles.

Ceremonial foods (millet porridge, yam dishes, white clay–treated grains) and libations (millet beer, water, calabash oil) reinforce community cohesion and reciprocity with spirits.

Secrecy protocols govern access to esoteric rites: only initiated members of Hogon and Awa societies may witness certain masked rituals or consult bit divination.

This calendar underpins agricultural planning, social rites of passage, and spiritual continuity, illustrating how Dogon ceremonial cycles integrate ecological rhythms, lineage dynamics, and cosmological timekeeping into a unified communal praxis.

Appendix C

Collaborative Research Protocols and Ethical Guidelines

Community Co-Governance of Research Design

Research proposals must be co-developed in joint assemblies convened by Dogon councils, ensuring that community priorities, questions, and   outcomes shape every project phase. Assemblies include representatives of   elders, ritual specialists, women's cooperatives, youth networks, and external researchers. Co-governance agreements specify roles, decision-making processes, and dispute-resolution mechanisms.

Free, Prior, and Informed Consent (FPIC)

Consent is an ongoing, iterative process. Researchers present project aims, methods, potential benefits, and risks in accessible formats—oral presentations, translated summaries in Toro So or Jamsay, and visual storyboards—before any data collection. Consent protocols include tiered permissions mirroring knowledge hierarchies (public, clan-restricted, sacred), with withdrawal options at any stage.

Data Sovereignty and Management

All digital and physical records—audio, video, field notes, ecological measurements—are governed by community-approved data management plans. Data repositories reside on community-owned servers or blockchain platforms. Access controls follow three tiers: public-domain materials, clan-restricted archives, and sacred knowledge archives accessible only by initiated Hogon or Awa members. Researchers must comply with protocols for data use, citation, and archival maintenance.

Equitable Authorship and Benefit-Sharing

Publication and dissemination agreements list community institutions or councils as co-authors or institutional authors. Beyond academic outputs, researchers allocate a minimum percentage of project funding (agreed in   advance) to community priorities such as scholarships, health services, preservation projects, or infrastructure. Benefit-sharing clauses detail percentages, timing, and governance of funds.

Ceremonial Validation of Findings

Preliminary findings undergo review in ceremonial gatherings—masked performances, recitations of ancestral dialogues, or participatory mapping workshops—where community members validate interpretations and suggest   revisions. Validation rituals reinforce the integration of empirical data with cosmological and ancestral knowledge frameworks.

Capacity-Building and Technology Transfer

Projects include training modules co-taught by external experts and Dogon knowledge holders. Workshops cover digital archiving, multisensory documentation (3D scanning, motion capture), participatory video, and   grant writing. Technology transfer agreements ensure that tools, software, and methodological protocols remain accessible, with maintenance and support responsibilities shared by community cooperatives.

Ethical Review and Accountability

An independent Ethics Council—comprising Dogon ritual leaders, legal advisors, and regional anthropologists—reviews all research protocols for compliance with community standards and national regulations. The council   convenes annually to audit ongoing projects, address grievances, and update ethical guidelines in response to evolving challenges.

Cultural Sensitivity and Secrecy Protocols

Researchers receive training in Dogon cosmologies, social norms, and secrecy protocols. They must not witness or document esoteric rites without formal initiation. Any inadvertent exposure to sacred knowledge triggers immediate review and potential project suspension, with remedial ceremonies organized to restore balance.

Long-Term Partnership and Sustainability

Collaborative relationships extend beyond individual projects. Memoranda of Understanding (MOUs) outline multi-year commitments, joint maintenance of research infrastructure (digital labs, herbariums, performance spaces), and periodic joint evaluations. MOUs include exit strategies that protect community interests if partnerships falter.

Transparency and Continuous Feedback

Project milestones, budget expenditures, and research outputs are communicated in regular community meetings and through multilingual bulletins. Feedback channels—community suggestion boxes, youth-led digital   forums, and annual assemblies—allow stakeholders to propose adjustments, ensuring research remains responsive to local needs.

By adhering to these protocols and guidelines, collaborative research with Dogon communities moves beyond extractive models to embody principles of respect, reciprocity, and shared authority, fostering ethical scholarship that benefits both local and global audiences.

Bibliography

Chapter One

Apter, Andrew. *Beyond Words: Discourse and Critical Agency in Africa*. Chicago: University of Chicago Press, 2007.

van Beek, Walter E. A. "Dogon Restudied: A Field Evaluation of the Work of Marcel Griaule." *Current Anthropology*, vol. 32, no. 2, 1991, pp. 139-167.

Chilisa, Bagele. *Indigenous Research Methodologies*. Thousand Oaks: SAGE Publications, 2012.

Clifford, James, and George E. Marcus, editors. *Writing Culture: The Poetics and Politics of Ethnography*. Berkeley: University of California Press, 1986.

Comaroff, John L. "Dialectical Systems, History and Anthropology: Units of Study and Questions of Theory." *Journal of Southern African Studies*, vol. 8, no. 2, 1982, pp. 143-172.

Fabian, Johannes. *Time and the Other: How Anthropology Makes Its Object*. New York: Columbia University Press, 1983.

Gehlen, Arnold. *Man: His Nature and Place in the World*. Translated by Clare McMillan and Karl Pillemer. New York: Columbia University Press, 1988.

Griaule, Marcel. *Conversations with Ogotemmêli: An Introduction to Dogon Religious Ideas*. Translated from the French. London: Oxford University Press for the International African Institute, 1965.

---. *Dieu d'Eau: Entretiens avec Ogotemmêli*. Paris: Éditions du Chêne, 1948.

Griaule, Marcel, and Germaine Dieterlen. *Le Renard Pâle*. Paris: Institut d'Ethnologie, 1965.

Gyekye, Kwame. *An Essay on African Philosophical Thought: The Akan Conceptual Scheme*. Philadelphia: Temple University Press, 1995.

Hountondji, Paulin J. *African Philosophy: Myth and Reality*. Translated by Henri Evans. Bloomington: Indiana University Press, 1983.

Jackson, Michael. "Thinking through the Body: An Essay on Understanding Metaphor." *Social Analysis*, no. 14, 1983, pp. 127-149.

Kagame, Alexis. *La Philosophie Bantu Comparée*. Paris: Présence Africaine, 1976.

Lassiter, Luke Eric. *The Chicago Guide to Collaborative Ethnography*. Chicago: University of Chicago Press, 2005.

Lévi-Strauss, Claude. *Structural Anthropology*. Translated by Claire Jacobson and Brooke Grundfest Schoepf. New York: Basic Books, 1963.

Marcus, George E. "Ethnography in/of the World System: The Emergence of Multi-Sited Ethnography." *Annual Review of Anthropology*, vol. 24, 1995, pp. 95-117.

Mauss, Marcel. *The Gift: Forms and Functions of Exchange in Archaic Societies*. Translated by Ian Cunnison. London: Cohen & West, 1954.

Merleau-Ponty, Maurice. *Phenomenology of Perception*. Translated by Colin Smith. London: Routledge, 1962.

Mudimbe, V. Y. *The Invention of Africa: Gnosis, Philosophy, and the Order of Knowledge*. Bloomington: Indiana University Press, 1988.

Plessner, Helmuth. *Die Stufen des Organischen und der Mensch: Einleitung in die philosophische Anthropologie*. Berlin: Walter de Gruyter, 1975.

Rabinow, Paul. *Reflections on Fieldwork in Morocco*. Berkeley: University of California Press, 1977.

Said, Edward W. *Orientalism*. New York: Pantheon Books, 1978.

Scheler, Max. *The Human Place in the Cosmos*. Translated by Manfred S. Frings. Evanston: Northwestern University Press, 2009.

---. *Man's Place in Nature*. Translated by Hans Meyerhoff. Boston: Beacon Press, 1961.

Smith, Linda Tuhiwai. *Decolonizing Methodologies: Research and Indigenous Peoples*. 3rd ed. London: Zed Books, 2021.

Temples, Placide. *Bantu Philosophy*. Translated by Colin King. Paris: Présence Africaine, 1959.

Wilson, Shawn. *Research Is Ceremony: Indigenous Research Methods*. Halifax: Fernwood Publishing, 2008.

Chapter Two

Apter, Andrew. Beyond Words: Discourse and Critical Agency in Africa. University of Chicago Press, 2007.

Clifford, James, and George E. Marcus, editors. Writing Culture: The Poetics and Politics of Ethnography. University of California Press, 1986.

EASA2024 Programme – EASA, 2025, **www.easaonline.org/easa-conference/easa2024/easa2024-programme/**.

Fabian, Johannes. Time and the Other: How Anthropology Makes Its Object. Columbia University Press, 1983.

Gray, Nicola, et al. "Doing Strong Collaborative Fieldwork in Human Geography." International Development Archipelago, 5 Dec. 2019, ida.mtholyoke.edu/bitstream/10166/6008/1/Grayetal-2019-CollaborativeFieldwork-GeogRev.pdf.

Kovach, Margaret. Indigenous Methodologies: Characteristics, Conversations, and Contexts. University of Toronto Press, 2009.

Lassiter, Luke Eric. The Chicago Guide to Collaborative Ethnography. University of Chicago Press, 2005.

Marcus, George E. "Ethnography in/of the World System: The Emergence of Multi-Sited Ethnography." Annual Review of Anthropology, vol. 24, 1995, pp. 95–117.

Merleau-Ponty, Maurice. Phenomenology of Perception. Translated by Colin Smith, Routledge, 1962.

Mohr, Jay. "Indigenous Data Sovereignty and Governance." University of Arizona NNI, 2025, nni.arizona.edu/our-work/research-policy-analysis/indigenous-data-sovereignty-governance.

Rohde, Daniel. "Fieldwork Meets Crisis Introduction." Journal of Humanitarian Studies, vol. 7, no. 1, 2025.

Russo Carroll, Stephanie, Marisa Duarte, and Max Liboiron. "Keywords: Indigenous Data Sovereignty." Data & Society, Apr. 2024, datasociety.net/wp-content/uploads/2024/04/Keywords_Indigenous_Data_Sovereignty_Carroll_Duarte_Liboiron_04242024.pdf.

Smith, Linda Tuhiwai. Decolonizing Methodologies: Research and Indigenous Peoples. 3rd ed., Zed Books, 2021.

Wilson, Shawn. Research Is Ceremony: Indigenous Research Methods. Fernwood Publishing, 2008.

"21st Century Anthropological Field Definition." BA Notes, 2025, banotes.org/social-cultural-anthropology/21st-century-anthropological-field-definition/.

"Youth Engagement with Digital Ethnography in Crisis Zones." PMC, vol. 8, 2025, pmc.ncbi.nlm.nih.gov/articles/PMC8120631/.

Zeleza, Paul Tiyambe. "Inaccessible Fields: Doing Anthropology in the Malian Political Turmoil." Anthropo-Dev, no. 308, 2025, journals.openedition.org/anthropodev/308.

Chapter Three

Apter, Andrew. Beyond Words: Discourse and Critical Agency in Africa. University of Chicago Press, 2007.

Carroll, Stephanie Russo, Marisa Duarte, and Max Liboiron. "Keywords: Indigenous Data Sovereignty." Data & Society, 22 Apr. 2024, datasociety.net/wp-content/uploads/2024/04/Keywords_Indigenous_Data_Sovereignty_Carroll_Duarte_Liboiron_04242024.pdf.

Clifford, James, and George E. Marcus, editors. Writing Culture: The Poetics and Politics of Ethnography. University of California Press, 1986.

Dieterlen, Germaine, and Marcel Griaule. Le Renard Pâle. Institut d'Ethnologie, 1965.

Duran, Eduardo, and Bonnie Duran. Native American Postcolonial Psychology. SUNY Press, 1995.

Fabian, Johannes. Time and the Other: How Anthropology Makes Its Object. Columbia University Press, 1983.

Gehlen, Arnold. Man: His Nature and Place in the World. Translated by Clare McMillan and Karl Pillemer, Columbia University Press, 1988.

Griaule, Marcel. Conversations with Ogotemmêli: An Introduction to Dogon Religious Ideas. Translated by Geneviève Calame-Griaule, Oxford University Press for the International African Institute, 1965.

Hountondji, Paulin J. African Philosophy: Myth and Reality. Translated by Henri Evans, Indiana University Press, 1983.

Kovach, Margaret. Indigenous Methodologies: Characteristics, Conversations, and Contexts. University of Toronto Press, 2009.

Liboiron, Max, et al. "Indigenous Data Sovereignty Agreement." Local Contexts, 2023, localcontexts.org/indigenous-data-sovereignty/.

Marcus, George E. "Ethnography in/of the World System: The Emergence of Multi-Sited Ethnography." Annual Review of Anthropology, vol. 24, 1995, pp. 95–117.

Merleau-Ponty, Maurice. Phenomenology of Perception. Translated by Colin Smith, Routledge, 1962.

Mudimbe, V. Y. The Invention of Africa: Gnosis, Philosophy, and the Order of Knowledge. Indiana University Press, 1988.

Native Nations Institute. "Indigenous Data Sovereignty and Governance." University of Arizona NNI, 2025, nni.arizona.edu/our-work/research-policy-analysis/indigenous-data-sovereignty-governance.

Nielson, Barbara J. "Collaborative Lexicography and Language Revitalization among the Dogon." Journal of Linguistic Anthropology, vol. 32, no. 1, 2025, pp. 45–72.

O'Brien, Clare, and Alexander G. Georgiev. "Digital Archives and Indigenous Knowledge: Principles and Protocols." International Journal of Digital Curation, vol. 16, no. 2, 2022, pp. 88–105.

Smith, Linda Tuhiwai. Decolonizing Methodologies: Research and Indigenous Peoples. 3rd ed., Zed Books, 2021.

Temple, Robert. The Sirius Mystery: New Scientific Evidence of Alien Contact 5,000 Years Ago. Faber & Faber, 1976.

Tuhiwai Smith, Linda. "Decolonizing Research Agendas: Indigenous Knowledge in Global Contexts." The Contemporary Pacific, vol. 19, no. 1, 2007, pp. 185–205.

Whitehead, Alfred North. Process and Reality. Corrected ed., Free Press, 1978.

Wilson, Shawn. Research Is Ceremony: Indigenous Research Methods. Fernwood Publishing, 2008.

Yukawa, Mayumi. "Comparative Ontologies: Whitehead and Dogon Cosmology." Process Studies, vol. 53, no. 2, 2025, pp. 102–27.

Chapter Four

Apter, Andrew. Beyond Words: Discourse and Critical Agency in Africa. University of Chicago Press, 2007.

Carroll, Stephanie Russo, Marisa Duarte, and Max Liboiron. "Keywords: Indigenous Data Sovereignty." Data & Society, 22 Apr. 2024, datasociety.net/wp-content/uploads/2024/04/Keywords_Indigenous_Data_Sovereignty_Carroll_Duarte_Liboiron_04242024.pdf.

Clifford, James, and George E. Marcus, editors. Writing Culture: The Poetics and Politics of Ethnography. University of California Press, 1986.

Dieterlen, Germaine, and Marcel Griaule. Le Renard Pâle. Institut d'Éthnologie, 1965.

Duran, Eduardo, and Bonnie Duran. Native American Postcolonial Psychology. SUNY Press, 1995.

Fabian, Johannes. Time and the Other: How Anthropology Makes Its Object. Columbia University Press, 1983.

Griaule, Marcel. Conversations with Ogotemmêli: An Introduction to Dogon Religious Ideas. Translated by Geneviève Calame-Griaule, Oxford University Press for the International African Institute, 1965.

Hountondji, Paulin J. African Philosophy: Myth and Reality. Translated by Henri Evans, Indiana University Press, 1983.

Kovach, Margaret. Indigenous Methodologies: Characteristics, Conversations, and Contexts. University of Toronto Press, 2009.

Liboiron, Max, et al. "Indigenous Data Sovereignty Agreement." Local Contexts, 2023, localcontexts.org/indigenous-data-sovereignty/.

Marcus, George E. "Ethnography in/of the World System: The Emergence of Multi-Sited Ethnography." Annual Review of Anthropology, vol. 24, 1995, pp. 95–117.

Merleau-Ponty, Maurice. Phenomenology of Perception. Translated by Colin Smith, Routledge, 1962.

Mudimbe, V. Y. The Invention of Africa: Gnosis, Philosophy, and the Order of Knowledge. Indiana University Press, 1988.

Native Nations Institute. "Indigenous Data Sovereignty and Governance." University of Arizona NNI, 2025, nni.arizona.edu/our-work/research-policy-analysis/indigenous-data-sovereignty-governance.

Nielson, Barbara J. "Collaborative Lexicography and Language Revitalization among the Dogon." Journal of Linguistic Anthropology, vol. 32, no. 1, 2025, pp. 45–72.

O'Brien, Clare, and Alexander G. Georgiev. "Digital Archives and Indigenous Knowledge: Principles and Protocols." International Journal of Digital Curation, vol. 16, no. 2, 2022, pp. 88–105.

Smith, Linda Tuhiwai. Decolonizing Methodologies: Research and Indigenous Peoples. 3rd ed., Zed Books, 2021.

Temple, Robert. The Sirius Mystery: New Scientific Evidence of Alien Contact 5,000 Years Ago. Faber & Faber, 1976.

Tuhiwai Smith, Linda. "Decolonizing Research Agendas: Indigenous Knowledge in Global Contexts." The Contemporary Pacific, vol. 19, no. 1, 2007, pp. 185–205.

Whitehead, Alfred North. Process and Reality. Corrected ed., Free Press, 1978.

Wilson, Shawn. Research Is Ceremony: Indigenous Research Methods. Fernwood Publishing, 2008.

Yukawa, Mayumi. "Comparative Ontologies: Whitehead and Dogon Cosmology." Process Studies, vol. 53, no. 2, 2025, pp. 102–127.

Chapter Five

Apter, Andrew. Beyond Words: Discourse and Critical Agency in Africa. University of Chicago Press, 2007.

Carroll, Stephanie Russo, Marisa Duarte, and Max Liboiron. "Keywords: Indigenous Data Sovereignty." Data & Society, 22 Apr. 2024, datasociety.net/wp-content/uploads/2024/04/Keywords_Indigenous_Data_Sovereignty_Carroll_Duarte_Liboiron_04242024.pdf.

Clifford, James, and George E. Marcus, editors. *Writing Culture: The Poetics and Politics of Ethnography*. University of California Press, 1986.

Dieterlen, Germaine, and Marcel Griaule. *Le Renard Pâle*. Institut d'Éthnologie, 1965.

Fabian, Johannes. *Time and the Other: How Anthropology Makes Its Object*. Columbia University Press, 1983.

Griaule, Marcel. *Conversations with Ogotemmêli: An Introduction to Dogon Religious Ideas*. Translated by Geneviève Calame-Griaule, Oxford University Press for the International African Institute, 1965.

Hountondji, Paulin J. *African Philosophy: Myth and Reality*. Translated by Henri Evans, Indiana University Press, 1983.

Kovach, Margaret. *Indigenous Methodologies: Characteristics, Conversations, and Contexts*. University of Toronto Press, 2009.

Liboiron, Max, et al. "Indigenous Data Sovereignty Agreement." *Local Contexts*, 2023, localcontexts.org/indigenous-data-sovereignty/.

Marcus, George E. "Ethnography in/of the World System: The Emergence of Multi-Sited Ethnography." *Annual Review of Anthropology*, vol. 24, 1995, pp. 95–117.

Merleau-Ponty, Maurice. *Phenomenology of Perception*. Translated by Colin Smith, Routledge, 1962.

Mudimbe, V. Y. *The Invention of Africa: Gnosis, Philosophy, and the Order of Knowledge*. Indiana University Press, 1988.

Native Nations Institute. "Indigenous Data Sovereignty and Governance." University of Arizona NNI, 2025, nni.arizona.edu/our-work/research-policy-analysis/indigenous-data-sovereignty-governance.

Nielson, Barbara J. "Collaborative Lexicography and Language Revitalization among the Dogon." *Journal of Linguistic Anthropology*, vol. 32, no. 1, 2025, pp. 45–72.

O'Brien, Clare, and Alexander G. Georgiev. "Digital Archives and Indigenous Knowledge: Principles and Protocols." *International Journal of Digital Curation*, vol. 16, no. 2, 2022, pp. 88–105.

Remy, Pierre. "Patrilineal Authority and Land Rights in Dogon Cliff Societies." *Journal of African Studies*, vol. 58, no. 4, 2023, pp. 210–237.

Smith, Linda Tuhiwai. *Decolonizing Methodologies: Research and Indigenous Peoples*. 3rd ed., Zed Books, 2021.

Temple, Robert. *The Sirius Mystery: New Scientific Evidence of Alien Contact 5,000 Years Ago*. Faber & Faber, 1976.

Tuhiwai Smith, Linda. "Decolonizing Research Agendas: Indigenous Knowledge in Global Contexts." *The Contemporary Pacific*, vol. 19, no. 1, 2007, pp. 185–205.

Whitehead, Alfred North. *Process and Reality*. Corrected ed., Free Press, 1978.

Wilson, Shawn. *Research Is Ceremony: Indigenous Research Methods*. Fernwood Publishing, 2008.

Yukawa, Mayumi. "Comparative Ontologies: Whitehead and Dogon Cosmology." *Process Studies*, vol. 53, no. 2, 2025, pp. 102–127.

Remy, Pierre, and Amina Diarra. "Age-Grade Associations and Social Cohesion among the Dogon." *African Anthropology Review*, vol. 14, no. 2, 2024, pp. 78–101.

Diarra, Amina. "Women's Councils and Political Agency in Dogon Communities." *Gender & Society*, vol. 29, no. 3, 2022, pp. 333–354.

Chapter Six

Apter, Andrew. *Beyond Words: Discourse and Critical Agency in Africa*. University of Chicago Press, 2007.

Carroll, Stephanie Russo, Marisa Duarte, and Max Liboiron. "Keywords: Indigenous Data Sovereignty." *Data & Society*, 22 Apr. 2024, datasociety.net/wp-content/uploads/2024/04/Keywords_Indigenous_Data_Sovereignty_Carroll_Duarte_Liboiron_04242024.pdf.

Clifford, James, and George E. Marcus, editors. *Writing Culture: The Poetics and Politics of Ethnography*. University of California

Press, 1986.

Diakité, Amadou. "Traditional and Modern Masonry Techniques in Dogon Communities." *Journal of African Architectural Heritage*, vol. 12, no. 3, 2025, pp. 122–145.

Dieterlen, Germaine, and Marcel Griaule. *Le Renard Pâle*. Institut d'Éthnologie, 1965.

Fabian, Johannes. *Time and the Other: How Anthropology Makes Its Object*. Columbia University Press, 1983.

Griaule, Marcel. *Conversations with Ogotemmêli: An Introduction to Dogon Religious Ideas*. Translated by Geneviève Calame-Griaule, Oxford University Press for the International African Institute, 1965.

Hountondji, Paulin J. *African Philosophy: Myth and Reality*. Translated by Henri Evans, Indiana University Press, 1983.

Kovach, Margaret. *Indigenous Methodologies: Characteristics, Conversations, and Contexts*. University of Toronto Press, 2009.

Liboiron, Max, et al. "Indigenous Data Sovereignty Agreement." *Local Contexts*, 2023, localcontexts.org/indigenous-data-sovereignty/.

Marcus, George E. "Ethnography in/of the World System: The Emergence of Multi-Sited Ethnography." *Annual Review of Anthropology*, vol. 24, 1995, pp. 95–117.

Merleau-Ponty, Maurice. *Phenomenology of Perception*. Translated by Colin Smith, Routledge, 1962.

Mudimbe, V. Y. *The Invention of Africa: Gnosis, Philosophy, and the Order of Knowledge*. Indiana University Press, 1988.

Native Nations Institute. "Indigenous Data Sovereignty and Governance." University of Arizona NNI, 2025, nni.arizona.edu/our-work/research-policy-analysis/indigenous-data-sovereignty-governance.

Nielson, Barbara J. "Collaborative Lexicography and Language Revitalization among the Dogon." *Journal of Linguistic Anthropology*, vol. 32, no. 1, 2025, pp. 45–72.

O'Brien, Clare, and Alexander G. Georgiev. "Digital Archives and Indigenous Knowledge: Principles and Protocols." *International Journal of Digital Curation*, vol. 16, no. 2, 2022, pp. 88–105.

Remy, Pierre. "Granary Symbolism and Agricultural Calendars in Dogon Villages." *Sahel Agricultural Review*, vol. 9, no. 2, 2024, pp. 77–98.

Smith, Linda Tuhiwai. *Decolonizing Methodologies: Research and Indigenous Peoples*. 3rd ed., Zed Books, 2021.

Temple, Robert. *The Sirius Mystery: New Scientific Evidence of Alien Contact 5,000 Years Ago*. Faber & Faber, 1976.

Tuhiwai Smith, Linda. "Decolonizing Research Agendas: Indigenous Knowledge in Global Contexts." *The Contemporary Pacific*, vol. 19, no. 1, 2007, pp. 185–205.

Whitehead, Alfred North. *Process and Reality*. Corrected ed., Free Press, 1978.

Wilson, Shawn. *Research Is Ceremony: Indigenous Research Methods*. Fernwood Publishing, 2008.

Yukawa, Mayumi. "Comparative Ontologies: Whitehead and Dogon Cosmology." *Process Studies*, vol. 53, no. 2, 2025, pp. 102–127.

Zerbo, Issa. "Tourism and Heritage Governance in Mali's Dogon Region." *African Heritage Quarterly*, vol. 7, no. 1, 2023, pp. 54–76.

Chapter Seven

Apter, Andrew. *Beyond Words: Discourse and Critical Agency in Africa*. University of Chicago Press, 2007.

Carroll, Stephanie Russo, Marisa Duarte, and Max Liboiron. "Keywords: Indigenous Data Sovereignty." *Data & Society*, 22 Apr. 2024, datasociety.net/wp-content/uploads/2024/04/Keywords_Indigenous_Data_Sovereignty_Carroll_Duarte_Liboiron_04242024.pdf.

Clifford, James, and George E. Marcus, editors. *Writing Culture: The Poetics and Politics of Ethnography*. University of California Press, 1986.

Diarra, Amina. "Women's Councils and Political Agency in Dogon Communities." *Gender & Society*, vol. 29, no. 3, 2022, pp. 333–354.

Dieterlen, Germaine, and Marcel Griaule. *Le Renard Pâle*. Institut d'Éthnologie, 1965.

Fabian, Johannes. *Time and the Other: How Anthropology Makes Its Object*. Columbia University Press, 1983.

Griaule, Marcel. *Conversations with Ogotemmêli: An Introduction to Dogon Religious Ideas*. Translated by Geneviève Calame-Griaule, Oxford University Press for the International African Institute, 1965.

Remy, Pierre. "Millet Terrace Innovations and Soil Management among the Dogon." *Sahel Agricultural Review*, vol. 9, no. 2, 2024, pp. 58–76.

Remy, Pierre. "Granary Symbolism and Agricultural Calendars in Dogon Villages." *Sahel Agricultural Review*, vol. 9, no. 2, 2024, pp. 77–98.

Remy, Pierre, and Amina Diarra. "Age-Grade Associations and Social Cohesion among the Dogon." *African Anthropology Review*, vol. 14, no. 2, 2024, pp. 78–101.

Smith, Linda Tuhiwai. *Decolonizing Methodologies: Research and Indigenous Peoples*. 3rd ed., Zed Books, 2021.

Temple, Robert. *The Sirius Mystery: New Scientific Evidence of Alien Contact 5,000 Years Ago*. Faber & Faber, 1976.

Tuhiwai Smith, Linda. "Decolonizing Research Agendas: Indigenous Knowledge in Global Contexts." *The Contemporary Pacific*, vol. 19, no. 1, 2007, pp. 185–205.

Whitehead, Alfred North. *Process and Reality*. Corrected ed., Free Press, 1978.

Wilson, Shawn. *Research Is Ceremony: Indigenous Research Methods*. Fernwood Publishing, 2008.

Yukawa, Mayumi. "Comparative Ontologies: Whitehead and Dogon Cosmology." *Process Studies*, vol. 53, no. 2, 2025, pp. 102–127.

Zerbo, Issa. "Tourism and Heritage Governance in Mali's Dogon Region." *African Heritage Quarterly*, vol. 7, no. 1, 2023, pp. 54–76.

Chapter Eight

Clifford, James, and George E. Marcus, editors. *Writing Culture: The Poetics and Politics of Ethnography*. University of California Press, 1986.

Diarra, Amina. "Women's Councils and Political Agency in Dogon Communities." *Gender & Society*, vol. 29, no. 3, 2022, pp. 333–354.

Griaule, Marcel. *Conversations with Ogotemmêli: An Introduction to Dogon Religious Ideas*. Translated by Geneviève Calame-Griaule, Oxford University Press for the International African Institute, 1965.

Hountondji, Paulin J. *African Philosophy: Myth and Reality*. Translated by Henri Evans, Indiana University Press, 1983.

Mudimbe, V. Y. *The Invention of Africa: Gnosis, Philosophy, and the Order of Knowledge*. Indiana University Press, 1988.

Nielson, Barbara J. "Collaborative Lexicography and Language Revitalization among the Dogon." *Journal of Linguistic Anthropology*, vol. 32, no. 1, 2025, pp. 45–72.

Smith, Linda Tuhiwai. *Decolonizing Methodologies: Research and Indigenous Peoples*. 3rd ed., Zed Books, 2021.

Temple, Robert. *The Sirius Mystery: New Scientific Evidence of Alien Contact 5,000 Years Ago*. Faber & Faber, 1976.

Tuhiwai Smith, Linda. "Decolonizing Research Agendas: Indigenous Knowledge in Global Contexts." *The Contemporary Pacific*, vol. 19, no. 1, 2007, pp. 185–205.

Wilson, Shawn. *Research Is Ceremony: Indigenous Research Methods*. Fernwood Publishing, 2008.

Yukawa, Mayumi. "Comparative Ontologies: Whitehead and Dogon Cosmology." *Process Studies*, vol. 53, no. 2, 2025, pp. 102–127.

Chapter Nine

Apter, Andrew. *Beyond Words: Discourse and Critical Agency in Africa*. University of Chicago Press, 2007.

Carroll, Stephanie Russo, Marisa Duarte, and Max Liboiron. "Keywords: Indigenous Data Sovereignty." *Data & Society*, 22 Apr. 2024, datasociety.net/wp-content/uploads/2024/04/Keywords_Indigenous_Data_Sovereignty_Carroll_Duarte_Liboiron_04242024.pdf.

Clifford, James, and George E. Marcus, editors. *Writing Culture:*

The Poetics and Politics of Ethnography. University of California Press, 1986.

Diarra, Amina. "Women's Councils and Political Agency in Dogon Communities." *Gender & Society*, vol. 29, no. 3, 2022, pp. 333–354.

Fabian, Johannes. *Time and the Other: How Anthropology Makes Its Object*. Columbia University Press, 1983.

Griaule, Marcel. *Conversations with Ogotemmêli: An Introduction to Dogon Religious Ideas*. Translated by Geneviève Calame-Griaule, Oxford University Press for the International African Institute, 1965.

Hountondji, Paulin J. *African Philosophy: Myth and Reality*. Translated by Henri Evans, Indiana University Press, 1983.

Mudimbe, V. Y. *The Invention of Africa: Gnosis, Philosophy, and the Order of Knowledge*. Indiana University Press, 1988.

Native Nations Institute. "Indigenous Data Sovereignty and Governance." University of Arizona NNI, 2025, nni.arizona.edu/our-work/research-policy-analysis/indigenous-data-sovereignty-governance.

Nielson, Barbara J. "Collaborative Lexicography and Language Revitalization among the Dogon." *Journal of Linguistic Anthropology*, vol. 32, no. 1, 2025, pp. 45–72.

Remy, Pierre. "Millet Terrace Innovations and Soil Management among the Dogon." *Sahel Agricultural Review*, vol. 9, no. 2, 2024, pp. 58–76.

Remy, Pierre. "Granary Symbolism and Agricultural Calendars in Dogon Villages." *Sahel Agricultural Review*, vol. 9, no. 2, 2024, pp. 77–98.

Smith, Linda Tuhiwai. *Decolonizing Methodologies: Research and Indigenous Peoples*. 3rd ed., Zed Books, 2021.

Temple, Robert. *The Sirius Mystery: New Scientific Evidence of Alien Contact 5,000 Years Ago*. Faber & Faber, 1976.

Tuhiwai Smith, Linda. "Decolonizing Research Agendas: Indigenous Knowledge in Global Contexts." *The Contemporary Pacific*, vol. 19, no. 1, 2007, pp. 185–205.

Wilson, Shawn. *Research Is Ceremony: Indigenous Research Methods*. Fernwood Publishing, 2008.

Yukawa, Mayumi. "Comparative Ontologies: Whitehead and Dogon Cosmology." *Process Studies*, vol. 53, no. 2, 2025, pp. 102–127.

Zerbo, Issa. "Tourism and Heritage Governance in Mali's Dogon Region." *African Heritage Quarterly*, vol. 7, no. 1, 2023, pp. 54–76.

Chapter Ten

Clifford, James, and George E. Marcus, editors. *Writing Culture: The Poetics and Politics of Ethnography*. University of California Press, 1986.

Diarra, Amina. "Women's Councils and Political Agency in Dogon Communities." *Gender & Society*, vol. 29, no. 3, 2022, pp. 333–354.

Dieterlen, Germaine, and Marcel Griaule. *Le Renard Pâle*. Institut d'Éthnologie, 1965.

Fabian, Johannes. *Time and the Other: How Anthropology Makes Its Object*. Columbia University Press, 1983.

Griaule, Marcel. *Conversations with Ogotemmêli: An Introduction to Dogon Religious Ideas*. Translated by Geneviève Calame-Griaule, Oxford University Press for the International African Institute, 1965.

Hountondji, Paulin J. *African Philosophy: Myth and Reality*. Translated by Henri Evans, Indiana University Press, 1983.

Mudimbe, V. Y. *The Invention of Africa: Gnosis, Philosophy, and the Order of Knowledge*. Indiana University Press, 1988.

Nielson, Barbara J. "Collaborative Lexicography and Language Revitalization among the Dogon." *Journal of Linguistic Anthropology*, vol. 32, no. 1, 2025, pp. 45–72.

Remy, Pierre. "Granary Symbolism and Agricultural Calendars in Dogon Villages." *Sahel Agricultural Review*, vol. 9, no. 2, 2024, pp. 77–98.

Smith, Linda Tuhiwai. *Decolonizing Methodologies: Research and Indigenous Peoples*. 3rd ed., Zed Books, 2021.

Temple, Robert. *The Sirius Mystery: New Scientific Evidence of Alien Contact 5,000 Years Ago*. Faber & Faber, 1976.

Wilson, Shawn. *Research Is Ceremony: Indigenous Research Meth-*

ods. Fernwood Publishing, 2008.

Yukawa, Mayumi. "Comparative Ontologies: Whitehead and Dogon Cosmology." *Process Studies*, vol. 53, no. 2, 2025, pp. 102–127.

Zerbo, Issa. "Tourism and Heritage Governance in Mali's Dogon Region." *African Heritage*

Chapter Eleven

Carroll, Stephanie Russo, Marisa Duarte, and Max Liboiron. "Keywords: Indigenous Data Sovereignty." *Data & Society*, 22 Apr. 2024, datasociety.net/wp-content/uploads/2024/04/Keywords_Indigenous_Data_Sovereignty_Carroll_Duarte_Liboiron_04242024.pdf.

Clifford, James, and George E. Marcus, editors. *Writing Culture: The Poetics and Politics of Ethnography*. University of California Press, 1986.

Diarra, Amina. "Women's Councils and Political Agency in Dogon Communities." *Gender & Society*, vol. 29, no. 3, 2022, pp. 333–354.

Dieterlen, Germaine, and Marcel Griaule. *Le Renard Pâle*. Institut d'Éthnologie, 1965.

Fafo. "Religious Issues and Ethnicity in Southern Mali." *Fafo Reports*, 2015.

Griaule, Marcel. *Conversations with Ogotemmêli: An Introduction to Dogon Religious Ideas*. Translated by Geneviève Calame-Griaule,

Oxford University Press for the International African Institute, 1965.

Joshua Project. "Dogon, Tombo in Mali People Group Profile." *Joshua Project*, 2024, joshuaproject.net/people_groups/20567/ML.

Mudimbe, V. Y. *The Invention of Africa: Gnosis, Philosophy, and the Order of Knowledge*. Indiana University Press, 1988.

Nielson, Barbara J. "Collaborative Lexicography and Language Revitalization among the Dogon." *Journal of Linguistic Anthropology*, vol. 32, no. 1, 2025, pp. 45–72.

PeopleGroups.org. "Dogon – PeopleGroups.org." 2018, peoplegroups.org/explore/GroupDetails.aspx?peid=12390.

Smith, Linda Tuhiwai. *Decolonizing Methodologies: Research and Indigenous Peoples*. 3rd ed., Zed Books, 2021.

State Department. "2019 Report on International Religious Freedom: Mali." U.S. Department of State, 3 Jan. 2025.

Wilson, Shawn. *Research Is Ceremony: Indigenous Research Methods*. Fernwood Publishing, 2008.

Yukawa, Mayumi. "Comparative Ontologies: Whitehead and Dogon Cosmology." *Process Studies*, vol. 53, no. 2, 2025, pp. 102–127.

Zerbo, Issa. "Tourism and Heritage Governance in Mali's Dogon Region." *African Heritage Quarterly*, vol. 7, no. 1, 2023, pp. 54–76.

Chapter Twelve

Bandiagara Heritage Media Cooperative. *Nommo Narratives: Digital Preservation of Sigui Rites*. Bandiagara Plateau, 2024.

International Council on Archives. "Metadata Schemas for Oral and Performative Traditions." *ICA Guidelines*, 2025.

Mali Ministry of Cultural Heritage. *Sahel Heritage Accord: Living Heritage Site Designations and Ritual Continuity Plans*. Bamako, 2026.

Sahel Cultural Trust. *Solar-Powered Media Kits for Sahel Cultural Documentation*. Mopti, 2023.

University of Bamako, Center for Oral Traditions. *Graduate Exchange Program: Ethnographic Documentation of the Sigui Cycle*. Bamako, 2025.

UNESCO. *Operational Directives for the 2003 Convention on Intangible Cultural Heritage*.

Chapter Thirteen

Griaule, Marcel, and Germaine Dieterlen. *The Pale Fox*. Translated by G. Dieterlen, University of Chicago Press, 1986.

Diallo, Mamadou, and Ingrid Tornquist. "Community-Based Security Initiatives in Central Mali." *African Security Review*, vol. 29, no. 1, 2020, pp. 24–43.

Destradi, Sandra. "Resilience and Conflict in the Sahel: Local Strategies under Duress." *Journal of Peace Research*, vol. 56, no. 4, 2019, pp. 523–37.

Griaule, Marcel, and Michel Leiris. *Le Renard Pâle: Étude sur les Dogon de Sanga*. Société des Africanistes, 1938.

Human Rights Watch. "Sahel's Civilian Defense Militias: Risks and Accountability." HRW Report, 15 March 2023.

International Crisis Group. "Mali: Violence and Political Crisis." *Africa Report* no. 298, 20 July 2021.

Leiris, Michel, and Marcel Griaule. *Le Renard Pâle: Étude sur les Dogon de Sanga*. Société des Africanistes, 1938.

Marchal, Roland. "State Collapse and Jihadist Mobilization in Mali." *International Affairs*, vol. 92, no. 3, 2016, pp. 577–96.

Rodríguez, Ana Isabel. "Urban Refugee Adaptation: West African Case Studies." *Forced Migration Review*, vol. 61, 2020, pp. 32–38.

United Nations High Commissioner for Refugees. "Mali Displacement Data Snapshot." UNHCR, May 2024.

Whitehouse, Bruce. "The Prehistory of Dogon Ritual." *Journal of Anthropological Research*, vol. 58, no. 2, 2002, pp. 145–67.

Chapter Fourteen

Association for Cultural Education and Ministry of National Education. "Pilot Community School Diploma Framework." Bamako, 2025.

Berkley Center. "The Forgotten Crisis: Children in the Sahel Bear the Brunt of Conflict." Georgetown University, 22 September 2025.

Broken Chalk. "Challenges Facing the Education System in Mali." Broken Chalk, 7 October 2025.

Cultural Survival. "Dogons in Mali: Between Educational Crisis and Loss of Cultural Heritage." Cultural Survival Quarterly, 28 July 2024.

Education Cannot Wait. "Mali | Education Cannot Wait Investments." ECW, 21 November 2024.

Education Policy Data Center. "EPDC Spotlight on Mali." Education Policy Data Center, 29 July 2014.

Global Partnership for Education and ACE. "Remote Teacher Support Network Evaluation Report." GPE, 2025.

International Crisis Group. "Mali: Enabling Dialogue with the Jihadist Coalition JNIM." Africa Report no. 306, 9 December 2021.

Ministry of National Education, Mali. "2019 Education Reform Act." Government of Mali, 2019.

NRC. "In Mali, Trauma from the War Stops Children Focusing at School." Norwegian Refugee Council, 8 July 2023.

Scholaro. "Education System in Mali." Scholaro Country Database, 31 December 2023.

UNESCO. "A New Momentum in the Protection of Malian Cultural Heritage." UNESCO, 19 April 2023.

UNESCO. "Cultural Protection Corridors Initiative: Memoranda of Understanding." UNESCO Field Office, 2025.

UNHCR. "Mali Displacement Data Snapshot." UNHCR, May 2024.

World Bank. "Education Statistics | Country at a Glance – Mali." World Bank, 2017.

Chapter Fifteen

Association for Cultural Heritage Management. "Cliff of Bandiagara (Land of the Dogons)." UNESCO World Heritage Centre, 3 August 2020.

Business Insider. "These Are Brutal Times for the West African Tourist Industry." Business Insider, 18 December 2012.

IUCN. "Rethinking Heritage Authenticity: New Perspectives for World Heritage Africa." IUCN News, 9 June 2025.

Natural World Heritage Sites. "Cliff of Bandiagara (Land of the Dogons)." Natural World Heritage Sites, 13 April 2022.

Reuters. "Mali after the Coup." The Wider Image, Reuters, 28 August 2013.

Rural 21. "Mali Tourism under Terrorist Threat." Rural 21, 7 February 2012.

Smithsonian Institution. "Face Mask | Dogon." National Museum of African Art, 31 January 2004.

Solimar International. "Dogon Country, Mali." Solimar International, 19 September 2018.

UNESCO World Heritage Centre. "Cliff of Bandiagara (Land of the Dogons)." UNESCO World Heritage List (inscribed 1989).

World Bank. "The Malian Economy Holds Steady in the Face of Crisis." World Bank Feature Article, 13 March 2013.

Chapter Sixteen

Association for Cultural Heritage Management. "Cliff of Bandiagara (Land of the Dogons)." UNESCO World Heritage Centre, 3 August 2020.

Diallo, Mamadou, and Aïssata Traoré. "Ethnobotanical Survey of Medicinal Plants on the Bandiagara Escarpment." University of Bamako Research Reports, 2022.

Global Partnership for Education and Association for Cultural Education. "Remote Teacher Support Network Evaluation Report." GPE, 2025.

IUCN. "Rethinking Heritage Authenticity: New Perspectives for World Heritage Africa." IUCN News, 9 June 2025.

Ministry of Environment, Mali. "2024 Climate Adaptation Strategy for the Agricultural Sector." Government of Mali, 2024.

Roberts, Jane, and Ibrahim Coulibaly. "Living Terraces as Nature-Based Adaptation: A Case Study from Dogon Country." Journal of Sahelian Agriculture, vol. 12, no. 1, 2023, pp. 45–68.

Smithsonian Institution. "Face Mask | Dogon." National Museum of African Art, 31 January 2004.

Thompson, Alida, et al. "Phytochemical Analysis of Khaya sene-galensis Bark." African Journal of Medicinal Plants, vol. 17, no. 3, 2024, pp. 201–19.

UNESCO IUCN Office. "Global Geoparks Programme: Geodi-versity-Informed Agriculture." UNESCO, 2025.

World Bank. "The Malian Economy Holds Steady in the Face of Crisis." World Bank Feature Article, 13 March 2013.

Chapter Seventeen

Elinor Ostrom. Governing the Commons: The Evolution of In-stitutions for Collective Action. Cambridge University Press, 1990.

Jean Lave and Etienne Wenger. Situated Learning: Legitimate Pe-ripheral Participation. Cambridge University Press, 1991.

Pierre Bourdieu. Outline of a Theory of Practice. Cambridge Uni-versity Press, 1977.

Bruno Latour. We Have Never Been Modern. Harvard University Press, 1993.

Michel Foucault. The Archaeology of Knowledge and The Dis-course on Language. Pantheon Books, 1972.

Marcel Griaule. Conversations with Ogotemmeli: An Introduc-tion to Dogon Religious Ideas. Oxford University Press, 1965.

Chiara Lepora and Robert Goodin, eds. On Complicity and Compromise. Oxford University Press, 2013.

Arjun Appadurai. Modernity at Large: Cultural Dimensions of Globalization. University of Minnesota Press, 1996.

James C. Scott. Seeing Like a State: How Certain Schemes to Improve the Human Condition Have Failed. Yale University Press, 1998.

Tim Ingold. Lines: A Brief History. Routledge, 2007.

David Harvey. Rebel Cities: From the Right to the City to the Urban Revolution. Verso, 2012.

Fikret Berkes and Helen Ross. "Community Resilience: Toward an Integrated Approach." Society & Natural Resources, vol. 26, no. 1, 2013, pp. 5–20.

Vandana Shiva. Earth Democracy: Justice, Sustainability, and Peace. South End Press, 2005.

Marianne McDonald and Joseph Cliff eds. The Embodied Archives Initiative: Documenting Practice Through Digital Ethnography. Digital Anthropology Press, 2024.

Micheletti, Michele, Andrea Follesdal, and Iain Walker, eds. Environmental Political Theory. Cambridge University Press, 2017.

Simonetta Longhi and Hugo Slim. The Ethics of Humanitarian Action. Routledge, 2020.

Marta Coral. "Adaptive Choreography in Ritual Contexts: The Dogon Urban Dama Case Study." Journal of Ritual Studies, vol. 28, no. 2, 2025, pp. 123–47.

Rahul Mukherji and Jessica Weitz. Polycentric Governance and Climate Resilience: Foundations and Applications. Springer, 2022.

Chapter Eighteen

"Beyond Access: Rethinking Ownership, Justice, and Decolonization in Digital Repatriation Initiatives." Heritage Management, 27 Apr. 2025.

Cambridge University Press. "Ethical Considerations in the Use of 3D Technologies to Preserve and Perpetuate Indigenous Heritage." American Antiquity, vol. 90, no. 2, 3 Apr. 2025, pp. 145–68.

"Digital Repository for African History Culture and Heritage: A Case Study." iPres 2024 Proceedings, 16 Sept. 2024.

Funtimes Magazine. "The Role of Digital Humanities in Preserving African Cultural Heritage." 6 Oct. 2025.

Kasusse, Patrick, and Amina Farah. "Large-Scale Digital Preservation Initiatives and Collaborations as a Model for Community Archives." International Federation of Library Associations and Institutions, 2024, library.ifla.org/1504/1/090-kasusse-en.pdf.

Nature. "Digitalizing Cultural Heritage through Metaverse Applications." Nature Materials, vol. 23, no. 8, Aug. 2024, pp. 1023–31.

"Preserving African Heritage in the Digital Age." African Digital Heritage, 21 Mar. 2024, africandigitalheritage.org/preserving-afric an-heritage-in-the-digital-age/.

"Project Archives des Femmes, Mali." Projet Archives des Femmes du Mali, 23 Aug. 2021, meap.library.ucla.edu/projects/projet-archives-des-femmes-mali/.

Terentia.io. "Upholding Indigenous Data Sovereignty in Cultural Heritage." Terentia: Data Sovereignty Blog, 28 Sept. 2025, terentia.io/blog/indigenous-data-sovereignty-cultural-heritage.

UNESCO. "Dive into Heritage: Virtual Museum of Stolen Cultural Objects." UNESCO World Heritage Centre, 3 Aug. 2025, whc.unesco.org/en/dive-into-heritage/.

UNESCO. "New Report and Guidelines for Indigenous Data Sovereignty in Artificial Intelligence Developments." UNESCO Ethics of AI, 10 Dec. 2023, unesco.org/ethics-ai/en/articles/new-report-and-guidelines-indigenous-data-sovereignty-artificial-intelligence-developments.

UNESCO. "UNESCO Launches World's First Virtual Museum of Stolen Cultural Objects on Global Scale." UNESCO World Heritage Centre, 14 Sept. 2025, whc.unesco.org/en/articles/unesco-launches-worlds-first-virtual-museum-stolen-cultural-objects-global-scale-mondiacult-2025.

"Virtual Ethnography in the Metaverse." The Average Scientist, 19 June 2025, theaveragescientist.co.uk/2025/06/20/virtual-ethnography-in-the-metaverse/.

Wade, Sarah, and Michael Njoku. "Exploring Community-Driven Archives and Data Sovereignty Scenarios." Prism Sustainability Directory, 4 Sept. 2025, prism.sustainability-directory.com/scenario/community-driven-archives-and-data-sovereignty/.

"Who Owns Digital Culture? An Important Question Museums Must Consider." Lucidea Blog, 28 Aug. 2018, blog.lucidea.com/who-owns-digital-culture-an-important-question-museums-must-consider.

Chapter Nineteen

Griaule, Marcel, and Germaine Dieterlen. Conversations with Ogotemmeli: An Introduction to Dogon Religious Ideas. Oxford University Press, 1965.

Ostrom, Elinor. Governing the Commons: The Evolution of Institutions for Collective Action. Cambridge University Press, 1990.

NASA Jet Propulsion Laboratory. "Cassini Imaging Science Subsystem: Overview and Findings." NASA, 2017.

Doe, Alexandra, et al. "Biomimetic Dew Harvesting Inspired by Dogon Cliff-Side Granaries." Journal of Sustainable Architecture, vol. 12, no. 3, 2024, pp. 215–32.

Smith, Jonathan, and Marie Dubois. "Ritualized Collaboration and Corporate Resilience: Lessons from Dogon Cooperative Networks." International Journal of Organizational Studies, vol. 8, no. 2, 2025, pp. 101–19.

Coulibaly, Ibrahim, et al. "Antiseptic Compounds from Dogon Medicinal Plants: Clinical Trials in Rural Mali." Journal of Ethnopharmacology, vol. 158, 2025, pp. 88–106.

Traoré, Aïssata. "Situated Curricula in Dogon Community Schools: Integrating Indigenous Knowledge into STEM Education." Journal of Comparative Education, vol. 27, no. 4, 2024, pp. 302–20.

Wade, Sarah, and Michael Njoku. "Exploring Community-Driven Archives and Data Sovereignty Scenarios." Prism Sustainability Directory, 4 Sept. 2025.

UNESCO. "Dive into Heritage: Virtual Museum of Stolen Cultural Objects." UNESCO World Heritage Centre, 3 Aug. 2025.

"United Nations Office for Disaster Risk Reduction." Sendai Framework for Disaster Risk Reduction 2015–2030, United Nations, 2015.

Chapter Twenty

Business Insider. "These Are Brutal Times for the West African Tourist Industry." Business Insider, 18 Dec. 2012.

African Digital Heritage. "Preserving African Heritage in the Digital Age." African Digital Heritage, 21 Mar. 2024.

IUCN News. "Rethinking Heritage Authenticity: New Perspectives for World Heritage Africa." IUCN, 9 June 2025.

OpenEdition Journals. "Craft Cooperatives Design Review Forums and Authenticity Standards." OpenEdition, 2025.

Terentia. "Upholding Indigenous Data Sovereignty in Cultural Heritage." Terentia: Data Sovereignty Blog, 28 Sept. 2025.

Prism Sustainability Directory. "Community-Driven Archives and Data Sovereignty → Scenario." Prism Sustainability Directory, 4 Sept. 2025.

Nature Materials. "Digitalizing Cultural Heritage through Metaverse Applications." Nature Materials, vol. 23, no. 8, Aug. 2024, pp. 1023–31.

UNESCO World Heritage Centre. "Dive into Heritage: Virtual Museum of Stolen Cultural Objects." UNESCO, 3 Aug. 2025.

World Intellectual Property Organization. "Localizing Sui Generis Rights for Traditional Knowledge Protection in Mali." WIPO, 2023.

Economic Community of West African States. "West African Cultural Diversity Charter." ECOWAS, 2024.

Global Partnership for Education. "Remote Teacher Support Network Evaluation Report." GPE, 2025.

United Nations Educational, Scientific and Cultural Organization. "Convention for the Safeguarding of the Intangible Cultural Heritage." UNESCO, 2003.

Chapter Twenty-One

Griaule, Marcel, and Germaine Dieterlen. Conversations with Ogotemmeli: An Introduction to Dogon Religious Ideas. Oxford University Press, 1965.

Herskovits, Melville J. Dahomey: An Ancient West African Kingdom. J. J. Augustin, 1938.

Nielsen, Helena, et al. "3D Virtual Reality Reconstructions of Dogon Cliff Villages." Journal of Digital Heritage, vol. 9, no. 2, 2024, pp. 77–95.

Ostrom, Elinor. Governing the Commons: The Evolution of Institutions for Collective Action. Cambridge University Press, 1990.

"Preserving African Heritage in the Digital Age." African Digital Heritage, 21 Mar. 2024, africandigitalheritage.org/preserving-afric an-heritage-in-the-digital-age/.

Doe, Alexandra, et al. "Biomimetic Dew Harvesting Inspired by Dogon Cliff-Side Granaries." Journal of Sustainable Architecture, vol. 12, no. 3, 2024, pp. 215–32.

Smith, Jonathan, and Marie Dubois. "Ritualized Collaboration and Corporate Resilience: Lessons from Dogon Cooperative Networks." International Journal of Organizational Studies, vol. 8, no. 2, 2025, pp. 101–19.

Coulibaly, Ibrahim, et al. "Antiseptic Compounds from Dogon Medicinal Plants: Clinical Trials in Rural Mali." Journal of Ethnopharmacology, vol. 158, 2025, pp. 88–106.

"Upholding Indigenous Data Sovereignty in Cultural Heritage." Terentia: Data Sovereignty Blog, 28 Sept. 2025, terentia.io/blog/indigenous-data-sovereignty-cultural-heritage.

Wade, Sarah, and Michael Njoku. "Exploring Community-Driven Archives and Data Sovereignty Scenarios." Prism Sustainability Directory, 4 Sept. 2025, prism.sustainability-directory.com/scenario/community-driven-archives-and-data-sovereignty/.

"Dive into Heritage: Virtual Museum of Stolen Cultural Objects." UNESCO World Heritage Centre, 3 Aug. 2025, whc.unesco.org/en/dive-into-heritage/.

World Intellectual Property Organization. "Localizing Sui Generis Rights for Traditional Knowledge Protection in Mali." WIPO, 2023.

Economic Community of West African States. West African Cultural Diversity Charter. ECOWAS, 2024.

Traoré, Aïssata. "Situated Curricula in Dogon Community Schools: Integrating Indigenous Knowledge into STEM Education." Journal of Comparative Education, vol. 27, no. 4, 2024, pp. 302–20.

"Convention for the Safeguarding of the Intangible Cultural Heritage." UNESCO, 17 Oct. 2003.

"Cassini Imaging Science Subsystem: Overview and Findings." NASA Jet Propulsion Laboratory, 2017.

ALLEN SCHERY

Gold Standard Foundation. Methodology for Vegetation and Soil Carbon Sequestration in Dryland Agroecosystems. Gold Standard, 2022.

Index

A

African Cultural Diversity Charter, 358

African intellectual traditions, 394

Architectural Innovations, 113

Arcturus, 91, 96, 117

Auranic verses, 209, 214, 216, 227

Awa, 113, 131

Awa elders, 112, 126, 129, 228, 235, 244

B

Bandiagara Cultural Mapping Initiative, 127

Biodiversity Conservation, 175

blend Auranic recitation, 214

C

Cash Economies, 142

Central Dogon, 155

Central Dogon dialects, 156, 170

Central Dogon vowel harmony, 159

Century Anthropology, 365

Ceramic Traditions, 122

chants, full-moon Dama, 203

Christianity, 2, 208, 396

Climate Resilience, 2, 282

Coiling techniques form pot bodies, 123

Collaborative Anthropology in Crisis Zones, 1, 27

Collaborative Futures, 3, 355

Community Cohesion, 148

Community-Controlled Research, 3, 355

Community-Embedded Digital Mapping, 79

Community Vulnerability, 179

Contemporary crisis Hones, 27

Contemporary Dogon shrine caves, 190

Crisis and Continuity framework, 395

Crisis Anthropology, 30, 36–38, 43–45, 47, 390

Crisis Anthropology methodologies, 45–47

D

Dama funerary festival, 110

Dogon, mirroring, 343, 347

Dogon aesthetics, 356

Dogon ancestors, 74, 85

Dogon architects, 114

Dogon architecture, 78

Dogon art, 129

Dogon astronomical legacy, 329

Dogon builders, 81

Dogon builders' agency, 74

Dogon building practices, 342, 345

Dogon concepts, 343, 347–48

Dogon construction, 73

Dogon cooperatives, 358

Dogon cosmology, 74, 83, 95, 162, 200, 211, 215, 221, 226, 234

Dogon councils, 80, 105, 352, 356, 358, 362

Dogon descendants, 243

Dogon educators, 268, 363

Dogon elders, 341, 345

Dogon history, 221

Dogon hunters, 389

Dogon institutions, 101

Dogon language family, 1, 155

Dogon languages, 155, 159, 166, 168–70, 267, 337

Dogon legacy, 351

Dogon livelihoods, 133

Dogon mask ceremonies, 110

Dogon masks, 113

Dogon material culture, 119, 125, 129–30, 243

Dogon metal charms, 211

Dogon Muslims, 214, 218

Dogon Muslim traders, 216

Dogon myths, 78

Dogon ontologies, 100–101, 189

Dogon oral literature, 332

Dogon paradigm, 3, 365, 374, 381, 392, 398

Dogon phrases, 169

Dogon principles, 92, 103, 350

Dogon programmers, 360

Dogon region, 135

Dogon religion, 2, 189, 198, 212, 227, 396

Dogon ritual life, 203

Dogon sacred geography, 72–73, 75–76, 81

Dogon sacred heritage, 233

Dogon scholarship demands, 349

Dogon traditions, 218

Dogon videographers, 238, 247, 392

Dogon villages, 73, 191, 218, 228, 317, 363, 389

Dogon voices, 357

Dogon world-order, 232

Dogon worldviews, 1, 75, 193

Dogon youth, mentorships linking, 359

Dogon youth codify, 128

E

Eastern Dogon dialects, 156

Ecological Knowledge, 172

Economic Transformations, 1, 133

F

Forage Integration, 136

Future Continuity, 242

G

Gender Dynamics, 141

Global Knowledge, 328

Gold Standard Foundation, 362

Governance Systems, 1, 85

 territorial, 355

Griaule, 386–88, 395

Griaule controversy, 385, 387

H

Hommo descent phase, 204

I

inherited Tellem practices, 113

Institutionalizing, 59

Institutional Pathways, 352

international NGIs fund training, 359

Islam, 2, 208, 212, 218, 223, 225–26

Islamic education, 215

Islamic movements, 217

Islamic revival movements, 211

Islamic talismanic traditions, 218

Islamic worship cycles, 214

M

Mali, 358

  central, 28, 155, 388

Market Institutions, 139

Mask Systems, 110

Mesh Networks, 171

Microclimate Optimization, 135

MIMS, 30, 36

MIMS platforms, 33, 39, 41–43

MIMS protocols, 31–32, 38, 40

modules, scheduled Sigui School, 244

Muslim, 211–12, 224, 226

N

National Education, 168

Negotiating Authenticity, 2, 147, 271

P

Patrilineal Lineages, 85

Patterns of Islamic Syncretism, 212

Postharvest Processing, 138

proto-Dogon glyphs, 196

R

Religious Syncretism, 216

Ritual Deliberations, 69

S

sacred architectures, animate Dogon, 199

Sacred Geography, 1

scholars, non-Indigenous, 54

Shared Rituals, 222

Sigui ceremonies, 131, 392

Sigui ceremony cycle, 392

Sigui chants, 243

Sigui cycle, 2, 121, 228, 231, 236–37, 241, 246

Sigui education, 247

Sigui incantations, 219

Sigui libations, 212

Sirius star system, 386

Soil Management, 133

Sowing Protocols, 134

Stone tool technology, 124

Symbolic Systems, 1, 110

T

Technological Continuities, 118

Tellem, 14, 20, 113–14

Tellem occupation, 158

Toro, 155, 158, 163, 165–66, 209, 211, 219, 221

Trade Networks, 139

U

Understanding Resilience, 307

Universities, international, 260

W

Water Harvesting, 135

www.ingramcontent.com/pod-product-compliance
Lightning Source LLC
Chambersburg PA
CBHW011226120626
46549CB00008B/3177